*International Political Economy Series*

Series Editor: **Timothy M. Shaw**, Visiting Professor, University of Massachusetts Boston, USA and Emeritus Professor, University of London, UK

The global political economy is in flux as a series of cumulative crises impacts its organisation and governance. The IPE series has tracked its development in both analysis and structure over the last three decades. It has always had a concentration on the global South. Now the South increasingly challenges the North as the centre of development, also reflected in a growing number of submissions and publications on indebted Eurozone economies in Southern Europe.

An indispensable resource for scholars and researchers, the series examines a variety of capitalisms and connections by focusing on emerging economies, companies and sectors, debates and policies. It informs diverse policy communities as the established trans-Atlantic North declines and 'the rest', especially the BRICS, rise.

*Titles include:*

Lourdes Casanova and Julian Kassum
THE POLITICAL ECONOMY OF AN EMERGING GLOBAL POWER
In Search of the Brazil Dream

Toni Haastrup, and Yong-Soo Eun (*editors*)
REGIONALISING GLOBAL CRISES
The Financial Crisis and New Frontiers in Regional Governance

Kobena T. Hanson, Cristina D'Alessandro and Francis Owusu (*editors*)
MANAGING AFRICA'S NATURAL RESOURCES
Capacities for Development

Daniel Daianu, Carlo D'Adda, Giorgio Basevi and Rajeesh Kumar (*editors*)
THE EUROZONE CRISIS AND THE FUTURE OF EUROPE
The Political Economy of Further Integration and Governance

Karen E. Young
THE POLITICAL ECONOMY OF ENERGY, FINANCE AND SECURITY IN THE UNITED ARAB EMIRATES
Between the Majilis and the Market

Monique Taylor
THE CHINESE STATE, OIL AND ENERGY SECURITY

Benedicte Bull, Fulvio Castellacci and Yuri Kasahara
BUSINESS GROUPS AND TRANSNATIONAL CAPITALISM IN CENTRAL AMERICA
Economic and Political Strategies

Leila Simona Talani
THE ARAB SPRING IN THE GLOBAL POLITICAL ECONOMY

Andreas Nölke (*editor*)
MULTINATIONAL CORPORATIONS FROM EMERGING MARKETS
State Capitalism 3.0

Roshen Hendrickson
PROMOTING U.S. INVESTMENT IN SUB-SAHARAN AFRICA

Bhumitra Chakma
SOUTH ASIA IN TRANSITION
Democracy, Political Economy and Security

Greig Charnock, Thomas Purcell and Ramon Ribera-Fumaz
THE LIMITS TO CAPITAL IN SPAIN
Crisis and Revolt in the European South

Felipe Amin Filomeno
MONSANTO AND INTELLECTUAL PROPERTY IN SOUTH AMERICA

Eirikur Bergmann
ICELAND AND THE INTERNATIONAL FINANCIAL CRISIS
Boom, Bust and Recovery

Yildiz Atasoy (editor)
GLOBAL ECONOMIC CRISIS AND THE POLITICS OF DIVERSITY

Gabriel Siles-Brügge
CONSTRUCTING EUROPEAN UNION TRADE POLICY
A Global Idea of Europe

Jewellord Singh and France Bourgouin (editors)
RESOURCE GOVERNANCE AND DEVELOPMENTAL STATES IN THE GLOBAL
SOUTH
Critical International Political Economy Perspectives

Tan Tai Yong and Md Mizanur Rahman (editors)
DIASPORA ENGAGEMENT AND DEVELOPMENT IN SOUTH ASIA

Leila Simona Talani, Alexander Clarkson and Ramon Pachedo Pardo (editors)
DIRTY CITIES
Towards a Political Economy of the Underground in Global Cities

Matthew Louis Bishop
THE POLITICAL ECONOMY OF CARIBBEAN DEVELOPMENT

Xiaoming Huang (editor)
MODERN ECONOMIC DEVELOPMENT IN JAPAN AND CHINA
Developmentalism, Capitalism and the World Economic System

Bonnie K. Campbell (editor)
MODES OF GOVERNANCE AND REVENUE FLOWS IN AFRICAN MINING

**International Political Economy Series**
**Series Standing Order ISBN 978–0–333–71708–0 Hardcover**
**Series Standing Order ISBN 978–0–333–71110–1 Paperback**

You can receive future titles in this series as they are published by placing a standing order. Please contact your bookseller or, in case of difficulty, write to us at the address below with your name and address, the title of the series and one of the ISBNs quoted above.

Customer Services Department, Macmillan Distribution Ltd, Houndmills, Basingstoke, Hampshire RG21 6XS, England

# Recipient States in Global Health Politics

## PEPFAR in Africa

Ricardo Pereira
*Scientific Officer, Foundation for Science and Technology, Portugal*

First published 2014 by
PALGRAVE MACMILLAN

Palgrave Macmillan in the UK is an imprint of Macmillan Publishers Limited, registered in England, company number 785998, of Houndmills, Basingstoke, Hampshire RG21 6XS.

Palgrave Macmillan in the US is a division of St Martin's Press LLC, 175 Fifth Avenue, New York, NY 10010.

Palgrave Macmillan is the global academic imprint of the above companies and has companies and representatives throughout the world.

Palgrave® and Macmillan® are registered trademarks in the United States, the United Kingdom, Europe and other countries

ISBN: 978–1–137–44296–3

This book is printed on paper suitable for recycling and made from fully managed and sustained forest sources. Logging, pulping and manufacturing processes are expected to conform to the environmental regulations of the country of origin.

A catalogue record for this book is available from the British Library.

A catalog record for this book is available from the Library of Congress.

*To my mother and father*

# Contents

| | | |
|---|---|---:|
| *Preface* | | viii |
| *Acknowledgements* | | ix |
| *List of Abbreviations and Acronyms* | | xi |
| 1 | Introduction: Agency in Global Health | 1 |
| 2 | Global Health Governance and Role of States | 15 |
| 3 | Recipient States in an Asymmetric System | 30 |
| 4 | International Developments of States in Africa | 47 |
| 5 | PEPFAR: Project of Global Transformation | 66 |
| 6 | Botswana: National Survival against HIV/AIDS | 92 |
| 7 | Ethiopia: Self-Help with External Support | 110 |
| 8 | South Africa: Changing HIV/AIDS Policies | 125 |
| 9 | Conclusion: Recipient States Being Sovereign | 142 |
| *Notes* | | 157 |
| *References* | | 161 |
| *Index* | | 179 |

# Preface

This book appears at a time of crucial renewal of global health agendas not just in the United States of America but also internationally. Considering the book's focus on US bilateral programmes, the US President's Emergency Plan for AIDS Relief (PEPFAR) was reauthorised for another five years in November 2013. Since 2003, PEPFAR has remained a decisive programme and remains a priority in US policy. At the same time, the countdown to 2015 precipitates discussions on the future of the United Nations Millennium Development Goals and the role countries around the globe are urged to play in the future. As Western countries flatten and reduce their aid budgets, developing countries, historical recipients of the former's assistance, encounter an enlarged array of actors with varying capabilities to partner with – in particular so-called emerging economies (China, India, Brazil). Despite the increasing literature on the relations between developing and emerging countries, in the specific area of global health intervention, the intensity and implication of 'emerging countries' in the developing world from a *comparative* point of view, that is, when compared to historical Western countries, remain to be assessed.

Ten years into its launch, PEPFAR is increasingly coming under scholarly scrutiny on generated results at the epidemiological and sociopolitical level. Is PEPFAR improving health indicators in comparative terms at the country and regional scale? How are data backing PEPFAR's upcoming commitments being produced and employed? Questions such as these are fundamental and demand an answer. This book looks at the political dynamics that the massive stream of programmes broadly nurtures from the recipient country's perspective. It is a contribution to an understanding of the interplay of global health politics, in general, and contextualised political practice of countries under intervention, and the agency they exert in that regard.

# Acknowledgements

The opportunity to publish this book presented itself during the proceedings of the 2011 International Studies Association Conference in Montreal, Canada. Having learnt about Professor Timothy Shaw's interest in including titles on global health governance for Palgrave Macmillan's series on International Political Economy, I explored the possibility of submitting a book proposal in that area at some point in the future. In 2013, Palgrave Macmillan editors Christina Brian and Ambra Finotello helped with setting the milestones for the project that unfolded. The role played by anonymous reviewers is equally crucial as the project was driven by their insightful comments and valuable suggestions.

I would like to acknowledge several persons and institutions for their direct and indirect contributions to the book project, as well as to the research that backs it. I would like to thank Professor Paula Elyseu Mesquita, Director of Foundation for Science and Technology, for her confidence in my abilities to write a book in the area of health-related science and technology coordination between Africa and Europe. I am grateful to my colleagues at the same institution with whom I have shared my anxieties and hopes while completing this book. I would also like to thank Professor Joana Pereira Leite and Professor Clara Carvalho, who gave me opportunities to deliver guest seminars on PEPFAR and global health governance at ISEG-University of Lisbon and ISCTE-University Institute of Lisbon in March and April 2013, respectively. These seminars provided a platform to discuss some of the central ideas examined in this book with students and researchers who were a part of the audience.

I would like to express my gratitude to Professor Paula Duarte Lopes, from the University of Coimbra – the institution which hosted my research. I am also thankful to the directors and colleagues at other institutions where the project was implemented, including the Health and Economics AIDS Research Division (HEARD), University of KwaZulu-Natal, South Africa; Centre for the Study of HIV and AIDS (CSHA), University of Botswana; Organization for Social Science Research in Eastern and Southern Africa (OSSREA), Addis Ababa, Ethiopia; and Department of Peace Studies, University of Bradford, United Kingdom. I would like to acknowledge the Foundation for Science and Technology which entirely funded my research.

Finally, I would like to express my gratitude to my parents, sister and grandmother for standing by me always.

# List of Abbreviations and Acronyms

| | |
|---|---|
| ABC | abstain, be faithful, condomise |
| ACHAP | African Comprehensive HIV/AIDS Partnership |
| AFRICOM | Africa Command |
| AGOA | African Growth and Opportunity Act (United States) |
| AIDS | Acquired Immunodeficiency Syndrome |
| ANC | African National Congress |
| ARV | antiretroviral |
| BDP | Botswana Democratic Party |
| BEE | Black Economic Empowerment |
| BRICS | Group of Brazil, Russia, India, China and South Africa |
| BSAC | British South Africa Company |
| CARE Act | Ryan White Comprehensive AIDS Resources Emergency Act |
| CDC | Centers for Disease Control and Prevention |
| CIA | Central Intelligence Agency (United States) |
| COP | country operational plan |
| CSIS | Center for Strategic and International Studies |
| CSO | civil society organisation |
| DoD | Department of Defense (United States) |
| EPRDF | Ethiopian People's Revolutionary Democratic Front |
| FBO | faith-based organisation |
| FDA | Food and Drug Administration (United States) |
| GAO | Government Accountability Office (United States) |
| GHI | Global Health Initiative (United States) |
| Global Fund | Global Fund to Fight AIDS, Tuberculosis and Malaria |
| HAPCO | Ethiopian HIV/AIDS Prevention and Control Office |
| HDI | Human Development Index |
| HIV | human immunodeficiency virus |
| HRW | Human Rights Watch |
| IHR | International Health Regulations |
| MCA | Millenium Challenge Account (United States) |
| MDGs | Millenium Development Goals (United Nations) |
| NAC | National Aids Council (Botswana) |
| NACA | National AIDS Coordinating Agency (Botswana) |

| | |
|---|---|
| NEPAD | New Partnership for Africa's Development |
| NGO | nongovernmental organisation |
| OVC | orphan and vulnerable children |
| PEPFAR | President's Emergency Plan for AIDS Relief |
| PPP | public-private partnership |
| SANAC | South African National AIDS Council |
| SAP | structural adjustment programme |
| SARS | severe acute respiratory syndrome |
| TAC | Treatment Action Campaign |
| TB | tuberculosis |
| TPLF | Tigray People's Liberation Front |
| UNAIDS | Joint United Nations Programme on HIV/AIDS |
| UNDP | United Nations Development Program |
| USAID | United States Agency for International Development |
| VCT | HIV/AIDS voluntary counselling and testing |
| WHO | World Health Organization |

# 1
# Introduction: Agency in Global Health

## Introduction

Traditionally, states – and the conflicts that have been associated with them in terms of military, economic and ideological expansion – have been the major topic of study in the discipline, as the classical literature by Edward H. Carr (1939), Hans Morgenthau (1948) or Kenneth Waltz (1979) shows. However, the emergence of research agendas diverging from a strict focus on the state have started to gain currency since the 1990s to the point where they are now challenging the relevance of the state as a major factor in international affairs.

Arguably this is a consequence of the rise of the human security policy paradigm with the publication of the first United Nations Human Development Report (1994). Defined as 'freedom from need' and 'freedom from want' it points to a whole range of phenomena that pose direct and indirect threats to the integrity of the individual and populations, such as hunger, disease, social disruption and violence. Born within the United Nations system it gradually spilt onto the foreign policy agendas of a number of governments in the late 1990s, particularly in Western Europe and so-called 'Middle Powers', as Canada or Japan (Behringer, 2005; Debiel and Werthes, 2006).

This policy shift took place parallel to socio-economic developments associated with the demise of the Soviet Union, the concomitant end of the Cold War bipolar confrontation and perceived hegemony of the United States of America. As a process of integration of markets, territories and populations at a worldwide scale, globalisation was exacerbated from the 1980s onwards thanks to increasingly sophisticated means of communication and information. The relevance of non-state actors in that process, namely private companies and nongovernmental organisations (NGOs), conglomerated around an idea of 'retreat of the state' and supremacy of 'social and economic forces' in terms of core objects of study. At the same time, ideological structures and forces such as liberalism and neoliberalism became increasingly at the heart of analysis rather than individual states (Cox, 1981). Certainly, states remained very important actors, yet not as sovereign policy-making entities as they used to be (Jessop, 2003). In a context of expanding mechanisms of social, political and economic organisation based on public-private partnerships, states are rendered the role of facilitators and mediators of an assemblage of public and private actors (Jessop, 2003).

As a result, the focus on human security, globalisation and social forces has resulted on the growing primacy of populations over states in terms of major actors of analysis. Eminently, population-related topics such as international development, migrations, epidemics, or human rights, became absolutely central in the day-to-day policy and analysis of international affairs. This character of the post-Cold War international world is exemplified by the realm of global health, in which this book's analysis is situated. Global health constitutes the space where manifold actors (states, international organisations, nongovernmental organisations, private companies, populations) and phenomena (for example, epidemics) interact according to their different conflicting agendas, which nevertheless are subject to no central government. Often the powerful actors correspond to funders of global health initiatives of different sorts, whereas the weak are generally the recipient of such initiatives. Still, the idea of population – its needs, duties and rights – lies at the core of global health debates, often hindering the issue of interstate asymmetry.

Prominence of populations is visible in the recent readings, mostly by critical authors across the social sciences, of the practice of development or human rights based on the frameworks of biopower and biopolitics (Foucault, 1978; 1984), which reflect precisely on the issue of the population, and the management that it is subjected by global social forces (Douzinas, 2007; Duffield, 2007; Jabri, 2007). These social forces have macro and micro dimensions that, altogether, demonstrate a transfused sovereign power among diverse units, as several works in anthropology have been suggesting in the area of development, health and HIV/AIDS (Escobar, 1984/1985; Ferguson, 1994; Nguyen, 2010). Sovereignty is not solely characteristic of state institutions, but of different actors, whose power 'to give life or impede it to the point of death' (Foucault, 1984) is absolutely crucial.

Some critical scholars of postcolonial theory inspiration (Richmond, 2010; Ginty, 2010; De Goede, 2010) have researched agency inside states, at the population level, as expressions of local resistance against a hegemonic liberal structure. Smaller, weaker states appear as plain facilitators of the hegemonic structure of major states and other institutions. Alternatively, those smaller, weaker states are rendered the category of 'rogue,' 'failed' and other assertions. Nevertheless, one finds this assertion troublesome, since it often suggests that states, including so-called 'weak states', typically from the developing world, are already embedded in that hegemonic structure. In fact, this book argues that, despite being highly constrained by the external structure, states are characterised by agency when behaving with other states, including smaller, weaker states when dealing with stronger ones. Even in a context of international asymmetry, states retain their ability to take decisions of their own and pursue strategies and policies autonomously, with a view to the accomplishment of national interests. As it is shown throughout the book, they are not necessarily 'hijacked' (Richmond, 2010) by the structural hegemonic powers in terms of policies and practices.

In fact, such reading of the post-Cold War liberal order is found wanting for the fact that it does not allow for a perspective of human agency in it (Chandler, 2009a). In this book, human agency is formulated in terms of a deliberative power of states as political communities, no matter how complex they might be domestically, to institute its own policy *vis-à-vis* the constraints that affect their action. Eventually, this invites a reassessment of current population-centred approaches and shifts analytical focus back to states, particularly states more prone to subordination to the international powers. For the purpose of this book, this comprises recipient states of global health programmes and their ability to exert their agency when dealing with their donors. To an extent, this implies revisiting some traditional tenets of international politics on interstate behaviour and how they respond to the problem of absence of agency.

## Method and framework of analysis

This book aims at demonstrating that recipient countries hold the capacity to autonomously define and purse their own strategies and policies, and ultimately attain political goals, even if highly constrained in their choices internationally. However, so this objective can be meaningful and to some extent successful, it requires a method of analysis that takes those smaller states as *normal* states in international relations. This means engaging seriously with the prolific, powerful literature enumerated above, but also to propose another analytical framework. This is one that combines some key tenets of International Relations theory, particularly the neorealist theory of Kenneth Waltz, yet with concern for both internal and external spheres of the states involved and social forces that affect them as well.

Concepts of agency and structure in International Relations were originally theorised by Kenneth Waltz (1979) in *Theory of International Relations*. States are the units in the international structure, and they hold agency when acting with other units. In that regard, they are sovereign; however, no matter how powerful the state, such sovereignty is constrained by the structure. Later authors in the same theoretical tradition as Waltz, that is, structural neorealism (Keohane, 1984; Mearsheimer, 2001), as well as in other traditions (Bickerton, 2007), have argued that from the 1980s onwards the structure has become the hegemony of the United States of America, allies in Western Europe, and Japan. However, just like there is no absolute sovereignty, there is no absolute hegemony either. This means that a country, no matter how weak it can be in economic and military terms, still enjoys a degree of agency, especially when behaving with powerful states. However, this understanding of agency needs to bear in mind the context of asymmetry between powerful, hegemonic states and weaker states. One needs to recognise weaker states' 'subalternity' (Ayoob, 2002). This asymmetry is primarily understood in function of the disparities of wealth and human development between regions, but also the origin of influential epistemologies and policies consubstantiating the actual relationship. In the particular case of postcolonial sub-Saharan African states in this book, the question of context is very crucial.

Moreover, one ought to connect both external and internal dimensions of states in order to understand their behaviour with powerful states, reversing the neorealist postulate that both spheres should remain detached (Rosenberg, 1990; 1994). States' actions need to be informed by their historical and sociological experience. Furthermore, despite their specificities associated with the European colonial project, states in sub-Saharan Africa are certainly part of the international system, and should be subject of analysis in the discipline like states anywhere else (Brown, 2006).

Therefore, weaker, smaller states act as *normal* states, that is, as units in the international system featured with agency, in which their behaviour in theory is not any different when compared to stronger states in the same system. In practice, even if subject to a large degree of subordination to strong states' policies, they are capable to autonomously identify their own policy issues, strategise against them and ultimately pursue political goals. In other words, they act in terms one could qualify as *rational*.

## Case study

The book's argument is explored in the realm of international development relations, specifically global health programmes, featured by intense donor-recipient exchange. Among the plethora of global health initiatives, the United States President's Emergency Plan for AIDS Relief (PEPFAR) stands out quite strongly. For one, it is an initiative which has enjoyed large-scale political and financial attention – arguably the largest bilateral programme aimed at a single disease ever. Furthermore, it has been driven by significant high-level political dialogue between the United States (US) administration and representatives in countries hosting projects, beyond plain HIV/AIDS relations. Indeed, PEPFAR is the product of different interrelated security and humanitarian concerns that emerged among the William 'Bill' Clinton administration (1993–2001), crystallised around the political elite led by George W. Bush (2001–2009) and continued under the current Barack Obama presidency (since 2009). It constitutes a striking example of United States foreign policy in the area of global health and development and diplomacy, in which asymmetric relations between the United States of America and countries under implementation stand out. Moreover, given its all-encompassing character in terms of types and quantity of organisations involved and sectors of activity approached, PEPFAR holds a cross-cutting impact on recipient countries' external, internal and local dimensions of governance.

Launched in 2003, PEPFAR was inserted in the context of the United States' 'War on Terror', and more broadly within the emerging nexus linking epidemics to security that came to the fore through several intelligence and think tank reports (National Intelligence Council, 2000; Gordon, 2002; Schneider and Moodie, 2002). The fear of an expanding global jihad exploiting social vulnerabilities provoked by AIDS in the worst-affected territories of Muslim majority or of Muslim 'large minorities', such as Nigeria, South Africa and Ethiopia, constitutes a serious motivation for action and scaling up the response (Lyman and Morrison, 2006). Yet, linkages to security precede, not only 11 September 2001 terrorist attacks, but also the very Bush administration (Pereira, 2009).

Nevertheless, preventing global jihads and local instability through HIV/AIDS implementation does not represent, as such, the sole justification for PEPFAR, which has allocated for its first phase (2004–2008) close to 15 billion US dollars. Other reasons were important too. First, there were domestic dynamics, that is, arguably the need faced by the Bush administration to respond to its pressuring Christian conservative constituency (the so-called Christian Right) vastly engaged in HIV/AIDS politics and broadly in development in the Third World (Dietrich, 2007). Second, in the latest period of his mandate, President Bush has arguably 'necessitated' to deposit a positive policy-making legacy *vis-à-vis* very low popularity levels at home and abroad (Feffer, 2008). Nevertheless, as United States Global AIDS Coordinator between 2006 and 2009, Mark Dybul (2009) aptly highlighted during the 2009 presidency's transitional period, the United States' reputation was very high across PEPFAR's focus countries and should be maintained.

Finally, philanthropy – often expressed as 'compassion' – has guided both fund allocation and implementation by a wide range of nongovernmental organisations across the 15 focus countries and a number of others where the United States Agency for International Development (USAID) carries out activities in the field too. Various respondents with United States government implementing agencies have emphasised this aspect.

PEPFAR constitutes the largest financial bilateral initiative to fight a single disease ever. Building on the experience of the Ryan White Comprehensive AIDS Resources Emergency Act of 1990, whose scope was the growing AIDS epidemic in the United States (Bowen et al., 1992), PEPFAR was established by the United States Leadership Against HIV/AIDS, Tuberculosis, and Malaria Act of 2003. Five years later, it was continued by the Tom Lantos and Henry J. Hyde United States Global Leadership Against HIV/AIDS, Tuberculosis, and Malaria Reauthorization Act of 2008, and currently functions under the framework of the PEPFAR Stewardship and Oversight Act of 2013. PEPFAR is managed by the Office of the United States Global AIDS Coordinator and gathers several implementing US government agencies: USAID, Peace Corps, and Departments of State, Defence, Trade, Labour, and Health and Human Resources.

Channelled through United States government agencies (primarily USAID) and diplomatic missions, PEPFAR has virtually reached the vast majority of countries where USAID is present. However, in the beginning, it focused on 15 countries which accounted for half of the global number of infections by HIV, according to the Joint United Nations Programme on HIV/AIDS (UNAIDS), most of them in Southern and Eastern Africa.[1] Irrespective of the particularities associated with the individual countries, all were generally presented by Dybul (2009) as the 'future' of United States-led global order.

According to the Government Accountability Office (GAO) (2008: 10), budgetary allocations for the 2004–2008 five-year period had mostly been oriented towards antiretroviral (ARV)-based treatment (55 per cent), the rest being dedicated to palliative care (15 per cent), prevention (20 per cent) and orphans and vulnerable children (10 per cent). For most of its first phase, PEPFAR treatment funding, rather than contracting preferably less expensive, generic ARVs (and thus expanding scale-up efforts), was oriented for the purchase of US 'Big Pharma' branded ARVs, comparatively more expensive (Thompson, 2007). As such, PEPFAR worked as a governmental protectionist scheme for US pharmaceutical companies to enter African markets, despite the reported inclusion over time of generic drugs in PEPFAR-funded programmes.

It is important to underscore that, as a public-private partnership, host countries' institutions are equally very relevant. As any annual report to the United States Congress demonstrates, 'partnership' has been a buzzword in the process of PEPFAR (2011a). PEPFAR policy documents have always been very keen in terms of 'horizontalising' relations, showing that, in these difficult times of AIDS, the United States government and proud NGOs stand together with the world's least advantaged populations. Illustratively, photographs line side by side President Bush or a United States ambassador with their counterparts or 'civil society members', especially children and young people. In turn, the flag of the United States of America stands side by side with the host country's flag. However, despite this rhetoric of horizontal relations, it becomes clear that the United States government maintains the material hegemony over the partnership, the host governments, and nongovernmental organisations, remaining the weakest link in it.

Over the years, PEPFAR has advanced different models of partnership. However, the year 2009 witnessed the consolidation of a concept of partnership that has featured relations between the United States global AIDS coordination and its numerous stakeholders around the world. 'Partnership compact' gives meaning to the proposals of partnership that have been offered ever since to governments of affected countries. After several years under emergency mode, the 2009 annual report to the United States Congress launches the concept of 'partnership compact':

> To build on the success the American people's partnerships have achieved to date and reflect the paradigm shift to an ethic of mutual partnership, the USG [United States Government] is working with host countries to develop Partnership Compacts: agreements that engage governments, civil society, and the private sector to address the issues of HIV/AIDS. The goal of Compacts is to advance the progress and leadership of host nations in the fight against HIV/AIDS, with a view toward enhancing country ownership of their programs. ... PEPFAR

will continue to be part of this new era of development that champions friendship and respect, mutual understanding and accountability – and trusts in the people on the ground to do the work. (PEPFAR, 2009a: 58)

This piece is historically decisive as it marks transition towards PEPFAR's second phase (2009–2013) and launches five-year, co-joint, strategic partnership frameworks between the Unites States Global AIDS Office and its programmes' host countries. Such frameworks are to fulfil principles of country ownership, flexibility, transparency, accountability, and the active participation of other key partners from civil society, the private sector, other bilateral and multilateral partners, and international organisations, and should support and strengthen national HIV/AIDS strategies. This includes support to the Global Fund to Fight AIDS, Malaria and Tuberculosis and UNAIDS. Yet, PEPFAR is also articulated with the African Growth and Opportunity Act of 2000. According to its 2008 report, such trade-related initiative 'has helped African firms become more competitive internationally, thereby bolstering sub-Saharan African economic growth and helping to alleviate poverty in one of the poorest regions of the world' (Office of the United States Trade Representative, 2008: 7). In this regard, PEPFAR is made part of a larger effort of reducing poverty and enhancing economic chances for Africans, while trying to enlarge a consuming market for US products as well.

With the Obama administration, the major novelty has been the Global Health Initiative, which aims at harmonising the different global health programmes, such as PEPFAR and the President's Malaria Initiative, and incorporating other epidemics with a focus on health systems and gender in eight focus countries (Office of the United States President's Spokesman, 2010).[2] In a context of budgetary constraints, the administration has decreased the pace of funding to the global health programmes, including PEPFAR. This is a phase of shifting the emergency mode towards sustainability and country ownership, in which host countries are increasingly encouraged to engage in the leadership and finance of United States-initiated projects.

This book looks specifically at the experience of PEPFAR's implementation in three countries in sub-Saharan Africa with 'focus country' status during the emergency phase. Aside from this fact, they were primarily selected for being representative of different strategic rationales regarding security, development and overall political and economic reform. On the one hand, Botswana's relevance is explained by the fact that it is considered a 'success story' of African development in

US foreign policy. In the latest decades, Botswana's governments are considered exemplary for their commitment to economic growth, good governance, stability and liberal institutions. Eventually, the country is put forward as a 'model' that the rest of the continent should emulate and aspire to. In a context of persistent conflict and underdevelopment across the continent, Botswana is diplomatically presented as the country everyone should strive for. Consensually, available literature presents this country as a major case of successful and peaceful postcolonial national development under a liberal framework based on partnership between the state and private interests (Mbabazi et al., 2002: 38–39; Mogae, 2006). Such success is much enhanced when this country is compared with other sub-Saharan countries, mostly those whose economies rely on mineral resources. The example of HIV/AIDS further centralises that aspect, as the national government has been generally commended for its committed and 'country-owned' (Whitfield and Maipose, 2008) response to advice on the social and economic impact of the epidemic (Osei-Hwedie, 2001; Bar-On, 2002; Noorbaksh, 2008; Gossett, 2010). In fact, the country has been severely affected by the epidemic, as the estimated number of people living with the disease is 340,000 (UNAIDS, 2013: 123), that is, 16 per cent of the total population (WHO, 2013: 156). On the other hand, Ethiopia and South Africa were chosen for their status as 'anchors' of strategic policy of the United States of America, in their corresponding regions, Horn of Africa and Southern Africa, and the African continent as a whole (Jefferson, 2006). As the United States Africa Command (AFRICOM) is launched with the aim of stabilising the continent in more diplomatic and humanitarian forms (Esquire, 2008), they reflect a harder version of power politics embedded in United States foreign policy. As far as Ethiopia goes, its regional location has been featured by manifold threats such as state failure, epidemics, Islamic extremism, refugee movements and armed conflicts. In a context of complex relations between the United States of America and the countries in the Horn of Africa, Ethiopia emerges as the main United States local ally in the effort of stabilisation inside Ethiopia and around the region (Somalia, Northern Kenya, Eritrea and South Sudan) (Lyons, 2006). Forty-five to 50 per cent of the Ethiopian population is Muslim (Permanent Mission, 2007), and therefore it is deemed worrisome. Concerning HIV/AIDS, although the estimate percentage of people living with AIDS is quite small in the face of the total population – not even one per cent (WHO, 2013: 158) – the absolute figure is still prominent: 760,000 (UNAIDS, 2013: 123). With regard to South Africa, the large size of the HIV/AIDS epidemic – 6.1 million people living with the disease (UNAIDS, 2013: 124) – poses itself security concerns from a United States foreign policy perspective. Most studies relating AIDS and security in South Africa (and Southern Africa in general) reflect upon impact in the military structures (Heinecken, 2003; Rupiya, 2006), war (Cheek, 2001), urban juvenile criminality (Schönteich, 1999) and recruitment of youths for extremist activity against Western interests (Lyman and Morrison, 2006: 56–57). Even though deeply integrated in the global capitalist economy and characterised by the rule of liberal political institutions and a vibrant civil society sector, the specificity of domestic dynamics on urban insecurity, violence, social exclusion, and increasing inequalities, often mirrored by the experience of HIV/AIDS, demands careful attention from a security perspective.

Independent of the constructions of US policy around interests associated to Botswana, Ethiopia and South Africa, the comparative analysis of PEPFAR's implementation in the three countries over the years seeks to explain that the motivations driving individual action are quite singular. Nonetheless, they share the commonality of displaying underlying political goals and strategies aimed at clear policy problems. Eighty-five semi-structured interviews with representatives of PEPFAR-implementing organisations – US and host countries' governments and NGOs – and third parties constitute fundamental vehicles of information that gave shape to the analysis and ensuing conclusions. They were carried out at a crucial juncture for PEPFAR's implementation, that is, from September 2009 through November 2010, as it was transiting from first phase (emergency) to second phase (sustainability and country ownership).[3] Additionally, other usual sources provided crucial elements: academic literature, policy documents (PEPFAR; US government as a whole; and Botswanan, Ethiopian and South African governments), and media reporting on PEPFAR and the governments of all countries involved.

## Chapter's roadmap

Taking the case of the implementation of major global health programme PEPFAR in three relevant loci (Botswana, Ethiopia and South Africa), this chapter has put forward the argument that recipient states hold a proactive behaviour with view of attaining national interests that stretch beyond the scope of those programmes. Accordingly, recipient states are not mere facilitators of major states' agendas and policies, yet active, autonomous entities that pursue their own strategies, policies and political goals. Despite Western hegemony, they have a life of their own, and in this regard they are as 'normal' and 'rational' as any state. This argument is situated within the current discussions on the role smaller, weaker states are supposed to play in the context of Western hegemony and increasing centrality of populations in international analysis, and the consequences to the research of agency in international relations.

Chapter 2 investigates the context upon which the analysis the recipient states' behaviour is analysed: global health relations. It reviews the leading narratives that consolidated this field of international relations, as they impact on the terms of analysis of broader relations between the United States government through PEPFAR and the national governments of the countries where PEPFAR has been implemented. It starts off by introducing the idea of contemporary global health intervention as a function of the emergence of the human security, population-centred paradigm of the international community in the post-Cold War. Then, it looks more specifically at the dimension of social change inside the West in the last three decades under the influence of the sociology of risk; David Fidler's liberal-institutional approach to global health governance based on the centrality of the World Health Organisation's (WHO) International Health Regulations' (IHR) revision of 2005; and the post-Foucauldian explanation of liberal power transmitted by medical intervention inside and outside the West. Building on the idea that there is no government for global health relations, this chapter appraises the question of states in this domain of action, with a particular concern for recipient, weaker states in the international system faced with the facilitator/rogue duality.

Chapter 3 elaborates further the proposition of the book of putting forward an alternative analytical lens to assess recipient states' behaviour in international relations in general and global health governance in particular. It discusses in detail two bodies of scholars: on the one hand, the so-called 'Africanist critique of International Relations' that questions the viability of a state-based framework for the study of African politics; on the other hand, critical authors who have argued along the lines of a West-led hegemonic international structure in which agency is absent at the level of interstate relations. This chapter adopts an analytical lens which takes back original concepts developed by classical, neorealist author Kenneth Waltz, yet incorporates a notion of asymmetry in the international system, complemented by a historical-sociological approach to interstate relations, in which the state is regarded as a social relation. Recipient states are indeed *normal, rational* agents that have policy dilemmas, devise strategies and aim at political goals, and that is not nullified by the subordination to heavy external programmes.

Once the imperative of adopting a historical-sociological approach to the study of international relations is accepted, it is important to investigate the trajectory of Botswana, Ethiopia and South Africa, since it helps understanding individual behaviour to the implementation of PEPFAR. Chapter 4 begins by discussing the character of the postcolonial settlement between the newly African state and the former colonising powers, followed by the period of the 1980s and 1990s. Despite the powerful influence of the neoliberalising structural adjustment programmes of the time, African states sought to preserve autonomy through their survivalist modes in very adverse circumstances. The first decade of the 21st century witnesses the renewal of a purportedly active state setting out to attain different agendas, according to individual country's choices and old and new issues that they face, including social/human development and health-related ones. Yet, it should be remarked that this latter period has witnessed in the African scene an emergence of new and powerful actors, apart from Western governments and organisations.

Chapter 5 dives into the process of construction of the global health programme that serves as a case study for this book: PEPFAR. It presents the origins, political rationales, key policies and organisational design that PEPFAR has undergone since its establishment in 2003. The purpose of most parts of this chapter is to describe those manifold aspects, so PEPFAR's ambition to act as a powerful influence among individuals, communities and countries where supported projects are implanted is demonstrated. This stretches from domestic preparedness – in terms of both constituencies and organisation of state institutions ('whole-of-government' approach) – down to actual models of incorporating external organisations, especially those based in the host countries. This division of labour is especially immanent of PEPFAR's 2003–2009 phase. Nevertheless, it is also careful about the prospects of generating ownership of projects among host countries that features the second phase (2009–2013) and largely drives the analysis of the responsiveness of Botswana, Ethiopia and South Africa to PEPFAR.

Chapters 6, 7 and 8 investigate not only *how* the three PEPFAR host countries at stake in this book have been experiencing that global health programme but for *what purpose* they have accepted to participate, or even looked for it. This means that the approach to the individual cases has to expand beyond strict HIV/AIDS issues, including broader historical (proceeding from the fourth chapter), governance and political concerns. As such, it applies an understanding in which these three countries, though recipient and subordinate to an external programme, act as normal and rational states towards the strategic achievement of political goals in the face of policy issues of their own. As it will be seen, the direct implication of PEPFAR in that logic of behaviour varies according to the importance that the overall HIV/AIDS epidemic constitutes for the governments of those recipient countries.

The chapter on Botswana demonstrates that the country's acceptance and involvement in a major programme such as PEPFAR is directly linked to a concern for population's survival by the national government in light of the tremendous prevalence of HIV/AIDS. Extensive interviews validate the idea that the Botswana government has sought to own the external programme through an encompassing government-led response to the epidemic and its consequences. The capacity to guide and fund the national programme is based on the state developmentalism of the post-independence era, in turn fed by the impressive economic growth experienced by the country in the last couple of decades. However, it is precisely because of the prospects of developmental collapse that Botswana's government is very keen to decidedly act on this matter.

In turn, Ethiopian government's interest in PEPFAR has primarily to do with a broader geopolitical and developmental vision, in which the HIV/AIDS epidemic plays a role among other social pressing issues. In a context of very low human development and contestation to the Ethiopian federal regime and the Ethiopian People's Revolutionary Democratic Front (EPRDF)-led governments, intervening socially, including in HIV/AIDS through PEPFAR, contributes to the endurance of the political regime. This process is characterised by contradictions, in which it is also in the interest of the United States government, in light of the broader political situation in the Horn of Africa, to help with the consolidation of that regime. As such, HIV/AIDS cannot be regarded as a striking problem on its own terms in Ethiopia from a comparative perspective; however, it is a catalyser for strategic relations between both countries.

At last, in South Africa the politics of the HIV/AIDS epidemic has contributed to the policy of transmitting ideas and values domestically and abroad by the governmental leadership since the Mbeki administration till today. Whereas the immediate post-apartheid government under Nelson Mandela opted out of engaging with the then-emergent epidemic in the name of social pacification, the following administrations were increasingly forced to do it. The launch and implementation of PEPFAR has undergone two phases – Mbeki and Zuma – that reflect the domestic tensions and changes that affected the realm of HIV/AIDS intervention in that country, both in terms of questioning and complying with leading international regimes of intervening in HIV/AIDS. As contradictory as it might seem for many observers in the West, particularly in Mbeki's phase, pursuit of international prestige – in 'Black Africa' to begin with – has been a driver of South African behaviour.

The concluding chapter is divided into three parts. Firstly, as a result of the analysis carried out, it puts forward a comparative discussion of the three cases. In the face of a common global health programme, individual countries behave differently yet with autonomy and aiming broader political goals in which the HIV/AIDS epidemic plays a more or less defining role. Secondly, it initiates a discussion on theoretical consequences for further investigation of national agency beyond strict programming in the area of health and development. Thirdly, it connects to the practice of health and development today, particularly what country ownership represents from the perspective of traditional, recipient, host states, as well as those countries' role in the provision of 'global public goods' such as HIV/AIDS-related treatments.

# 2
# Global Health Governance and Role of States

## Introduction

This chapter discusses the realm within which PEPFAR is implemented and recipient states play a role, that is, global health. The engagement to be pursued throughout this chapter departs from an exercise of reflection on the leading narratives on this topic by scholars, activists and policy makers. In this regard, context is very crucial: global health was elaborated in parallel with the emergence of human security as a paradigm of Western foreign policy for the post-Cold War, and this has held consequences in terms of the 'securitisation' of health-related issues. This intertwines with dimensions of social change inside the West in the last three decades under the influence of the sociology of risk, yet also juridical-institutional changes at the level of the World Health Organisation's (WHO) International Health Regulations (IHR), which underwent revision in 2005. Nonetheless, the governance of global health remains faulty, as the plethora of national and international, public and private entities involved in global health are subject to no kind of world government. Global health governance's incoherent status ultimately invites the appraisal of the role of traditional actors – states – in this domain, including weaker, smaller ones.

These narratives frame the analysis of global health and hold an impact on the terms of analysis of broader relations between the United States government through PEPFAR and the national governments of the countries where PEPFAR has been implemented. By looking at and discussing these narratives one aims at a more critical understanding of the role PEPFAR recipient states are meant to play.

## Human security and the construction of global health

The realm of health affairs outside the domain of individual states is traditionally denominated as international health. Since 1948, with the establishment of WHO, it remained mostly confined to its inter-state framework and its IHR created in 1969. Another landmark was the signature in 1989 of the WHO's 'Health for All Declaration', also known as the Alma-Ata Declaration, in which member states committed to the attainment of the best health conditions to their populations. However, it also featured in development aid to the Third World and military agendas during the Cold War. Nevertheless, in retrospect, David Fidler (2005: 180) argues this was a field of 'low politics' compared to

larism that neorealist theories of International Relations prominently explained and reinforced.

The end of the Cold War in the late 1980s to early 1990s brought about foreign and security policy consequences that started to be conceptual-ised in another way, including in the domain of international health. One consequence was the rise of an understanding of security based on individuals and population groups rather than on states. Human secu-rity is the 'paradigm' that growingly started to be laid down onto the nascent European defence and foreign security policies and the Middle Powers Initiative, for instance. It derived from the intellectual labour that urged for attention to forms of violence and insecurity beyond the formal interstate warfare. It was also very influential among the United Nations system in conflict prevention, peacekeeping and post-conflict reconstruction missions. It was so defined by the United Nations Development Program (UNDP):

> Human security can be said to have two main aspects. It means, first, safety from such chronic diseases as hunger, disease and repression. And second, it means protection from sudden and hurtful disrup-tions in the patterns of daily life – whether in homes, in jobs or in communities. (UNDP, 1994: 23)

As a result, human-related phenomena such as epidemics, migration, trafficking in drugs or environmental damage began to be conceptual-ised as threats to stability inside countries, regions and even the world, in a context in which state confrontation was growingly understood as obsolete. So-called 'new threats' like those are far more disruptive and killing than wars between armies, and hold indirect consequences for the whole of the international community. As far as epidemics go, they deteriorate many populations' living standards in developing countries, particularly in Africa, and thus contribute to the damage caused by phenomena such as civil wars (Kaldor, 1999) and 'failed states' (Zartman, 1995), that is, states 'unable or unwilling' to offer the residents basic public goods such as food, access to health or public security. Human security appeared together with familiar agendas for the post-Cold War such as human rights, democratisation, the rule of law, and the market that, once implemented, could reduce instability and conflict in general. In addition to that, viruses emerge as threatening in terms of the globalisation of trade and travel at a larger geographical scale, particularly in the context of outbreaks.

As a result, while traditionally states attracted analytical focus, in the last ten years, entities such as viruses, and the diseases and epidemics that they provoke, were growingly elaborated as threats to security. Indeed, pathogenic agents only constitute threats to humans when they first infiltrate human ecology and afterwards penetrate and develop themselves within the human body. Viruses as such do not pose any threat. What is actually convertible to a threat status are peoples, societies and, in the last analysis, states, as part of a complex social and political impact that the multiplication of infected people feeds and arguably provokes in a context of fast global relations (Elbe, 2003; Ban, 2003; Brower, 2003; Saker et al., 2004; Owen and Roberts, 2005; McInnes and Lee, 2006). If one perceives detection, prevention, care and eventual cure of populations as the major measures against disease, one defines as security objective the contention of the multiplication of the number of people carrying the agent, despite the ethical problems it may entail (Elbe, 2006). The linking of viruses to security is consummated in the depiction of 'securitised people' as those 'at risk', 'vulnerable' and making up 'dangerous classes' (Hardt and Negri, 2004). In other words, they are a reflection of the epidemiological estimates on the several diseases, yet, particularly, the major epidemics. In the case of HIV/AIDS, in Southern and Eastern Africa they are the general population, while in China, India, Russia and the West, they are drug injectors, migrants, homosexuals and the general mass of the marginalised ones. Eventually, they led to the almost blurring of traditionally separate disciplinary fields such as International Relations and Public Health.

Together with an exercise of social constructivism, liberal-institutionalist approaches gained prominence in the analysis and policy recommendation of international/global mechanisms of response to the manifold viral and epidemic manifestations. The 'securitisation' of health and disease was embedded institutionally under the revised International Health Regulations of 2005, and is found in the rhetoric and rationale of multilateral and bilateral initiatives, such as the Global Fund, established in 2001, or PEPFAR, launched in 2003.

## Western risk society and the politics of technicalisation

Global health is eminently a Western invention with the aim of making sense of globalisation and a new paradigm of human security-based foreign policy. As remarked, the problems of health and disease were already subject to international discussion and resolution. However, the West-led hegemony of globalisation in terms of worldwide socio-economic relations fuelled by technological advances in information and communication created a landscape in which those problems, among other human/ population-related ones (migrations, environmental degradation, scarcity of energy resources, urban insecurity), were bound to have direct and indirect security consequences for the Western world and its lifestyle. In other words, 'threats' like those were undermining of what Anthony Giddens has called 'ontological security' (Giddens, 1990), building on the notion of 'risk society' (Beck, 1992) as a latest stage of Western modernity, in which, after wealth and power, risk and impotence emerge (Beck, 1995). Although in the industrial age, there was already a notion of risk, it was considered a price to pay for the material progress of societies through social protection systems and other compensatory mechanisms. Accordingly, Western societies do not aim at maximising risks, yet minimising them through the implementation of emergency measures against increasingly incontrollable risks, such as nuclear proliferation, global warming or even large-scale pandemics. For Beck (2006), the best response is 'precaution through prevention'.

This sociological reading has proved to be very influential in the way responses to epidemics and viral outbreaks started to be conceptualised by political analysts and policy makers of global health. Along with human security policies, the inevitability of the occurrence of direct and indirect effects at a global scale has led to a very large epistemological consensus around the definition of preventive and curative measures aimed at the sources of those risks. As a result, global health governance has become, in the words of James Ferguson (1994), an 'anti-politics machine'. Global health governance became an eminent 'technical' field, in which what largely is at stake is the formulation and implementation of 'good' policies, informed by 'good practices', and accompanied with disbursement and allocation of resources to projects serving those in need. In the case of the major epidemics (HIV/AIDS, tuberculosis and malaria), this is observed in the manner biomedical responses attained supremacy, although preventive measures were also clearly emphasised. Rather than an implication of the political communities, as it used to happen during the Cold War, global health governance bypasses political contingencies and aims at 'fixing' the 'issues'.

## Global health governance's constitutionalism

A major feature of the post-Cold War international environment, namely in the area of health and disease, is the dissemination of governmental alongside nongovernmental actors. Apart from states and WHO, international organisations such as the United Nations constellation and the World Bank joined in, followed by many old and new large developmental and humanitarian NGOs, philanthropic organisations and initiatives and private companies, such as pharmaceutical companies. Often many of these entities have sat together under the aegis of public-private partnerships, a model of governance that got boosted in the context of post-Cold War acceleration of neoliberal reforms led by the major Western states, the World Bank and the International Monetary Fund, as described in the previous chapter. In the domain of global health, two major examples of PPP are the multilateral Global Fund and the bilateral PEPFAR. After a previous phase of being rendered to 'low politics', influential David Fidler observes this change of landscape, in which health and disease concerns attain centrality in the foreign policy of major states and generate many actors and agendas, as a 'revolution' (Fidler, 2008).

However, for Fidler (2004) it was not until 11 September 2001 attacks in the United States of America, the so-called case of 'Amerithrax' soon after 11 September 2011 and the outbreaks of severe acute respiratory syndrome (SARS) in 2003 that global health governance's 'constitutionalism' was reconfigured. Eventually, the WHO's IHR were revised and incorporated with an element of security in it. From a juridical-institutional point of view (Pereira, 2008), Fidler understands the role of WHO and its IHR as the key contents of international health's constitutionalism, whose historiography, obviously, stretches way back in time. It kicked off in the 1830s, as the first international hygienist conference took place in search of a response to a cholera epidemic affecting Europe at the time. Afterwards, other international conferences alike occurred throughout the 19th and early 20th centuries. Finally, they paved the way for the League of Nations' Office of Health Affairs and

WHO. Founded in 1948, WHO has gained reputation for inculcating an international cooperation regime based on the 1969 IHR, consolidating what Fidler (1999) has called *Microbialpolitik*, that is, an international agenda fundamentally guided by allied fight against disease. In Fidler's view, the 2001–2003 events above and their corresponding structuring responses of contingency constitute a turning point in the understanding of epidemics as object of national and international security. This period inaugurates 'the new world order in public health', in which global health governance likens the United States federal model in the context of crisis in health at the global scale. The functions of that model are: provision of national security; regulation of international trade; preparedness support and response to epidemic crisis; and protection of human rights (Fidler, 2004). Broadly, such 'new order' reiterates the post-9/11 counterterrorist response, in which all areas of governance in the United States were merged towards a more efficient and engaged reaction. However, this shift is still troublesome. The 2005 revision of the IHR diverted WHO away from its mandate, since it may be specifically serving national and international policies.

> Less clear is whether the new IHR might embroil WHO in the politics of national and international security to the detriment of its core public health functions. Although it makes some experts uncomfortable, the potential for terrorism involving weapons of mass destruction connects public health to security concerns. (Fidler and Gostin, 2006: 92)

The 2005 IHR revision calls for the necessity to establish partnerships with other 'interested' sectors, notably the armed forces. At the same time, the new IHR allows the possibility of 'containment at the source', beyond the typical border controls for people and goods (WHO, 2007). Such situation allows foreign interventions to be triggered regardless of state sovereignty, namely with military means, for the sake of epidemic contention. In sum, these novelties reflect a real change in the purposes of the IHR.

Fidler's juridical-institutional explanation has been complemented by a more radical approach in terms of whom and what constitutes the governance of global health. This approach implies that a plethora of other defining actors, such as private companies, nongovernmental organisations, networks and partnerships and even Hollywood 'celebrities' (Drezner, 2007), needs to be inserted together with the traditional actors. Like major states and WHO, those agents maintain intense power agendas and regulating capacities, particularly under a framework which jeopardises national sovereignty given the possibility of 'containment at the source', as presupposed in the 2005 IHR. Moreover, since Fidler's constitutionalism seems to overestimate the role of epidemic crisis and response as contextual facts, that is, the outbreak event and the demanded quarantine measure, a complementing approach that embodies structural elements in the machinery of public health, such as surveillance and hygiene mechanisms administered by national and international agents, is required.

An historical analysis of disease surveillance stretches back to the 17th century, as epidemic surveillance departs nationally in metropolitan Europe, and increasingly expands onto the colonies. This regime is consolidated with the international hygienist arrangements of the 1830s (Bashford, 2006). As a result, it has helped to consolidate a system of security that one recognises today. Michel Foucault's (1984) work on the analytics of liberal political power from the 17th century onwards has been found highly helpful in this regard. Rather than simply deposited on domestic and international institutions of statehood, power permeates an insidious, comprehensive web of institutions and practices, governmental and nongovernmental, local and international, yet commonly affiliated to ideals of liberalism and free trade. Unlike in earlier absolutist regimes, power is conceived to both foster life and impede it to the point of death. The object of such power consists on human beings at the aggregate level, as well as life in general. Designated as 'biopower', it expresses the 18th century scientific effort of measuring and regulating all dimensions of life, such as birth, mortality, schooling, employment, criminality, and so on. This change has implied thinking the human being as an *être biologique*, a natural species, yet with political life and power. Biopower is therefore 'totalitarian' in the way that it is aimed at the totality of the population. Issues of health and disease become particularly pertinent in this framework of analysis of power.

Contrary to previous absolutist regimes, biopower, or biopolitics as it was later reformulated, necessitates to be rationalised and justified (Foucault, 1984: 258), and Foucault's later concept of governmentality embodies that necessity. It accounts for a discursive-material device (*dispositif*) of security embodying rationalities and technologies of government. They comprise 'discourses, institutions, architectural forms, regulatory decisions, laws, administrative measures, scientific statements, philosophical, moral and philanthropic propositions' (Foucault, 1980: 184). These technologies do not necessarily use violence to force people to do what the sovereign likes (Lemke, 2001). A major manifestation of the sovereign power's governmentality is found in the figure of the 'medical police' (Carroll, 2002). In fact, governmentality as rationalities and technologies of government largely corresponds to a general idea of police activity: 'practices of inspection and surveillance, information and intelligence gathering, and direct intervention (to the point of deadly force) in private, familial and commercial matters' (Carroll, 2002: 465). The medical police did not resort to deadly force; yet it pursued a variety of sanitary techniques in order to guarantee 'health and safety' among the population from now onwards (Carroll, 2002: 465).

A number of historical examples from the British Empire demonstrate the century-old political importance of medical intervention at a global scale. Alison Bashford (1999) has looked at the 1881 smallpox epidemic in Sydney, Australia, as an illustration of the more administrative facet of such medical policing through the establishment of the local health authority, that is, the Board of Health in the British Colony of New South Wales. Although smallpox epidemics were not 'uncommon' in the 19th century, that one precipitated key bureaucratic changes. Policing was primarily about carrying out activities animated by socio-political concerns rather than exhibiting state presence. Thus, one should mention the police role that charities pursued, as Carroll (2002) shows in the case of colonial Dublin, Ireland, hygienic activities in the 18th century. The ultimate function of health policing was to potentiate the general health status of the populations, not just for the sake of political economy but also to prevent scarring contagions and epidemics that could undermine the body politic. Bashford (2006) reports that, in function of the establishment of border epidemical check-ups and quarantine systems, surveillance mechanisms were installed at the global scale uniting metropolises and colonies. National surveillance and hygienist measures moved beyond from the national sphere on to the rest of the world, cementing Western power territorially and biologically, as the 1881 smallpox epidemic in Sydney above illustrated. As mentioned, a cholera epidemic affecting the European powers in the 1830s paved the way for the several international hygienist conferences during the 1800s that led to the establishment of the international sanitary institutions in the two world wars' interval.

Yet, in that period, health issues were essentially taken as technical matters by the League of Nations' Health Office, a predecessor of WHO. According to Bashford, its mission was to collect information from the national administrations, in order to control diseases such as malaria, smallpox and sleeping sickness, in close collaboration with the Economics Office of the organisation. General population-related dossiers tended to be studied in their migratory and trade dimensions, excluding issues such as birth control and sexual and reproductive health. The author provides several examples on how, despite direct enquiry, those latter matters were untouched by the League of Nations under the basis of not being part of the organisation's mandate.

An important role in the systems of information on populations between colonies and metropolises was played by the educational transnational institutions of tropical medicine of the British Empire. Founded in the late 19th century, the schools of tropical medicine in London and Liverpool were instrumental in the research and dissemination of epidemiological facts and practices at the field level. Supported by organisations such as the Rockefeller Foundation, the Red Cross, the business community of Liverpool (with vested interests in the Caribbean, West Africa and Latin America), the schools' agendas ranged 'from the medical concerns of a fading Empire to a national and international school of public health, moving towards integration of domestic and global health concerns' (Wilkinson and Power, 1998: 288). Tropical medicine as a distinctive discipline in the curricula of medical studies was born with the objective of facilitating the settlement of Britons and other Europeans in threatening environments characterised by pests such as smallpox, malaria or yellow fever (Arnold, 1997). But it also held the mission of improving the lives of natives engaged in the colonial businesses, therefore pursuing the 'benevolent' task assigned to imperialism. Nevertheless, Cameron-Smith identifies tropical medicine across the British Empire 'as a discourse that constructed the space of the tropics as Other and thus as racially pathological' (Cameron-Smith, 2007: 16). In turn, Jama Mohamed (1999) shows how colonial rule on medicine in Somaliland during the first half of the 20th century benefited from health interventions, vaccination namely, as it improved public health. The medical mission was therefore to '[popularise] the Government, and [to identify] the administration with the people's welfare' (Mohamed, 1999).

The integration of tropical medicine's culture and history when linked to the rise of 'medical police' is particularly illustrative of both the character of this early securitisation of infectious diseases and the apparatus of biopolitical instrumentalisation at the global level. Beyond international and national political institutions, culture, science and medical practice informatively contribute to the historical power regime. In more recent times, hygienism remained notably instrumental with regard to the implementation of powerful white-supremacist regimes such as the one South Africa experienced during the apartheid period

(Youde, 2005). According to Youde, the legacy of public health inter-vention as historically anti-black population transpires from the 2000 conflict between South African government, notably President Thabo Mbeki, and the international AIDS community. Mbeki claimed that the international community's AIDS discourse was a Western neocolonialist discourse expressing Africans' inferiority as a race to tackle their own problems (Youde, 2005). This episode was particularly dramatic since South Africa was holding, as it still does, the highest rate of HIV infections in the world.

The conceptualisation started by Foucault on liberal power – as driven by political-economic ideology and not institutions – leads to an image of an assemblage of various entities. '*Nébuleuse*' is an apt alternative word to assemblage that one borrows from Robert W. Cox (2005) to model the 'constitutionalism' in global (health) governance, contrasting with Fidler's adoption of the United States federal model. The end of the Cold War and the rise of global neoliberal agendas performed by an enlarged quantity of institutions in many different sectors of activity (trade, development, humanitarian, and so on) and at different scales (local, national, regional, global) confirmed the reformulation of the state as sovereign political unit and accelerated the networking of biopolitical-like modes of power. This '*nébuleuse*' builds on strong political density, where many networks of governmental and nongovernmental agents interact formally and informally at a global level. Global public health constitutes a quite solid domain for the analysis of those phenomena and the power relations they embody. They feature grand public-pri-vate, bilateral and multilateral funding, managing and implementing programmes, initiatives and entities: WHO, PEPFAR, Global Fund, World Bank, UNAIDS, Clinton Initiative, Bill and Melinda Gates Foundation, and a vast range of international NGOs in the field. Once inserted in the broader global governance, the health system as a regime of global surveillance consolidates the supremacy of an international arena domi-nated, not by anarchical relations of individual units of sovereignty in the form of states, as put by the neorealist tradition of International Relations (Waltz, 1979), but by a hegemonic world system of liberal sovereignty (Bickerton et al., 2007). In the field of 'global health', ulti-mate examples of such endeavour stretches as far as the project of medi-calisation of populations, as explored by Stefan Elbe (2010). If it is true that this explanation is not fully applicable to the whole world, namely in terms of the 'modern world' of powerful states of regional promi-nence, such as India, China and Russia (Cooper, 2004), this is particu-larly compelling with regard to the postcolonial world.

## Contradictions of global health governance

While the narratives around post-Cold War Western foreign policies rooted on human security and globalisation have arguably dominated the global health governance literature, another narrative, focusing on the contradictions that the international-political economy of health has exposed, has gained its own currency.

Adrian Kay and Owain Williams (2008) have drawn attention to the fact that global health governance is highly part of the larger processes of global governance, based on liberalisation and commodification. The results of global liberalisation and commodification are particularly noticeable in a number of instances. Since the market of health professionals has opened itself up to 'globalisation' it has allowed an easier transfer of human resources from lower-paying countries to better-remunerating ones. As a result, countries and regions already with very low scores in terms of health care find themselves struggling even more with the loss of medical and nursing personnel. In turn, as far as the manufacture and distribution of drugs go, particularly antiretroviral ones, the protection of patents pursued by, mostly, West-based pharmaceutical companies and their states, in order to maintain high levels of profit, constitutes another front undermining access to better health in poorer countries. For Kay and Williams, the leading global health governance literature fails to take contradictions like those into account.

> The current literature on GHG [global health governance] constructs a concept of global health that implicitly naturalises the neoliberalisation process and pushes analysts to seek technocratic and political solutions to adverse trends in population health across the globe. (Kay and Williams, 2008: 21)

Another set of incongruences have been put forward by authors that aggregate around the ethics of human rights and social justice, concerned with the social determinants of health, that is, by having a structural perspective of health condition's political economy (Williams and Rushton, 2009: 11–12). Mainly disseminated by the activist nongovernmental community and some academics, mostly from North America and Western Europe, this discourse is eminently targeted at Western countries as donors and leaders of globalisation (MSF, 2008; Schrecker, 2009). This ethics appeals to further international regulation of negative practices (such as contracting health staff from the Global South or protecting resolutely pharmaceutical patents) and further financial commitment to global health programmes. This stance fails to have a lasting influence in terms of actual political change. Yet, even if they could have it, their terms of the debate are located under a population-centred framework, in which affected political communities, particularly poorer, developing states, are supposed to have little or no autonomy in the face of larger states and private companies.

As a result, global health governance started to be regarded as a domain of failure, since the alluded contradictions and disputes do not suggest coherence of policies (Williams and Rushton, 2009). The idea of governance of the 'global' does not mean that there is an actual governmental form for that 'global', although the social constructivism that permeates much of the analysis suggests it. Here, Fidler's (2004) post-Westphalian, liberal-institutional 'constitutionalism' is found wanting, since the international system is still primarily driven by a more traditional set of actors, namely states.

## Global health governance and role of state

The failure of global health governance as a domain of coherence among the many actors that struggle inside it invites a reassessment of the character of such domain, by looking precisely at the most stable and consistent in the international arena: states. In an article, James Ricci (2009) criticises an overemphasis by global health governance authors on the propelled reduced relevance of the state in the field. He cautions against the overreliance on the pulverisation of non-state actors of different types as redefining the post-international juridical feature of governance. He argues that, despite the prominence of such organisations as the Bill and Melinda Gates Foundation, states are still main funders of global health initiatives, PEPFAR being a case in point (Ricci, 2009: 7).

The leading narratives on global health governance largely reduce the African state to the status of recipient of external funding in exchange for compliance with the policies recommended by the funder, multilateral or bilateral. However, it should be remarked that there are differences between multilateral and bilateral arrangements in terms of participation.

Multilateral structures such as the Global Fund and the broader United Nations system tend to favour the inclusion of representatives and citizens of recipient countries in technical and even leadership positions. For instance, at this time of writing, Michel Sidibé of Mali is the head of UNAIDS, and Tedros Adhanom Ghebreyesus of Ethiopia was the chair of the Global Fund until September 2011. In turn, bilateral programmes are majorly led by the donor country, as it happens in the case of PEPFAR. Although recipient countries are made part of a 'partnership', it is clear, as it will be discussed in the case of PEPFAR in Chapter 5, that the relationship is vertical, rather than horizontal. In either case, the national governments of recipient countries in Africa are urged by major governments and NGOs from donor countries and international organisations to behave with 'responsibility' and 'leadership' in the adoption of recommended institutions and policies. As a result, several governments in Africa, namely those of the countries under analysis in this book, with the exception of South Africa for a certain period, have responded positively to the external pressures toward observance of international community's policies and have engaged in a relationship with those institutions, even if in asymmetric terms. In this framework, the state is assigned the role of mediator and facilitator in the process of providing goods and services for the populations in need. In turn, this role as mediator or facilitator is enhanced and ameliorated through policies of direct assistance to state agencies and their representations (for example, clinics, hospitals and health-extension programmes) and 'capacity building' in several organisational areas.

The assumption of a highly obedient state to the international community opens up the possibility of an inverse case. By not being (entirely) compliant with, if not opposed to, good policies and practices, the state is attributed features of 'rogueness' by the international community. As discussed in detail in Chapter 8 on South Africa, a striking case of 'rogueness' concerns the reduction and suspension of antiretroviral treatment programmes in South Africa by the African National Congress-led (ANC) government of former President Thabo Mbeki and his Minister of Health Manto Tshabalala-Msimang. Due to his self-proclaimed dissidence in unequivocally buying into the drug-based response to the HIV/AIDS epidemic in his country and around Africa, he was considered a denialist by many home and international activists and his country's regime a 'rogue democracy' (Baker and Lyman, 2008).[1]

In a broader sense, another major example of 'rogue' recipient state behaviour is the real or perceived deviation of funds disbursed for policy implementation for what is considered illegitimate ends. Often framed in Western circles as 'corruption', this practice sits along other troubling practices associated with the functioning of the social and political fabric, namely electoral misconduct, abuse of state violence and disrespect for the rule of law. As a result, donor countries are often uncomfortable with assisting governmental structures directly (although they still do it) and prefer NGOs, even if, in some cases, the locally based ones, in some way or another, belong to the state/governmental division of labour, as it happens in the case of Ethiopia. As Chapter 5 on PEPFAR's political origins and political rationales discusses, one major reason for opting out for bilateral mechanisms at the expense of multilateral ones (even though also participating in them) concerns precisely the will to augment surveillance over the expenditure of the recipient state.

Two seemingly different antagonistic types of state emerge out of the literature and policy debates in global health governance. One is the facilitator state, in which the recipient state behaves according to what is expected by the community of funders and policy makers. Another type is the 'rogue' state, in which states deviate from compliance in several regards, from adoption of the 'right' policies to tackle health issues to management and employment of received funds according to pre-established purposes. Certainly, the proposed types are idealised categories within the framework, and therefore subject to debate over the addition of further categories and gradations. Nevertheless, they are applicable to the postcolonial African state, in particular, as opposed to donor countries. This ought to be clearly remarked since suggestions about playing roles as facilitators and/or 'rogues' have also been suggested for donor countries and their policy choices and stances. Moreover, these ideal types do not exclude their coexistence within a single country, that is, the same country can incorporate both types.

## Conclusion

Global health governance as a specific realm of relations in the international arena appears in the discipline of International Relations in function with broader post-Cold War developments associated with human security-based foreign policies in Western powers, globalisation-provoked 'new threats' to international security, neoliberalism, and human rights agendas. Given the diversity of interests and agendas by the manifold actors that compose this field, analysts so far have been concurring in arguing about the failure of achieving coherent 'governance' of phenomena as disparate as viral outbreaks and epidemics, with different incidences across the globe. Addressing a gap in the global health governance literature, this chapter explored the role of recipient states and their governments in this realm.

From a reflexive point of view, one could argue that the intellectual constitution and development of 'global health governance' as a distinguishable realm of relations within the discipline of International

Relations offers an example of how liberal and social constructivist theories came to dominate the analysis of the international arena. Global health governance is certainly influenced by the explosive proliferation of governmental and nongovernmental, national and transnational, not-for-profit and for-profit actors in the field, which are seductive for liberal-institutionalist, cosmopolitan approaches to International Relations in the post-Cold War era. In turn, social constructivism is strikingly visible in the construction of causalities (for instance, the link between epidemics and security) that give sense to the enhancement of the international-political study of health programmes, the same applying to the post-Foucauldian use of it, mentioned previously.

The understanding of the role of states in global health governance requires a relational approach, in which its historical and sociological development is pursued under the framework of relations with other countries, particularly powerful ones. This is arguably the cornerstone in the case of states in Africa, in which the question of international asymmetry is striking. Despite emphasising the state, Ricci does not account for the problem of asymmetry as crucial feature of the international system, particularly between the Western and African states, instrumental for any meaningful discussion in global health governance; by the same token, the discussion on African states' participation in global health security talks by Lenias Hwenda and colleagues (2011). Accordingly, even when considering African states as honourable diplomatic players, the international realm of the issue of structural asymmetry is left underdeveloped. They hold that African countries' health-related interests have been overwhelmed by the positions of developed countries. They point at debates on health security initiated by Europe and North America under WHO to demonstrate the need for serious political African engagement in such discussion. However, their recommendation does not consider the issue of asymmetry, either, finding themselves stranded in the idealism of institutional equality. It thus becomes necessary to explore the character of the intervened state, namely in the context of sub-Saharan Africa, bearing in mind the asymmetric state structure of relations in global health governance.

# 3
# Recipient States in an Asymmetric System

## Introduction

This book departs from the perspective that leading analyses of weaker, recipient states in the international system are limited by default as they ontologically refuse to take those states as normal states in International Relations. 'Normality' is hereby defined by the idea of a state that, regardless of world region, is capable of defining political goals and underlying strategies of pursuit of such goals. In other words, recipient states in sub-Saharan Africa are taken – both theoretically and empirically – as characterised by the same attributes as any other states, including Western, donor states.

The debate between the universality and singularity of the state, particularly in postcolonial Africa, has been very vivid to the point of generating consolidated schools of thought across Political Science, as it is noted throughout the following pages. This book does not hold the ambition of coming any closer to the settlement of this debate. Nonetheless, it aims at proposing an analytical framework that, while bearing in mind the historical and sociological particularities of any state involved, advances an understanding that can serve a comparative exercise of studying the experience of three countries with a major global health programme under broader international development relations. This requires a lens which reclaims the analytical centrality of the state and its relations with other states, yet is sophisticated enough to accommodate their theoretical and empirical nuances. Thus, such framework builds on traditional theoretical approaches within International Relations, while coming to terms with a more critical understanding of such relations. By accounting the asymmetric character of West-Africa relations, it is complemented with a historical-sociological understanding of the states involved and their international relations as well.

However, in order to proceed with the elaboration of such framework to some degree of success, a necessary engagement needs to be carried out *vis-à-vis* a leading body of literature on relations between the West and the developing world that points at an unabated hegemonic character of the West. In this regard, it is crucial to discuss the consensus of a structural hegemony led by the Western world, in which the postcolonial African states are featured by such low degree of agency to the point of being entrenched in the international structure itself.

## State agency and international system

Considering the centrality of states as agents, it is quite advisable to revise classical literature in International Relations, particularly the propositions by Kenneth Waltz, who first advanced a scientific depiction of the international system as composed of structure and units (Waltz, 1979: 79–80).[1] Accordingly, international political systems are composed of 'self-regarding units' (Waltz, 1979: 91) – that is, states – and liken free markets led by the principle of self-help. The self-help of states is driven by a basic goal of survival in the international system, since that is the basis for any other pursuit 'from the ambition to conquer the world to the desire merely to be left alone' (Waltz, 1979). The idea of self-help is paramount to understand states' behaviour no matter the capabilities it owns. Formally endowed by sovereignty attributed by the international system (even if in some cases without enjoying complete acknowledgement by some fellow states), states constitute cores that act with a rationale that seeks primarily its survival, although expansion might be a goal too.

Though not the only actors in the international system, for Waltz, states are the most important ones, as they 'nevertheless set the terms of the intercourse, whether by passively permitting informal rules to develop or by actively intervening to change rules that no longer suit them' (Waltz, 1979: 94). A remark made by the same author is particularly relevant for one's discussion of the African state. Positing that the states' predominance will be long ranging, Waltz famously wrote:

> The death rate among states is remarkably low. Few states die; many firms do. Who is likely to be around 100 years from now – the United States, the Soviet Union, France, Egypt, Thailand and Uganda? Or Ford, IBM, Shell, Unilever, and Massey-Ferguson? I bet on the states, perhaps even on Uganda. (Waltz, 1979: 95)

Certainly, today the Soviet Union – chief part of Waltz's thesis on the balance of power among major state-units as condition for world peace – is no longer around. However, the resilience Waltz attributed to an African state should be emphasised, particularly considering the elitism that cuts across his work, that is, the primary attention he gives to the world's more powerful states.

Another aspect to be highlighted on Waltz's work is his understanding of state sovereignty, which is not synonymous with absolute independence from others' constraints. In this important passage, Waltz has framed the terms of how state agency sets out:

> Sovereign states may be hardpressed all around, constrained to act in ways they would like to avoid, and able to do hardly anything just as they would like to. The sovereignty of states has never entailed their insulation from the effects of other states' actions. To be sovereign and to be dependent are not contradictory conditions. (Waltz, 1979: 96)

Ability to act with choice occurs in a relational manner, in which sovereignty is never an absolute property of states and requires conducts of interdependence. This means that, even though states have different capabilities (Waltz, 1979: 105), in principle, all of them – United States of America or Ethiopia – enjoy agency, that is, an ability to act autonomously within different gradations of constraint in the structure.

Considering the discussion on hegemony and what it means for West-Africa relations, the distinction between hierarchy and anarchy should be discussed too. For Waltz, whereas the state-units are featured by hierarchy (Waltz, 1979: 81–88), the international system is characterised by anarchy, that is, absence of central authority (Waltz, 1979: 102–116). In a clear separation between internal and external, Waltz argues that states have domestic levels of leadership enforcing the country's law, while outside them there is virtually no entity with that ability.

> A government, ruling by some standard of legitimacy, arrogates to itself the right to use force – that is, to apply a variety of sanctions to control the use of force by its subjects. If some use private force, others may appeal to the government. A government has no monopoly on the use of force, as is all too evident. An effective government, however, has a monopoly on the legitimate use of force, and legitimate here means that public agents are organised to prevent and to counter the private use of force. Citizens need not prepare to defend

themselves. Public agencies do that. A national system is not one of self-help. The international system is. (Waltz, 1979: 103–104)

However, Waltz's claim has been questioned in the last 30 years, especially since the end of the Cold War, and what that event meant in terms of the expansion of United States power worldwide. Hegemony-based approaches to international politics, including neorealist ones, have stressed the particular powerful feature of the United States of America and major allies (Western Europe and Japan) in the leadership of the international system and its consequences for the external anarchy-internal hierarchy debate.

## Reverting traditional international relations postulate

The concept of hegemony has been thoroughly used by International Relations scholars within the different mainstream theoretical strands (neorealism and neoliberalism) since the 1980s. Neorealist authors such as Robert Gilpin (1987) or John Mearsheimer (2001) have explored hegemony in terms of a stabilising power of the United States of America in a broader context of anarchy in the international system – that is, a system characterised by the absence of central authority – in opposition to hierarchy within the domestic realm of the units of that structure, the nation-states, as described by Waltz above. Neorealist authors, such as Mearsheimer, tend to be pessimistic about this character, since they might motivate 'adventurist' foreign policies by the hegemonic power. This interventionist feature of great powers has become particularly acute since the end of the Cold War, and perhaps constitutes the major point of contention between neorealists and their neoliberal colleagues, who, like Robert Keohane (1984), have regarded United States hegemony as an opportunity for leading international cooperation. Much political analysis of United States-driven global health and development initiatives derives from Keohane's inputs on international cooperation. Concepts such as 'soft power', or 'smart power' (Armitage and Nye, 2007), that is, power transmitted through international development assistance and international trade, appear as an alternative to military coercion in order to establish and consolidate an advantageous position for the United States of America. Unlike neorealist authors, who are generally amoral with regard to states' international relations, neoliberal authors are rather idealistic about foreign policy. Although recognising the anarchic international system, they animate the belief that the implementation of Western domestic liberal values worldwide – liberal representative democracy, market capitalism, civil society, limited government, human rights – will ameliorate the prospects of international security, stability and peace (Armitage and Nye, 2007). The taming of anarchy is not envisaged merely for the external sphere of relations between nation-states but also for the domestic sphere. This has happened both in practice and, increasingly, in theory, especially after the Cold War, as narratives about 'new threats to security' appeared throughout the 1990s. International security is not merely a function of great powers' balance of power, as put by Waltzian theory, but also of the impact of marginal, impoverished countries in the developing world. Issues around state failure, alluded to in the previous chapter, illustrate the concern mainstream theorists of International Relations have started to show about the domestic sphere of sovereign states and the need to contain the threats emanating from inside them (Bickerton, 2007).

The actual practice of this soft power-based policy – in which PEPFAR is a clear example of in many countries – conjugated with the maintenance of 'hard power', that is, military power in such contexts as Iraq and Afghanistan – has had relevant theoretical consequences. The broader policy of prevention of state failure and promotion of statebuilding led to a renewed understanding of the international system as one characterised, not by anarchy or interdependence, but by hierarchy as central government (Bickerton, 2007). Conversely, the domestic sphere of postcolonial states is featured by anarchy, that is, absence of central government (Bickerton, 2007). Christopher Bickerton has summarised it in these terms:

> The highly influential theory of state failure led to a reworking, perhaps even an inversion, of the basic categories of International Relations (IR). Traditional IR theory was built on the assumption that state sovereignty was the precondition for social and political order within domestic society. In the absence of any ultimate political authority, the international realm, by contrast was seen as a domain of strife, where all political and legal order was undermined by the ever-present possibility of conflict. Thus one of the traditional problems for liberal theories of international politics in the last century was how to 'domesticate anarchy': that is, how to make the world order more like the domestic order. (Bickerton, 2007: 94)

In the case of interstate West-Africa relations, this claim has been animated by authors such as Kevin C. Dunn and Timothy M. Shaw (2001) encompassing a body that William Brown (2006) calls 'the Africanist critique of International Relations'.

The discussion of the 'intrusiveness' of the international liberal order in domestic realms has been expanded by the application throughout the last ten years of Michel Foucault's concepts of biopower, biopolitics and governmentality, originally developed to explain the historical rise of liberal power in France and Germany. In his 1975–1976 *Collège de France* lecture 'Society Must Be Defended', Foucault (2006) contradicts Carl von Clausewitz, claiming that 'politics is the continuation of war by other means', and not the other way around, as the celebrated war strategist put it. This remark has been found instructive in terms of the shifts of conceptualising power – liberal rather than absolute – from the 18th century onwards, with the end of the religious wars and the rise of what later became known as capitalism and liberal democracy. This sense of politics is less territorial and juridical and increasingly more deterritorialised and intensively political (Foucault, 2006). Accordingly, the nature of liberal power lies less on the utmost capacity and willingness of the sovereign of taking life as such but on the possibility of 'either fostering life or impede it to the point of death' (Foucault, 1984).

This characterisation of sovereign power – biopower – builds on the idea presented prior to that lecture in the first volume of *The History of Sexuality* that a new type of power centred in human beings at the aggregate level and in life in general was emerging (Foucault, 1984). This power emanates from the parallel expansion of scientific thought and shrinking of the religious influence, as a result of the Nietzschean 'death of God'. Foucault dedicated an entire volume – *The Birth of the Clinic* (Foucault, 1994) – to the particular role of medicine and its branches in this revolution in human knowledge about human beings and others, and nature around him, particularly in Europe. Biopower was exercised through the effort of measuring and regulating all dimensions of both biological and social life through biology, medicine, sociology: birth, mortality, criminality, education, employment. Biopower is pungently 'totalitarian' since it is targeted at the totality of the population and life manifestations. Liberal power is particularly complex in comparison with its former form, absolutism. It requires rationalisation and justification so it can be accepted, although, sometimes – as the very case of medicine, for instance, demonstrates – it is applied by force. Thus, power described by Foucault is presented as 'power/knowledge' in order to explain the striking influence, namely a moral one, of epistemic communities, that is, groups of scientists and others legitimated by the scientific 'truth' and agreeing on the measures to be taken to tackle with a specific issue (Haas, 1992), as the case of the politics of HIV/AIDS

(Youde, 2007) exemplify – basically meaning the agent of biopower, the later concept of biopolitics (Lemke, 2001) was introduced, to which one shall add up the concept of governmentality. Described as 'conduct of the conduct', it is a discursive-material apparatus of security embodying rationalities and technologies of government, which account for 'discourses, institutions, architectural forms, regulatory decisions, laws, administrative measures, scientific statements, philosophical, moral and philanthropic propositions' (Foucault, 1980: 184). These technologies are indeed designed to avoid the employment of violence to compel (Lemke, 2001). In a liberal, or liberalising, context that would be very complicated to achieve from the perspective of the management of the system's own sustainability. As such, frequently control is exerted through 'ideological manipulation or rational argumentation, moral advice or economic exploitation' (Lemke, 2000: 5).

These elaborations have been consistently used to explain the voracity of Western powers to intervene in non-Western settings, and enforce security (Jabri, 2007), human rights regimes (Douzinas, 2007) and development through security (Duffield, 2002; 2005; 2007). For Mark Duffield, post-Foucauldian concepts are virtuous in the formulation of a radical view of the security-development nexus looking at the case of humanitarian/development organisations.

> Following the lead of Foucault and the international political sociology of the Paris School..., the development-security *nexus* can be understood as a *dispositif* or 'constellation of institutions, practices, and beliefs that create conditions of possibility within a particular field'.... The nexus constitutes a field of development and security actors, aid agencies and professional networks, complete with their own forms of subjectivity, that call forth the conditions of need and insecurity to which collectively, and in competition, they seek to provide solutions. In this process, however, not only is risk normalised, but the origins and causes of the absences and instabilities these actors hope to rectify are also obscured and occluded. (Duffield, 2010: 56; italics in the original)

Critical authors such as those continue an avenue of research which, in the last analysis, was initiated at the Frankfurt School in its post-Auschwitz phase. Holding modernity and its perverse developmentalist creed arguably on the basis of the Nazi horrors as object of critique, it founded post-development as a field of social critique, namely with regard to the Third World and development aid and rationales pushed by the international establishment (International Monetary Fund, World Bank, major governmental donors and large North-based NGOs. Initiated in the early to mid-1980s by Colombian anthropologist Arturo Escobar (1984/1985), it has influenced a number of authors in several fields seeking to demonstrate that development, rather than a process, is both means and end, heading to no other tangible outcomes than violence and subjection (DuBois, 1991; Brigg, 2002).

International development is subject to 'governance at a distance' (Duffield, 2005: 208–210) through technologies of management such as the logical framework. These tools build on a presumption of neutrality of developmental and anti-poverty work, taking the shape of professional-technical intervention impinged to overcome political rigidities, as influential anthropological works of the mid-1990s by Arturo Escobar and James Ferguson (Dar and Cooke, 2008). Partnerships, notably transnational ones, integrate elements of reciprocity, mutuality and pluralism (Brinkerhoff and Brinkerhoff, 2004: 255; Kettl, 2008: 10). However, that does not mean they are more democratic (Roelofs, 2009), both in terms of interpartner relations and between the partnership framework and a whole public lying at the margins: from taxpayers, who fund the partnership, to clients, who are subject to their activities' ambitions and interventions. Flexibility does not mean more simplicity of relations, rather on the contrary: large partnerships tend to generate grand complexity, and are admittedly difficult to take hold from a theoretical perspective (Kettl, 2008; Roelofs, 2009; Milward and Provan, 2000). Similarly, goals based on empowerment and country ownership – subjectivities connected to hope, responsibility and self-reliance – are advanced too.

Country ownership is what recipient countries obtain when 'urged to take ownership of development policies and aid activities in their country, to establish their own systems of coordinating donors, and only to accept aid that suits their needs' (Renzio et al., 2008: 1). According to Bill Cooke (2003), this system of ownership provision – promoted, for instance, by the World Bank and repeated by other donors – discloses close vicinity with colonial forms of administration, namely 'indirect rule', in which colonial administration was tentatively more profitable when transmitted to native elites in order to prevent contestation. However, it is also important, as Katharina Welle (2001) has demonstrated, to bear in mind that partnership as an organising model of transnational collaboration has had different meanings in contemporary development discourse and practice. In her examination of a collaborative project of water management in Ghana, Welle made the distinction between partnership as 'discourse of solidarity' and as 'discourse of efficiency' (Welle, 2001: 4). Whereas initially (that is, early 1970s) partnership would stand for a commitment of solidarity as a mode of alternative development (Welle, 2001: 7) involving, primarily, nongovernmental partners in the North and South, later – from the mid-1980s until today – as large financial institutions started to implicate NGOs in their development financing (Welle, 2001: 9), partnerships started to be understood as means of achieving 'good government' (Welle, 2001: 10) – or 'good governance', as the current jargon put it – from an efficiency point of view.

The shift of level of analysis from the external to the internal obviously had an impact in terms of the scrutiny of agency within the structure of hegemony and empire. According to Oliver Richmond (2010), the national states and democratic institutions that receive the neoliberal policies of the great powers were 'hijacked and captured' (Richmond, 2010: 3), and therefore agency is left to be searched within the modes of local resistance to external neoliberal policies.

> In these struggles [generated by the hegemonic liberal project], a possibility of a post-liberal peace emerges, in which everyday local agencies, rights, needs, custom and kinship are recognised as discursive 'webs of meaning'. This might herald a more realistic recognition of the possibilities of, and dynamics of, contextual and local peacebuilding agencies within international peacebuilding, development and institutional architecture and policies. This move away from 'imperious IR' and a willingness to emphasise local context and contingency lays bare those paradoxes and tensions derived from territorial sovereignty, the overbearing state, cold institutionalism, a focus on rights over needs, distant trustee-style governance and a hierarchical international system in which material power matters more than everyday life. (Richmond, 2010: 4–5)

Informed by postcolonial-theoretical perspectives and by focusing on sectors of postcolonial populations, this agency/resistance has increasingly constituted a research agenda aimed at identifying forms of power hybridity (Richmond, 2010; Ginty, 2010). This agency/resistance to the liberal project of statebuilding and peacebuilding is presented as a local phenomenon of subversion and appropriation, capturing some nuances mentioned throughout Chapter 2, namely neopatrimonialism and the way it exemplifies a form of hybrid power (De Goede, 2010).

## Hegemony-based approaches and problem of agency

African states and governments act on their own under the auspices of their agency, that is, they hold the capacity of taking decisions independently, even if constrained and pressured by other states/governments and the structural social forces. This agency is a consequence of the postcolonial sovereign status achieved since the wave of independences. However, in order to properly analyse state action, one needs a more traditional approach to conceptualise agency and structure, as the first section suggested. In other words, the analysis should depart from the premise that the international arena is driven by anarchy and the unitary parts (states) are organised in a hierarchical way. As such, this book contends with the hegemony-based claims made in the previous part. One concedes that hegemony-based approaches are very appealing, as they are unambiguous about the asymmetries that characterise the world of states, in which the United States government's hegemony often leads to intervention within the domestic realms of less powerful states. However, those arguments are problematic for two reasons. On the one hand, they assume that the mere intellectual construction of the state in the African context is *per se* a colonial act by the Western world, that is, an external imposition to regulate postcolonial relations. On the other, they essentialise the membership of weak African states to the structure of United States hegemony, and thus negate their agency.

In the first case, one follows Brown (2006) in his critique of the authors he calls 'the Africanist critique of mainstream International Relations':

> Implicit in the Africanist critique is an idea that 'western IR' helps to reinforce Western dominance in the international system through, for example, aid donors' insistence on the adoption of particular reforms in Africa, centred on Western conceptions of the nation-state. (Brown, 2006: 126)

For Brown, the understanding of the African state as under absolute domination displays an essentialisation, at the knowledge level: the comparative history of Europe, where state-centric theory was born, and Africa. Underneath the Africanist critique's positions lies 'the notion of a one-way process of imposition of the Western ideal-state onto Africa as if Africans themselves had little to do with it' (Brown, 2006: 128). Brown further adds that, unlike the 'Africanist critique' often suggests, 'not only was the course of colonisation shaped by the interaction between Africans and Europeans but decolonisation and the foundation of independent states was a process in which Africans were actors, not simply acted upon' (Brown, 2006). This is consistent with Christopher Clapham's (1996) account of the post-independence arrangement under the Organisation for African Unity, in which the tenets of Westphalia (respect for state sovereignty; non-violation of state integrity; and state independence) were clearly remarked.

In the second case, the question of state agency, or the lack of it, is visible in the way authors such as Oliver Richmond (2010) conceptualise human agency, in which the state is deliberately bypassed. Accordingly, the state is an entity that is observed either as an external machination of potential oppression, often deriving from the colonial era, or as a plain superficiality. As such, these authors move straight away into the internal realm of the state. The search for agency within the domestic sphere of states in the developing world is symptomatic of an understanding of the national state as being not only unresponsive to citizens, and equivalently more attached to the prescriptions and guidance of the international community, but also violent and oppressive of those populations on behalf of the external project.

However, it is questionable to what extent the critique is directed at external policies and their consequences, namely at the level of national state violence or at liberalism itself. David Chandler has alluded to liberalism within the critique of international intervention as a 'field of adversity'. As such, rather than elaborating an alternative address to the putative impact of liberal interventionism in the developing world, those critics focus on the perniciousness of liberalism as practice.

> It would seem that at the core of the policy and radical critiques of the liberal peace is a critique of liberal aspirations rather than a critique of international interventionist policies and practices. The critique reflects the ease with which liberalism has become a 'field of adversity', through which both policy reform and critical claims for theoretical advance can both be made. The construction of a liberal 'field of adversity' seems to have little relation to policy realities. This is reflected in the fact that, while there is a consensus on the view that Western policies are problematic in that they are too liberal, there is much less attention to how the problems of the postcolonial world might be alternatively addressed. (Chandler, 2010: 16)

Chandler's remarks follow from his critique of post-Foucauldian authors, particularly Mark Duffield, who arguably do not theorise, or even exclude, human agency that emanates from neoliberal policies. For Chandler, Duffield's approach

> in effect, essentialises or naturalises the concept of biopower to argue that 'liberal' discourses of progress are essentially new forms of governing and controlling population (and moreover) appears to throw the baby of human agency out with the bathwater of development, rejecting modernising aspirations towards democracy and development for recreating oppressive neoliberal biopolitical frameworks of control and regulation (Chandler, 2009a: 99)

Furthermore, Jan Selby (2007) and David Chandler (Chandler, 2009a; 2009b) have contested the search for the existence of an alternative political solution to liberalism within Foucauldian accounts.[2] Chandler compares the contemporary post-Foucauldian approach, which he calls the 'poststructuralist critique' to the 'liberal cosmopolitans' of the 1990s – that is, authors such as Daniele Archibugi or Mary Kaldor – who arguably set up the Western interventionist framework of today. The radical discourse of poststructuralist post-territorial political community sought to critique this international order as a product of global liberalism, but the nature of the critique was in content and form arguably little different from that of 1990s cosmopolitanism (Chandler, 2009a: 68).

The dismissal of the state, and its agency, in the developing world, or its rendering to a rather passive part of a hierarchical international system, is problematic not because the study of emancipation in international politics from an anticolonial perspective is unimportant but because, by radicalising the argument about states as violent and therefore oppressive, it excludes the prospect of reducing international inequalities through interstate relations. Despite the multitude of social forces in the international realm, states are still the centres of political power in that realm and, as such, the attenuation or even change of hegemonic political power is a process that necessarily implicates states. However, it is relevant, first of all, to acknowledge the character of the African postcolonial state, in particular the relationship with the former colonising powers. As postcolonial states are created, often ties with the former colonial powers were not disrupted. Actually, they were retained, and, in the case of social policy (education, health), were intensified through mechanisms of development aid and cooperation. Despite the rhetoric of independence and sovereignty, often it was in the national elites' best interest to nurture these ties, which indeed constituted relevant means in light of the politics of neopatrimonialism. This aspect should be strongly emphasised, as it may be easily perceived as postcolonial 'politics of neocolonialism'.

## Agency, asymmetry and 'state as social relation'

Whereas Waltz's conceptualisation of agency and structure are useful for the analysis of postcolonial African relations, one does not advocate a complete return to Waltzian neorealist theory. Despite serving well as a 'problem-solving theory' (Cox, 1981) for the objectivity of its definitions, a full engagement with neorealist theory is empirically limited (Ayoob, 2002).

Although a confessed neorealist, Mohammed Ayoob underlines the elitism of Waltz's proposals, as they draw on the experience of major world powers (United States of America and Soviet Union), and their impact on the post-Second World War settlement in Europe. For Waltz, weaker states are almost inevitably inclined towards bandwagoning with the stronger powers, and there they remain: 'As soon as someone looks like the winner, nearly all jump on the bandwagon rather than continuing to build coalitions intended to prevent anyone from winning the prize of power' (Waltz, 1979: 126). However, Ayoob has made the same criticism for neoliberal authors alike, whose 'thesis on cooperation under anarchy skews the data in favour of affluent, industrialised democracies of the global North that form a small minority of the total membership of the international system' (Ayoob, 2002: 36). Concentration on North America, Western Europe, Japan and a few more countries/regions excludes, or inhibits, the vast majority of states, which are generally much poorer and less developed and industrialised. This problem of exclusion is found in the specific field of global health governance. As mentioned in the previous chapter, James Ricci (2009) has called for a rescue of the state in that area. After all, states are the major financial contributors and defining policy makers. However, Ricci's introduction of International Society theory does not take into due account the character of asymmetry, and thus invisibility, of the recipient state. As such, his theoretical approach is mired in the same elitism that liberal-institutional and globalisation scholars of global health mentioned above exhibit. This asymmetry is primarily understood in function of the disparities of wealth and human development between regions, but also the origin of influential epistemologies and policies that consubstantiate the actual relationship. Although Ricci's call for a renewed attention to the state is very pertinent, his International Society-based proposal as a fitter analytical framework suffers from the same theoretical problem that affects neoliberal and neorealist approaches, and that will be scrutinised in more detail in Chapters 6, 7 and 8. By leaving it in silence, Ricci's alternative, state-based proposal does not conceptualise the issue of asymmetry between states in global health governance. His allusion is mainly, if not exclusively, to donor countries – mostly Western and large, powerful states such as China. His mention of the Indonesian government's refusal to share A/H5N1 flu virus samples offers an example of how a smaller country conflicts with the major states; however, the background question of asymmetry within such (international) society is not addressed. It should be added that the segregation faced by postcolonial African states lies at the core of the 'Africanist critique of International Relations', which one has discussed in the previous section. Accordingly, this silencing is handed as evidence that International Relations theory just does not serve the realities of regions such as sub-Saharan Africa. This fact implicates an understanding of the contingencies that render those states generally a condition of subalternity and asymmetry *vis-à-vis* the major players in the international scene, who also happen to have been former colonial masters.

As a response, Ayoob proposes a version of neorealism he has called 'subaltern realism', which departs from a position in which the state is the central figure in the international arena, 'despite the prolifera- tion of nonstate actors and their increased capacity, in relative terms, to influence international and national outcomes' (Ayoob, 2002: 39). However, so it can have any significance, the state has to be effective and markedly Westphalian in order to achieve any real equality with the far more powerful states in the system. 'Only by approaching the Westphalian ideal more closely can the postcolonial states provide stable political order domestically and participate on a more equal footing in writing and rewriting the rules of international order' (Ayoob, 2002: 40). Ayoob prescribes these states as 'strong states' (Ayoob, 2002) that can guarantee development and economic growth, even if contrary to the international establishment.[3] But Ayoob's proposal is not radical in its rejection of the (postcolonial) state as a violent demon. He regards postcolonial violence as a contingency following the proclamation of juridical sovereignty and recognition as members of the United Nations. 'In many cases, establishing effec- tive statehood, to whatever extent this was possible, entailed the exer- cise of violence and counterviolence by the state and its opponents' (Ayoob, 2002: 43–44). As Hobbesian as he is about the need of central authority to regulate what alternatively would be a 'brutish way of life' among humans, violence is possibly necessary in order to build a nation that can prosper in the future. Ayoob's rejoinder to neorealist theory is valuable as it reiterates the centrality of the state – and therefore its agency – in the international system while, at the same time, considering the subalternity most states, including those in sub-Saharan Africa, have been experiencing since their existence as sovereign states.

However, as a committed neorealist theoretical perspective, Ayoob detaches external from internal spheres, and that is particularly limitative as a lens that captures the fullest possible levels of relations a state can have. Considering the porosity of the postcolonial state in terms of areas such as social development or health – mostly at stake in this book, after all – it is necessary to establish a framework that connects external and domestic dimensions of interstate action.

An envisaged framework that deals with the limits of neorealist theory for explaining the realities of postcolonial relations, while acknowledging its clarity in the definition of structure and agency, is one that is sociologically informed by the work of Justin Rosenberg (1990; 1994). Taking states as social relations, Rosenberg argues that such state-specific property as sovereignty, and the very international system, is partially the product of interstate relations. Reflecting on the emergence of the nation-state in Europe after the Peace of Westphalia in 1648, Rosenberg argues that internal and external developments to states combine and consolidate the international system of relations.

> We are viewing, in the emergence of sovereign nation-states, the consolidation of a structure of political power whose core institution (sovereignty) is a point of continuity between the domestic and the 'international.' The mustering of administrative power domestically is inescapably bound up with relations between states – and viceversa. (Rosenberg, 1990: 254)

Although the author reflects on the specific case of Europe, it is worth applying to relations with states in sub-Saharan Africa, which, despite their nuances are members with agency in the international system. In another piece, Rosenberg repeats his appeal for an attention to the social component of states and their relations beyond a dogmatic separation between external and internal. Yet, here he addresses the problem of the risk of treating any state as a mere Western construction, hollowed out of its specificities.

If one cannot look at those social relations, then one must treat the state as an irreducible actor. And to do this is to invest the specifically modern Western form of the state with an elemental status which abstracts it from its social and historical reality. (Rosenberg, 1994: 94)

Understanding the state as a social relation implies that the existing hierarchy found inside the state/units is the result of relations between political, social and economic forces, internal and external to the unit. This sociologically informed theory of the state allows for the comprehension of a sophisticated public-private partnership, PEPFAR (under analysis here), and its process of implementation in different national settings. And this applies not only to the recipient governments but also to the donor one. Likewise, the structure upon which states sit and interact is also historically and socially informed by social forces.

## Conclusion

In order to understand the ambition, scope and intensity of West-led statebuilding and development policies and initiatives, several theoretical perspectives suggested an inversion of the 'classical' structure-agency relationship as originally described by Kenneth Waltz. Accordingly, the structure appears hierarchical rather than anarchical, and the state-unit is anarchical rather than hierarchical, and this is particularly visible in the case of relations between the Western world and Africa. However, they have been challenged in two regards subscribed to in this book. First, in the face of 'the Africanist critique of International Relations' one reinforced that Africans were also part of the process of colonisation and postcolonisation, and thus the integration of Africa in the world of states is also their responsibility. Second, building on Chandler, one found problematic the jeopardy, or even negation, of agency among postcolonial African states by critical theorists, namely when employing Foucauldian frameworks.

As a result, one advanced a conceptual proposal that recovers the concepts of agency, structure, anarchy and hierarchy in light of Kenneth Waltz's (1979) *Theory of International Relations*. States are the key units of the international system, and are characterised by internal hierarchy, with the primacy of central government. In turn, the international system is featured by anarchy, that is, the absence of central government who enforces law in the international realm. Nevertheless, though basically useful for explaining states' ability to act autonomously, that is, with agency, in the world system, Waltzian theory of International Relations is limited in so far as it was primarily elaborated to explain major states' behaviour. It thus is argued that a sociologically informed understanding of the state as a social relation allows for a more inclusive grasping of the recipient state's behaviour *vis-à-vis* the structure.

# 4
# International Developments of States in Africa

## Introduction

Even though the book looks at three specific countries (Botswana, Ethiopia and South Africa), one departs from a generalised idea of the 'African state'. The purpose of framing the debate around a generalisation has to do with a usual methodological approach to the study of African politics, which departs from generalisations towards specific countries or issue areas. According to leading Africa scholar Jean-François Bayart, this should not imperil the research 'since geographical proximity has none the less brought about a relative commonality of historical destiny, of which the colonial interlude is only of secondary importance' (Bayart, 2009: 34). As the same author further claims, '[this] allows us to construct a scientific object, to circumscribe a political area in a comparative perspective, even to talk of an "African" civilisation in the sense intended by Braudel as a reality of "great, inexhaustible length"' (Bayart, 2009).

However, this choice is also explained by the regional character of the broader foreign policy that informs the launch and implementation of the PEPFAR since 2003 in Botswana, Ethiopia and South Africa. Although it is part of a policy with a worldwide scope, PEPFAR has particularly been implicated in the broader United States foreign policy towards sub-Saharan Africa. As discussed later, PEPFAR's rationale departs from a generalising approach to issues around security and stability, irrespective of the country at stake. The synthesis of these two drivers of analysis – the methodological 'tradition' in the political study of African affairs and the character of policy making in the United States of America – leads to an approach to general sub-Saharan African relations with the United States of America and the Western world at large. To be more precise, one discusses the role of international aid and loan giving over time in such relationship, yet in linkage to a changing landscape of the possibilities of the traditional recipient countries in those processes.

## Postcolonial Settlement

Although framed by a nationalist rhetoric, strong ties with the former colonial powers were generally maintained by the leaders of the former colonies. With a relatively small number of exceptions (Angola, Mozambique, Guinea-Bissau, Algeria, Zimbabwe and Namibia), transition towards formal independence occurred in a fairly smooth manner, in which power was formally delegated from the colonial administrators to the leadership of the nationalist parties that had reclaimed sovereignty. Regarding the major colonial powers in Africa, the United Kingdom and France, there generally were no incentives to contend by force those demands of independence, arguably because resources allocated to the colonies were small and therefore did not justify military interventions. However, they sought a close relationship with the post-independence political regimes.

> The most sensible solution...was to leave with every appearance of willingness, while establishing as good a relationship as circumstances allowed with the successor regimes – many of which were in any event led by politicians who were closely associated with the colonial power. (Clapham, 1996: 37)

The postcolonial elites essentially inherited the bureaucratic apparatus established during the colonial period, and thus reproduced the rational logic of a nation-state as the Weberian tradition puts it. Additionally, the porous character of state institutions, namely in technical areas such as education or health – largely realms of Western knowledge inculcation – is explicable by the continual connections to the formal administrative and political power (Swidler, 2007). The character of the relationship between the newly independent sub-Saharan African states and their former colonial powers was as intense as asymmetric. It 'carried with it a constant reminder of the colonial past, and could never be entirely divorced from a sense of subordination' (Clapham, 1996: 77). In this regard, it is interesting to observe the role of the development apparatus in the postcolonial age.

> Expatriate workers from the former metropolis frequently increased in number after the independence, especially in the francophone

states, and provided a strong inducement for their home governments to help guarantee peaceful conditions and friendly relations
with the African state. (Clapham, 1996: 78)

In fact, the former colonial elites maintained an interest in keeping good
relations with what they saw as 'their Africa' (Clapham, 1996: 79).

Although the key relationship tended to be with the former colo-
niser, close links were maintained by the postcolonial elites with the
superpowers, usually with one of the two world rivals (United States
of America and Soviet Union). Nonetheless, even though the average
African postcolonial state is indeed porous, subaltern and to an extent
subordinated, it does not mean that it does not have the capacity of
taking independent actions, and as such does not necessarily conform
permanently to the system's structural constraints and guidance. Here
one looks particularly to the last three decades (1980–2010).

## The 1980s-1990s: structural adjustment programmes and survivalism

The immediate post-independence period of the 1960s was heralded
with optimism. Many African countries sought to attain levels of
economic growth as part of a nascent developmental strategy driven by
the state. This strategy aimed at building industries that would facilitate
transition from a primary sector-based economic stage, contribute for
the consolidation of sovereignty, and concomitantly reduce dependency from the former colonial rulers. At the same time, social welfare
concerns were also incorporated in the development strategy. According
to Africa historian J.D. Fage,

[with] independence...the new leaders of these countries almost
without exception embarked on development strategies which
involved increasing production for export of primary agricultural and
mineral products, and taxing, and borrowing against, the resultant
income from the world markets to provide funds for the development and diversification of the economy and the improvement of
society. (Fage, 1988: 499)

However, those early achievements proved to be non-lasting, as it
became increasingly visible in the 1970s. Progressively larger import
deficits at the average African country started to coexist with a spiral of
negative economic growth and depreciation of living conditions among

the population. Both external and internal factors were pointed out. Externally, the lack of, or insufficient, integration by national economies in the global marketplace despite post-independence efforts was signalled. Also, the great increases in oil prices in the 1970s certainly affected for the most part the small number (at the time) of non-oil-producing countries, which required energy to fuel the nascent industries (Fage, 1988: 501). Furthermore, the increase in the burden of interest rates on the national economy was another obstacle.

> Payments of the interest due on the foreign loans they had acquired to help finance their development programmes – let alone any repayments of the capital that had been borrowed – were becoming a very high proportion of their GNPs [gross national products], and were eating up more and more of their diminishing foreign earnings. (Fage, 1988: 505–506)

At the internal level, factors such as urbanisation and population growth were identified as explanatory of an increasingly difficult situation. As put by the same historian,

> From 1973 onwards, the problem of growing enough food in Africa to feed its growing and increasingly urbanised population was made much worse because there were a series of successions of years in which the amounts of rain received, particularly in the arid and semi-arid zones between 10° and 30° either side of the equator, were markedly less than the average. (Fage, 1988: 504)

But a second explanation lies on the character of the African state. The African state has been described as eminently neopatrimonial and clientelist, characterised by a system of 'giving and granting of favours, in an endless series of dyadic exchanges that go from the village level to the highest reaches of the central state' (van de Walle, 2001: 51). This system functions in a hybrid manner, in which that practice of favour exchange takes place behind the façade of a modern state structure. The nature of the state in Africa has been thoroughly studied in the last couple of decades (Bayart, 2009; Chabal and Deloz, 1999), but for the purposes of this chapter, one will refer to Nicolas van de Walle's description.

> Outwardly, the state has all the trappings of a Weberian rational-legal system, with a clear distinction between the public and the private realm, with written laws and a constitutional order. However, this

official order is constantly subverted by a patrimonial logic, in which officeholders almost systematically appropriate public resources for their own uses and political authority is largely based on clientelist practices, including patronage, various forms of rent-seeking, and prebendalism. (van de Walle, 2001: 51–52)

One critical feature of this neopatrimonial system is that 'it results in a systematic fiscal crisis' (van de Walle, 2001). The same author argues that this crisis – fundamental to understand the relation maintained for so long with the international lenders – has not to do with a 'big state', as believed by the leaders of the financial institutions, but with the revenue side.

Despite extensive state intervention in the economy [after the independence], cronyism and rent-seeking have siphoned off potential state revenues. Taxes are not collected, exemptions granted, tariffs averted, licenses bribed away, parking fines pocketed. As a result, revenues always lag behind expenditures. (van de Walle, 2001: 53)

In a context of external difficulties, and given the domestic political characteristics, countries turned to the international financial institutions and Western Europe to provide them with funding. However, funding through structural adjustment programmes (SAPs) under the auspices of the International Monetary Fund, the World Bank, and national donors came with a set of conditionalities that has enlarged over time.

Aid conditionality means that the granting of aid is tied to whether recipient countries adopt, or promise to adopt, certain recommended policies. At first only the granting of new short-term balance-of-payments aid was linked to policy conditionality, but over time most new programme and project aid became so linked. The policy conditions to which the granting of aid was linked initially concerned only macroeconomic matters but were soon extended into attempts to restructure the state-market relation. (Engberg-Petersen et al., 1996: 15)

The leading school of thought backing conditionality policies was eminently neoliberalism, which was re-emerging in Western Europe and North America in the late 1970s and early 1980s, and advocated drastic reductions of state bureaucracy and state interventionism in the economy. This school thrived in several governments of the time, whose main concern was to control inflation in their countries. The purpose was to release societies from the constraints imposed by the state through liberalisation of public-owned enterprises, so countries could respond more effectively to global market signals (Engberg-Petersen et al., 1996: 401).

Despite the narrower political manoeuvre room imposed by the design of the international interventions, national political elites have remained largely untouched, as they sought to navigate these conditionalities. As van de Walle shows in his discussion of the structural reforms, 'measures have been partially undertaken, reserved, diverted, compensated for, and manipulated so they do not threaten leaders' control over discretionary state resources' (Engberg-Petersen et al., 1996: 274). Moreover, given the neopatrimonial character of the African state,

> overall government consumption does not appear to have declined significantly over two decades of reform and, once aid resources to states are included, the total amount of resources controlled by governments has probably risen by several percentage points of GDP in the last twenty years. (van de Walle, 2001: 274)

This behaviour constitutes what Christopher Clapham (1996) has coined the 'politics of state survival'. Accordingly, survivalism has taken many shapes and forms from appealing to foreign funding aimed at resolving issues of poverty and underdevelopment to facilitating foreign direct investment, in a context in which state institutions and government elites generally coincide. As part of the growing privatisation of international relations throughout the 1990s, those appeals are targeted both at foreign governments and most prominently perhaps NGOs, which exploded in their visibility and influence, and private companies (Clapham, 1996: 244). The governmentality of the liberalising structural adjustment programmes was confronted with another governmentality: the governmentality of neopatrimonialism (Bayart, 2009: 268).

Aid has arguably helped to assure the elites the status quo. However, it did so at a very high cost in terms of domestic state structures being able to improve human development. Even liberal reformist observers such as van de Walle concede that the reduction of the state functions resulted in 'a progressive withdrawal of governments from key developmental functions they had espoused in an earlier era' (van de Walle, 2001: 276). In other words, states lost capacity to address conveniently the critical issues of social welfare and improvement that heighten development. Conversely, the provision of social services started to be provided by donors and NGOs who occupy those areas. At that level, the dependency of countries have augmented, and while it is fair to emphasise the neopatrimonial character of governments, it has to be stressed the extent to which those adjustment programmes are responsible for such outcomes too.

By the end of the 1990s and into the early 2000s, the international establishment altered its perspective by shifting policy focus away from a reduced state to a 'capable' one. Rather than reducing the African state, the purpose became to rebuild it, empower it and make it act 'responsibly' towards the international community.

## The 2000s: securitisation, statebuilding and developmental state

Both the international financial establishment and its body of critics acknowledged that the structural adjustment interventions across Africa did not bear the ultimately intended results. However, they evidently put forward different reasons to explain the situation. The former generally refers to a conditionality which was not hard enough in terms of enhancing private investment and liberalising public and parastatal[1] companies (Engberg-Petersen et al., 1996: 8). In turn, critics focus on problems of translating neoliberalism into practice. For some, the problem of neoliberalism is that it is too 'simplistic and misleading' (Engberg-Petersen et al., 1996: 8). For others, who do not share the same radical stance, the neoliberal paradigm is 'basically correct', but it ought to be adapted to local realities (Engberg-Petersen et al., 1996: 8). But perhaps the greatest divide in opinion between the former and the latter group has to do with how poor societies were before and after the programmes. For the critics, the average people became much poorer, while the supporters claim the very opposite. The supporters also allude to a lack of a counterfactual in the critics' discourse; they claim one just would not know 'what would have happened without structural adjustment' (Engberg-Petersen et al., 1996: 8).

In any case, the statistical fact is that, in terms of human development, the continent has remained in the lowest ranks of the Human Development Index (HDI). In 2000, the United Nations Millennium Summit established eight targets to be ideally achieved by 2015. The goals of the United Nations Millennium Development Goals (MDGs) were: to eradicate extreme poverty and hunger; to achieve universal education; to promote gender equality and to empower women; to reduce child mortality rates; to improve maternal health; to combat HIV/AIDS, malaria and other diseases; to ensure environmental sustainability; and to develop a global partnership for development. The MDGs constituted the basis of action for multilateral initiatives such as the 2001-established Global Fund to Fight AIDS, Tuberculosis and Malaria (henceforth Global Fund). However, major bilateral initiatives have been launched, such as the United States Millennium Challenge Account (MCA) and theme-specific programmes such as PEPFAR or the President's Malaria Initiative. Relevant bilateral initiatives were also widely found across Europe and elsewhere in the Western world (Japan, Canada, Australia), and more recently among some 'emerging countries' (Brazil, China, India).

But these initiatives occurred in a fairly different policy context compared to the late 1970s and 1980s described above. Since the end of the Cold War, commentators and policy makers have referred to a need of linking developmental efforts to what they perceive as new threats to international security (Krasner and Pascual, 2005; Klingebiel, 2006; Adelman and Eberstadt, 2008; Patrick, 2008). They refer to the amalgamated phenomena that jeopardise the unprecedented wave of liberal power after the demise of the Soviet Union and throughout the 1990s, that expanded across the world through trade and travel. It included the easier proliferation of migrations, and concomitantly epidemics; trafficking in drugs and weapons of mass destruction; and sophisticated transnational networks of terrorists. The purpose of external intervention, preferably through soft power means (Armitage and Nye, 2007), that is, aid and business opportunities, but also through military solutions, ought to consist on containing phenomena like those.

The idea of linking security to development of populations is far from new, as has been shown in the case of epidemic interventions in colonial settings.

> The genealogy of securitisation of infectious disease can be considered as old as the rise of liberal political regime in Europe since the 17th century, and whose global expansion and consolidation were favoured by international public hygienist surveillance as of the 1830s. (Pereira, 2008: 8)

However, this time around, the novelty had to do with the observation that development had become a strategically defined question of security as classically it used to be with regard to enemy states. This framework has been radically described as a governmentality in which the neoliberal economics embedded in the Structural Adjustment Programmes of the 1980s and 1990s was complemented by issues of denying life opportunities for the populations (Duffield, 2002; 2005).

Rather than serving purposes of progress and emancipation, development has become a tool of contention of 'surplus' postcolonial populations, and the pressures they put on global capitalism since the wave of decolonisation in the aftermath of the Second World War (Duffield, 2007). This pressure has become more intense from the 1990s onwards, particularly after the attacks in New York and Washington, DC, on 11 September 2001, as contention is required for more specific goals rooted on security challenges, such as international terrorism and other perceived threats to the Western world. Development interventions are constructed in rhetorical and policy terms as preventing such threats and managed by sophisticated mechanisms of 'governance at a distance' (Duffield, 2005: 208–210). These tools build on a presumption of neutrality of developmental work, driven by professional experts and aimed at overcoming stringencies that political struggle generates (Dar and Cooke, 2008). This body of critiques of development often constructs analyses through the employment of frameworks of biopower and biopolitics developed in the 1970s by Michel Foucault, as previous chapters discuss in more detail.

A burgeoning literature with strong impact on Western foreign policy circles has placed the problems of 'new threats' to security and development, not only but particularly in Africa, to the nature of the state in the developing world (Krasner and Pascual, 2005; Reno, 1995; Zartman, 1995; Ghani and Lockhart, 2008). Those states are described as eminently weak or even failed, and thus rendered dangerous. Robert Rotberg has defined two very academically and policy-influential working definitions of weak and failed states.

> Weak states (broadly, states in crisis) include a broad continuum of states: they may be inherently weak because of geographical, physical, or fundamental economic constraints; or they may be basically strong, but temporarily or situationally weak because of internal antagonisms, management flaws, greed, despotism, or external attacks. (Rotberg, 2004: 4)

In turn,

> Failed states are tense, deeply conflicted, dangerous, and contested bitterly by warring factions. In most failed states, government troops battle armed revolts led by one or more rivals. Occasionally, the official authorities in a failed state face two or more insurgencies, varieties of civil unrest, different degrees of communal discontent, and

a plethora of dissent directed at the state and at groups within the state. (Rotberg, 2004: 5)

In the aftermath of 11 September 2001 attacks, United States Policy Advisor Stephen Krasner and United States Ambassador Carlos Pascual argued that

> [in] today's increasingly interconnected world, weak and failed states pose an acute risk to the United States of America and global security. Indeed, they present one of the most important foreign policy challenges of the contemporary era. States are most vulnerable to collapse in the time immediately before, during, and after conflict. When chaos prevails, terrorism, narcotics trade, weapons proliferation, and other forms of organised crime can flourish. Left in dire straits, subject to depredation, and denied access to basic services, people become susceptible to the exhortations of demagogues and hatemongers. It was in such circumstances that in 2001 one of the poorest countries in the world, Afghanistan, became the base for the deadliest attack ever on the United States homeland, graphically and tragically illustrating that the problems of other countries often do not affect them alone. (Krasner and Pascual, 2005: 153)

As incongruent and possibly ironic as it might be, the reduction of the state advanced by the SAPs of the previous decades have diminished the capacity of states to assure its territorial authority, let alone the provision of social goods and services, as noted above. It has long been asserted that many African postcolonial states, which inherited the administrative divisions of the colonial period, face an endogenous weakness regarding their identity and therefore their predisposition to internal and cross-boundary conflicts (Clapham, 1996). Yet, the reduction of the state – and, consequently, its neopatrimonial character – has arguably enhanced the tendency towards fragmentation, as the struggle for resources became more intense. Rather than prescribing the reduction of the state as during the 1980s and 1990s, Western policy makers emphasised the role of a strong state in the developing world as facilitator of a successful comprehensive foreign policy. Krasner and Pascual thus conclude

> Today, stability requires more than maintaining a balance of power among strong states. Safety both here and abroad now depends on

the ability of the United States and the international community to make sovereignty work – to establish democracies that improve the lives of ordinary individuals rather than of the ruling elite. The first step in this process must be to prevent conflict if possible, or to ensure a meaningful peace when conflict does occur. The world can do more to help those countries at risk of unrest or recovering from war. If successful, then over the longer term the United States will have enabled more people to enjoy the benefits of peace, democracy, and market economies. That can only be in everyone's best interest. (Krasner and Pascual, 2005: 163)

As for the practice of this foreign policy of statebuilding, this has been based on an evermore intense tenet of partnership between governments and international organisations, constructed around 'mutual understandings' and 'mutual goals'. Countries in the developing world are encouraged to pursue 'good governance' and 'accountability', thus, remaining more responsive to the international community. The purpose is to raise a sense of responsibility within a liberal logic of respect for civil society, markets and human rights, and eventually 'own' the donor-induced policies and the donor-driven programmes. Establishing a successful, effective indigenous state is a precondition for international security and prosperity.

David Chandler (2006) has argued that this foreign policy, in which large-scale, development-related interventions promoted by Western countries are part of a general politics of statebuilding in non-Western regions, is one of an 'Empire in denial'. This process is characterised by a marked depoliticisation of relations, both between the international community and the countries under intervention, and between these latter and their societies. Whereas the national elites, given their dependence on the international community, work toward the fulfilment of international community's requirements, the latter, rather than connected to the state institutions for public goods, increase their dependence on the system of international NGOs, private companies and often criminal activity too. Relations are operated according to 'a narrow and functionalist framework' (Chandler, 2006: 5–6). This depoliticisation is a symptom of the Western empire's 'denialism' of its power behaviour and accountability *vis-à-vis* their societies and, of course, the regions where it intervenes (Chandler, 2006: 8–22). For Chandler, as far as relations with Africa are concerned, imperial denialism is visible in the establishment of partnerships in opposition to the 19th century-type overt discourse and practice of government.

> The new administrators of empire talk about developing relations of 'partnership' with subordinate states, or even of African 'leadership,' at the same time as instituting new mechanisms of domination and control. Gone is the language of Western dominance and superiority; replaced by the discourses of 'capacity-building' and 'empowerment' in the cause of the non-Western Other. ... They are eager to deny that they have any interests or deciding influence at the same time as instituting new mechanisms of regulation which artificially seek to play up to the authority, rights and interests of those subordinate to them. (Chandler, 2006: 9)

Indeed, this renewed form of empire is an ethical one in opposition to the traditional interest-based approach. Driven by liberalism, this is an empire concerned with implementing values such as those mentioned above, and not with conquering territories and founding colonies as it used to be. The ethics refer to a concern for the survival, development and security of the populations under intervention framed in terms of 'their (that is, non-Western) needs', and not 'our (that is, Western) needs'. 'The needs of non-Western states and societies have assumed centre stage' (Chandler, 2006: 71). Unlike in the past, the post-Cold War era of Western dominance seems to have cleared 'the context of "friend/ enemy:" the Other – the object of foreign policy – is more likely to be defined on the basis of needs' (Chandler, 2006: 73). In this context, 'Western states and international institutions appear less as external or coercive forces and more as facilitators, empowerers and capacity-builders' (Chandler, 2006: 77). This has been very visible in the case of PEPFAR as a bilateral programme of the United States government to provide primarily HIV/AIDS relief in a number of countries, but also in other overarching policy initiatives in and for Africa, such as the United States MCA or the United Kingdom's Commission for Africa (Chandler, 2006: 83–86).

Parallel to these policy developments in the West, a discourse on African Renaissance emerges in South Africa with resonance across the continent. It stretches back to the immediate post-apartheid foreign policy of South Africa through Deputy President Thabo Mbeki (Taylor, 2005: 33). Having generated a flourishing literature of debate and critique, African Renaissance essentially alludes to a 'third moment' of Africa's postcolonial existence, after decolonisation (1960s), followed

by democratisation (1990s), and featured by 'social, political democratisation, economic regeneration and the improvement of Africa's
geopolitical standing in world affairs' (Maloka, 2001). Although it was
alluding to Africa as a whole, it became questionable to what extent this
was a strategy of regional hegemony by the far most powerful economy
in Africa to engage profitably with the rest of the continent in a new
(post-apartheid) context (Cheru, 2002: xii; Lesufi, 2004; Owusu, 2006).
Still, it backed the latest pan-African plan for development in the continent, the New Partnership for Africa's Development (NEPAD), set up as
a result of collaborative efforts by a group of African countries (Algeria,
Egypt, Nigeria, Senegal, South Africa), supported by the Organisation
for African Unity and endorsed by the group of the eight most industrialised countries in the world (G8) (Maloka, 2001). Established in
2001, it promised a break away from the ineffective neoliberal policies imposed on African countries by structural adjustment policies and
serious improvements in national governance through further democratisation, openness to civil society, transparency and accountability
(Maloka, 2001).

This intellectual and policy event was further complemented by the
reintroduction of the theory and practice of the developmental state
in policy discussions about Africa (Stein, 2000). As mentioned, the link
between the state and development was relatively vivid in the immediate
post-independence phase, reduced drastically by the end of the 1970s
when African states turned to the neoliberal-driven financial institutions for funding. The idea of a dirigiste state that drives the economy
towards growth, yet respects the marketplace, found inspiration in the
fairly recent success stories of the so-called East Asian Tigers (Malaysia,
South Korea, Singapore) as well as in the more distant European cases
of post-Second World War Germany and the Scandinavian countries,
who sought to grow economically at a quite fast pace. In Africa, only
Botswana (White, 2006) and Mauritius (Meisenhelder, 1997) were
pointed as examples in this regard. It can be argued that this resurgence happened in reaction to three policy trends. First of all, as already
discussed, critics of the Structural Adjustment Programmes galvanised
the argument that giving the primacy to the market at the expense
of a minimal state led to disastrous results. Secondly, as also referred,
according to leading Western foreign policy strategists, the postcolonial experience has made evident that many African states have limited
capacity; they are weak or even failed, to the point of generating threats
to international stability and therefore require measures that rebuild
them and make them capable. Therefore, rebuilding them and making

them agents of development is an important prospect (Fritz and Rocha Menocal, 2007). Finally, several economic perspectives, converging on something one could call 'Afro-pessimism', argued that not only development in Africa was impossible but also its elites were inherently rent-seekers and corrupt. Yet, Thandika Mkandawire counterclaimed that there is firm historical evidence of developmentalist experiences that delivered positive results.

> Most arguments on the impossibility of developmental states in Africa are not firmly founded either on African historical experience or in the trajectories of the more successful 'developmental states' elsewhere. Africa has had examples of countries whose ideological inclination was clearly 'developmentalist' and that pursued policies that produced fairly high rates of growth and significant social gains and accumulation of capital in the postcolonial era. (Mkandawire, 2001: 309–310)

As Ian Taylor has convincingly argued in his comprehensive critique of NEPAD, not only this partnership has been a continuation of the previous hegemonic neoliberal framework (the 'Washington Consensus') – this time around initiated by Africans rather than by Washington, DC-based institutions – but also a renewal of the neopatrimonial and clientelist paradigm of the postcolonial era. Generally, NEPAD has been run by the same old elites and did not lead to the fresh start it alleges. By 2005, Taylor's commentary was put in these terms:

> In this light, grand pronouncements regarding the importance of good governance and democracy or of economic liberalisation are made redundant by the behaviour and actions of the very same people responsible for drawing up and/or committing themselves to such aims. Again, the divorce between rhetoric and reality is stark and more and more palatable. (Taylor, 2005: 275)

From a political-economic perspective, Ishmael Lesufi (2004) and Francis Owusu (2006) have corroborated Taylor's idea that African Renaissance-driven NEPAD was a tool of South African foreign policy toward expansion across the continent, thus following Mbeki's domestic policy of liberalisation in exchange for foreign direct investment. Yet, while acknowledging Taylor, Lesufi and Owusu's critiques, it is important to highlight that the 2000s era cannot be described in the same vein as the one before. Even though survivalism is still an arguable feature among many African countries today, the current period offers new, or renewed, intellectual but also policy choices. Thandika Mkandawire leaves a note of caution in that regard, as he appeals to a non-static view of the African polity.

> Having presented key actors as irredeemably greedy, corrupt and captured by rent-seekers and economies of affection and African states as preternaturally disposed to predation, the misreading denies us the opportunity to think creatively of modes of social organisation at both macro and micro-level that can extricate African countries from the crises they confront. (Mkandawire, 2001: 310)

The 2000s have indeed been witnessing interesting changes in the 'traditional' commentary about Africa. Impressive economic growth has spawned across some countries with spill-over effects in terms of improvements in human development. Among United States development analysis circles, this has been seen with large interest. Whereas for Steven Radelet with the Center for Global Development argues that some countries are already enjoying some 'emerging' status in the regional economy given their recent high rates of economic growth (Radelet, 2010), Daniel Kaufmann with The Brookings Institution gives it a 'tempered optimism':

> Many African countries are now recording positive (and sometimes substantial) growth, reducing poverty rates and attracting more foreign investment. However, it may be premature to declare success across the African region. ... Yet, most of the remaining SSA countries still face substantial governance and economic constraints to growth. It is important to recognise that performance is very varied across the African region and that many countries, like Gabon, still face daunting governance challenges. (Kaufmann, 2011)

Other analyses have pointed to the enlargement of the middle class as a very important indicator (Ncube et al., 2011).

There has also been a diversification of donors and lenders to look at. In fact, the first decade of the 21st century has been one where, first and foremost, China is holding an undisputed influence across the continent through direct investment and provision of loans for development projects (Lancaster, 2007; Kragelund, 2011). Intellectually, too, it is observable the renewed interest in several Asian models of growth, especially China, as many African students of development economics and other fields obtain opportunities to study in that country. Thirdly, Africa-focused international organisations, such as the United Nations Economic Commission for Africa and the African Union (2011), advocate an increasing dirigiste role for the state in order to achieve higher economic growth and development in a context of renewed optimism about the domestic state-based capabilities to deliver.

While there certainly are continuities from the previous decades, the first decade of the 21st century has undergone policy changes at the structural level of relations between the West and sub-Saharan Africa, especially as far as the role of the state in the latter region is concerned. As Western policy makers call for a merging between security and development and statebuilding as policies for African states in order to consolidate their goals of stability and peace, or 'Empire in denial' as suggested by Chandler, the latter in turn adopt, or re-adopt, policies of developmentalism based on the state. At the same time, as new donors and lenders, particularly China, come forth, some African states are achieving remarkable economic results.

## South Africa, Ethiopia and Botswana and the African state postcolonial experience

The previous sections delineated two periods of political-economic relations between African states and the international financial and development community, following a debate built on a generalised idea of the 'African state' that one aims at linking to the individual cases under scrutiny. Botswana, Ethiopia and South Africa offer distinct experiences not just between themselves but also regarding the characterisation given above. Yet, they certainly remain 'African' not only for their obvious geographical location, but also for the important part they play, in their different ways, within the debate of the postcolonial state in Africa.

Botswana is one of the two countries (the other is Mauritius) that had been presented as a democratic developmental state in the beginning of the 2000s. It is still part of the very small number of countries that are presented as 'models' of good governance, economic growth and improvement in human development by the international community. Yet, lasting repercussions of the state's commitment to development only started to trickle as a public-private partnership for the exploration of diamonds in the country, Debswana, was established between the state and the mineral giant company De Beers (Froitzheim, 2009). Ethiopia is assigned to the opposing majority of countries. Ethiopia is a historically very poor country, with low levels of development, ridden by long, violent, political conflicts. As such, Ethiopia corresponds to the leading descriptions made above about the African state, whereas Botswana does not. Interestingly, one of the promoters of Botswana as a model inside the continent was late former Ethiopian Prime Minister Meles Zenawi in his unpublished academic thesis 'African Development: Dead Ends and New Beginnings' (Zenawi, 2006), which includes a chapter dealing specifically with Botswana. Here Zenawi discusses Botswana as a successful case in the context of what he conceives as the failures of the liberal, or neoliberal, reforms in Africa in the 1980s and 1990s.

The basic issue that the Ethiopian leadership holds in hand in terms of a long, sustainable dynamic of development is the very low stage in which the country still finds itself. Despite recent propelled, double-digit growth annually, Ethiopia is still struggling with very strong dependence on subsistence agriculture, let alone limitations in infrastructure, human resources, and so on. In addition to that, problems of internal insurgencies undermine the prospects of development. Nevertheless, Ethiopia is part of the small group of African countries (together with South Africa and Liberia) with an 'idea of the state' (Clapham, 1996) outside the usual colonial structure. With the exception of the Italian occupation period and brief British administration that followed, at the turn of the mid-20th century, Ethiopia was never part of a European empire. Despite European influences for centuries, the modern state apparatus was initiated indigenously, even if according to a logic of internal colonial-like processes of domination, in which the Amhara ethnicity has predominated (Gilchrist, 2003). In turn, Botswana as a sovereign nation is not only recent, established in 1966, but also inherited the apparatus of the British Protectorate era.

The case of South Africa is very peculiar in the broader African context. It is so because it has been the far most economically advanced country in the continent, and therefore being in opposition to the average, poor, less developed African country. However, the persistence of a white minority regime of separate development (apartheid) during much of the postcolonial age rendered it problems of international recognition and acceptance, namely among African countries. Although South Africa did not share a pariah state status, that is, non-recognition, with the similar-minded regime of the former Republic of Rhodesia (today's Zimbabwe), this dual situation – being economically very advanced and influential yet in a context of exclusion of large sectors of its population – was observed by the end of the 1980s as 'a major threat hanging over the future of the continent, constituting a problem Africans had to continue to face and for which there seemed to be very little hope of finding any quick or peaceful solution' (Fage, 1988: 498). After the 1994 governmental elections and dismantlement of the apartheid, South Africa, with a multiracial government led by the African National Congress, has emerged as a vibrant influence across the continent, especially in Southern Africa. Remaining a 'regional hegemon' (Shillinger, 2006), South Africa has arguably reverted its negative reputation and is increasingly observed – not just in Africa but around the world – as a benign power both economically and militarily through engagement in the already mentioned NEPAD as well as in peacekeeping missions. It has become a liberal-idealist power, even if with flaws (Geldenhuys, 2008).

## Conclusion

From the late 1970s onwards, after a relatively short period of economic success subsequent to the first wave of independences (1960s), sub-Saharan African governments engaged in negotiations of development assistance funds from major donor countries and international financial institutions with the aim of resuming a path of economic growth and development. These negotiations not only implied the reproduction of a pattern of dependency to the Western donor countries and international financial organisations but also a subjection to conditionalities with socio-political effects. This neoliberally rooted approach was maintained throughout the 1980s and 1990s. However, from the early 21st century onwards it was supplemented with policies looking at specific unresolved problems structured around development, security and the state, in which interventions linking security goals to development appeared hand in hand with a necessity to – once again – reform state institutions. These are examples pointing at a striking hegemony of Western states and international organisations in sub-Saharan Africa, grounding an analytical shift from states to population.

However, the 'governmentality' of Western interventionism has been opposed by other governmentalities. Apart from the basic endowment that juridical-territorial sovereignty attributes, the neopatrimonial character of sub-Saharan African polity helped to retain important levels of independence. Despite the general context of underdevelopment of African societies, due to the reduction of investment in areas such as education or health, African elites sought to obtain external funding to retain their existence. As far as the attraction of external support is concerned, the 2000s heralded a diversification of sources. Although

Western donors remain relatively central, 'new partners', such as China, India and several Arab countries (for example, Saudi Arabia and United Arab Emirates), have appeared as significant alternatives. Nevertheless, a major novelty was the return of the development state as ideology and policy, parallel to pan-African initiatives aiming at growth and development such as NEPAD.

Despite reproducing traditional neopatrimonial practices and the serious negative impacts that might have on their national constituencies, these new developments in Africa appeared as instances of challenge to the perspective that sub-Saharan Africa is subject to a Western governmentality. In fact, the experience of the three last decades has been demonstrating the opposite, even with the asymmetry that persists between the West and sub-Saharan Africa, as well as between the latter region and the 'new partners'.

# 5
# PEPFAR: Project of Global Transformation

## Introduction

Since its inception PEPFAR has stood out as a global leader in HIV/AIDS intervention, with the aim of setting the agenda of delivering care and treatment emergently as well as, over time, working towards prevention of the disease and its interconnected issues. The latest proclamation has been made in 2011 by Secretary of State Hillary Clinton, who announced the ultimate goal of engendering 'an AIDS-free generation' for the world. Indeed, this programme, currently under a larger framework of global health, is a project of global transformation, particularly where the epidemic has its biggest impact, that is, in sub-Saharan Africa. Such transformation is aimed at the human and population level, yet also at the institutional and governance domains.

An emergent number of studies have focused on the actual practices and underlying subjectivities of the global health programmes on individuals and communities in the developing world in order to grasp the power exerted on those lives. Here the focus is on the frameworks that drive implementation, and thus this chapter looks into the origins, political rationales, policies and organisational design of PEPFAR, before proceeding to the analysis of the actual experience of implementation in Botswana, Ethiopia and South Africa.

## Origins of PEPFAR

The history of the US government's international intervention in HIV/AIDS started in 1986 with a USAID request to Congress for funding specifically for that area (Sheehan, 2008: 126). The main reason for doing it had to do with the developmental implications that the rising epidemic could originate. This was sensitive in the context of the late Cold War, particularly in Africa, where two models of development and modernity were challenging each other for influence: one market-based, of United States/Western inspiration, and another state-led, of Soviet/ Warsaw Pact support. This also happened in the context of the first international initiatives driven by WHO to establish programmes for monitoring and control of the epidemic (WHO, 2008). With the end of the Cold War in 1989, and despite an overall reduction of international development funding in the early 1990s, this intervention became part of a 'second phase' of United States-Africa relations and the progressive construction of

> concerns about under-development and humanitarian issues such as wars and armed conflicts, failed and collapsed states, poverty, HIV/ AIDS and environmental catastrophes such as drought and famine and their collective impact on United States national security. (Francis, 2010: 11)

Hence, progressively, HIV/AIDS started to be referred to as an issue of development with increasing security implications, as it came to be crystallised with the establishment of PEPFAR in 2003.

PEPFAR builds extensively on the experience of the Ryan White Comprehensive AIDS Resources Emergency (CARE) Act of 1990. It can be argued that PEPFAR constitutes a 'globalisation' of the early experience of a domestic programme. The CARE Act aimed at responding with a character of emergency to a disease that had already killed 50,000 people by 1990 in the United States of America (Rankin, 2009: 2). It had four components: primary care for those infected in major metropolitan areas; supportive services; early intervention and prevention programmes; and programmes for women, infants, children, youth and their families (Rankin, 2009: 5), and it was reauthorized four times: 1996, 2000, 2006 and 2009. This programme was the result of years of activism, namely by the person who gave name to the programme, Ryan White, an infected haemophiliac. This activism emerged in the face of years of neglect by the federal government, whose anti-gay stance had larger consequences to HIV/AIDS intervention in the country. Even though HIV can be transmitted in several ways, including blood transfusions, for a long time it was primarily associated to male homosexual practices, to the point of being called a 'gay cancer' in the early moments of discovery of the disease (Fee and Parry, 2008: 54).

The commonality between both programmes is visible in the way both have evolved. As it is discussed in more detail ahead in this chapter, both have started, as their titles make explicit, as emergency programmes for dealing with a crisis. Yet, they then pursued a strategy of transferring 'ownership' to the communities, which, in the case of PEPFAR, means largely the national governments and these countries' civil societies. The comments and examples that Leslie Rankin has put forward are informative on that regard.

> This approach is critical for HIV and AIDS services as localities are faced with many different issues. For example, an area that does not have coordinated public transit may allocate funding for van rides so that clients can be compliant with medical appointments, whereas an area with efficient public transit may chose to allocate funding for other purposes. By allowing localities the ability to prioritise rather than providing a standardised federal prioritisation, funding can be used efficiently to provide effective services. (Rankin, 2009: 44)

Over time, the CARE programme came to be confronted with the question of generating dependency. Considering that the programme's funding is largely spent on the provision of lifelong antiretroviral medications, the enrolment of new patients who could not, and cannot, turn to an alternative medical scheme in this programme has contributed to its increasing overall cost (Rankin, 2009: 45).

It should also be mentioned that the previous head of PEPFAR, Eric Goosby, was the first administrator of the CARE Act in 1991. Moreover, his career in the 1980s was spent in HIV/AIDS medical care (he is a medical doctor by training) primarily in the United States of America, and in the 1990s in the leadership of several other US domestic initiatives.

## From emergency to sustainability

As its name suggests, the first phase of PEPFAR has been particularly dedicated to emergency. Thus, it is no surprise that by 2007 slightly over half of PEPFAR's budget was going to treatment activities. According to GAO (2008: 12), the total allocation for treatment for the fiscal year 2007 alone was 1.16 billion USD. However, the acquisition of antiretroviral (ARV) drugs under PEPFAR is subject to strict rules. According to GAO (2005), all drugs that could be contracted by the recipient countries had to be approved by the United States Food and Drug Administration (FDA) and be of United States origin.

> Because the Emergency Plan is largely funded under the Foreign Assistance Act of 1961, the purchase of ARVs with these funds is subject to a provision of the act that prohibits the purchase of any medication manufactured outside the United States if the manufacture of that medication in the United States would be covered by a valid United States patent, unless the patent owner gives its permission. (GAO, 2005: 9–10)

As a result, in the beginning, and for a certain period, PEPFAR looked like it was functioning as a protection scheme for US pharmaceutical companies, which not only benefited economically from the programme but also sought to penetrate the most affected countries by the epidemic (Mann, 2003).

Nevertheless, the situation started to change over time, as GAO recommended an exploration of not only a larger palette of ARVs but also less expensive solutions in harmony with other donors' policies.

> The original ARVs provided under the plan are generally higher in price than the generic ARVs provided under the other initiatives. The differences in the prices, quoted to GAO during June and July 2004 by 13 manufacturers, ranged from $11 less to $328 more per person per year for original ARVs than for the lowest-priced corresponding generic ARVs provided under the other initiatives. At these prices, three of the four first-line regimens recommended by the World Health Organisation could be built for less – from $40 to $368 less depending on the regimen – with the generic ARVs provided under the other initiatives than with the original ARVs provided under the plan. Such differences in price per person per year could translate into hundreds of millions of dollars of additional expense when considered on the scale of the plan's goal of treating 2 million people by the end of 2008. (GAO, 2005)

Eventually, policy changed, and in October 2009 it was already permitting 100 drugs, including 71 generics (Medical: 2009). In this regard, a nongovernmental implementer in Ethiopia commented:

> In principle everything has to be American and licensed by the FDA [United States Food and Drug Administration]. However, experience

showed that was not very feasible. So we turned to Indian companies, especially for generics. Some companies in the US resisted (Abbott) but others were cooperative. With this move we could decrease the cost per patient from 1000 USD to 85 USD.

Indeed, PEPFAR started with a preoccupation of giving emergent relief in terms of making available treatment through ARVs and prevention of new infections. According to PEPFAR's first five-year strategy, the purpose was to 'rapidly mobilise resources' for 15 countries in order to 'provide treatment to 2 million HIV-infected people; prevent 7 million new HIV infections; and provide care to 10 million people infected and affected by HIV/AIDS, including orphans and vulnerable children' (PEPFAR, 2004). In addition to those core programmes, the programme would also develop supply-chain management systems, be driven by scientific evidence and build on public-private partnerships integrating both governmental and nongovernmental organisations, in which national 'bold leadership' is mandatory for success.

Although some specific research on PEPFAR has occasionally raised concerns about the quality of evaluation (Over, 2009), the PEPFAR coordination, the United States presidency and other higher level leadership has alluded to a great success in terms of saving 'millions of lives'. This tension was found in several interviews conducted, although the tendency is to speak rather positively about the impact. A respondent with a United States government agency in Ethiopia enthusiastically said '[before] PEPFAR there was just no assistance to HIV-infected people. Almost every patient visiting our medical facility was HIV-positive. PEPFAR has saved lives'. A respondent with an NGO in Botswana simply mentioned 'in many countries there was no response to AIDS.... And without PEPFAR countries would not be able to respond. I give a huge credit to PEPFAR'. In turn, a respondent with an international organisation in Ethiopia receiving PEPFAR funding gave a more balanced view:

> Since 2003 the assistance provided to the government has been improving, and the country is under way to reach universal access shortly. It was also good for tuberculosis and other opportunistic infections. There are more health centres too. The only shortcoming though is that it is only rooted on HIV/AIDS.

Another respondent with an international organisation in the same country referred, '[P]eople are now more informed. Although I do not know about the impact on infection and prevalence rates, I am aware PEPFAR has improved activities aimed at making people know their status'. In fact, the question of lack of measurement is found in another declaration, this time by an Ethiopian respondent with an Ethiopian NGO: 'PEPFAR has had a significant influence, but I do not have evidence about its efficiency'.

However, early assessments of impact on health systems so far are contradictory by PEPFAR. Although focusing on the 2000–2006 period, featured by the emergency mode, the comparison of PEPFAR focus and non-focus countries in light of WHO indicators 'demonstrates no significant difference in improvement in PEPFAR focus countries when compared with non-focus countries' (Duber et al., 2010: 8). In turn, global health initiatives such as PEPFAR have enhanced multisectoral coordination (Spicer et al., 2010). An interviewee with a PEPFAR-implementing NGO mirrors this duality.

> I would distinguish between positive intended consequences and negative unintended consequences. The former is that PEPFAR has reduced deaths and prolonged lives. In many places there was just no supply-chain and PEPFAR installed one. This is a benefit for the broad health system. The latter is that PEPFAR operates in a rather dysfunctional system. PEPFAR has pooled everything to HIV. It shifted resources allocated to TB, family planning and safe motherhood toward blood safety, ABC prevention, care and treatment and OVCs [orphans and vulnerable children].

The second phase was set up by the second five-year strategy plan that followed the Reauthorisation Act of 2008. Published in 2009, this document put forward an agenda aimed at achieving sustainability through country ownership in a spirit of 'shared responsibility' between the United States government and its partners in the host countries, especially the governments, and enlarging the scope of PEPFAR towards strengthening the health systems (PEPFAR, 2009a: 5–6). This policy shift from emergency to sustainability was reinforced by the proposal of the United States Global Health Initiative (GHI), an umbrella programme for all of United States governmental health-related programmes, in which PEPFAR maintains a leading role, while new dimensions, such as gender, are incorporated. The objective is to refrain from direct funding of service-providing activities to the populations, but to capacitate host countries' organisations to do it, as human resource capacity has long been identified as a major limitation to effective implementation (GAO,

2004). This is the definition of country ownership by Eric Goosby and colleagues:

> When the term 'country ownership' is used in the AIDS context, it is sometimes misunderstood to signal a complete absence of external support for a country's response. What it does mean, however, is that the overall leadership role belongs to the country, not to external partners. Every government has a unique responsibility to its people that flows from its sovereignty. (Goosby et al., 2012: 158)

More recently, the report *PEPFAR FY2013 Country Operational Plan (COP) Guidance* provides further resonance to the plan of achieving country ownership along those lines (PEPFAR, 2012). The report requests country teams to provide an update on dialogue and actions for transition, while advancing categorisation of host countries into long-term strategy: targeted assistance and technical collaboration, with co-financing as a principle of shared responsibility. This has been complemented by the passing of the PEPFAR Stewardship and Oversight Act of 2013 in November, which extends the programme's recently expired authorisation for another five years, followed by the nomination of Deborah Birx, former director of the Division of Global HIV/AIDS at the Centers for Disease Control and Prevention, as new US Global AIDS Coordinator.

Nonetheless, it should be mentioned that it does not merely represent a development in United States policy, but a rather international one. Prior to the Reauthorisation Act of 2008 and the 2009 five-year strategy report, the 2004 UNAIDS-sponsored Consultation on Harmonisation of International AIDS Funding's 'Three Ones' principles (one national HIV/AIDS strategy; one national AIDS coordinating authority; one national country-level monitoring and evaluation system) was already providing a policy framework in that direction (GAO, 2010: 4–6). This added to the 2002 United Nations International Conference on Financing for Development's 'Monterrey Consensus' and 2005 Paris Declaration on Aid Effectiveness. In order to materialise that strategic goal, PEPFAR constitutes partnerships with the host partner countries and non-state actors 'to ensure that PEPFAR programs reflect country ownership, with partner governments at the centre of decision making, leadership, and management of their HIV/AIDS programs and national health systems' (PEPFAR, 2012: 6). The Country Operational Plan (COP) provides 'the information for funding review and approval and serves as the basis for congressional notification, allocation, and tracking of budget and targets' (PEPFAR, 2012: 7). Moreover, COPs result in

> an opportunity to bring the United States country team together with partner government authorities, multilateral development partners, and civil society as an essential aspect of effective planning, leveraging resources, and fostering sustainability of programs. (PEPFAR, 2012: 8)

According to the GAO's (2010) study on the alignment of PEPFAR policies with the countries' strategies in four countries (two African, Uganda and Malawi; two Asian, Cambodia and Vietnam), which compared the national strategic and programmatic documents with PEPFAR's and consulted with PEPFAR implementers, 'PEPFAR activities generally support the goals laid out in partner countries' national HIV/AIDS strategies' (PEPFAR, 2012: 10). However, problems and limitations are also found. While some relate to 'differences between PEPFAR indicators and national and international indicators' and 'gaps in partner countries' access to PEPFAR information' (PEPFAR, 2012: 18–20), others concern 'unwillingness or inability to commit resources, public corruption and financial mismanagement, and lack of technical expertise' (PEPFAR, 2012: 20).

As referred above, one alleged reason for the unilateral stance of the United States of America *vis-à-vis* the multilateralism of many other donors has to do with tighter surveillance of spending by partner recipient governments in order to hamper corruption and mismanagement. As such, it is not surprising that, according to the latest PEPFAR report to Congress at the time of this writing, country ownership's 'key areas of focus included surveillance, planning, analysis, management, and budgeting, at key national ministries as well as other levels of government' (PEPFAR, 2011a). Yet, another major issue has precisely to do with how capable recipient countries, namely their governments, are to continue the current, PEPFAR-initiated and -funded efforts. National governments are embracing the idea and concept of country ownership as part of their developmental concerns. However, the levels of disbursing resources – the question of 'unwillingness or ability' quoted from the GAO's report – vary greatly according to the individual country's economic/developmental position. As far as the countries scrutinised in this book go, while Botswana and even South Africa are allocating national resources that account to about 80 per cent of the total expenditure in HIV/AIDS, Ethiopia is much lower.

To a large extent, the GHI, established soon after the inauguration of the Obama Administration in 2009, expands the ambition of the new policies on sustainability. This initiative seeks to pool together different ongoing plans (PEPFAR, the President's Malaria Initiative) and include areas such as maternal and child health, family planning, reproductive health and neglected tropical diseases, avian influenza and other epidemic threats (Kaiser, 2010). This thematic enlargement has also been noticeable for the apparent disappearance of the 'focus country' language in favour of a gradual enlargement of the number of countries benefiting directly from PEPFAR. This shift also happens at a time when PEPFAR's leadership has been forced to flatten or reduce the funding levels.

## Whole-of-government and partnership

PEPFAR is eminently rooted in a concept of partnership in which United States governmental and nongovernmental organisations are put together with host countries' counterparts, and possibly international organisations (such as WHO, UNAIDS, United Nations High Commissioner for Refugees, World Food Programme). The leadership of PEPFAR lies with the Office of the US Global AIDS Coordinator, and the United States government agencies involved are Department of State (namely embassies), USAID, Department of Defense (DoD), Department of Commerce, Department of Labor, Department of Health and Human Services (namely the Centers for Disease Control and Prevention [CDC]) and Peace Corps. There are two types of implementing partner: prime and sub-partner. The hierarchy is explained by the process of funding application, in which the prime secures the funding in the first place, and then channels it down to the sub-partner level. Generally prime partners obtain their funding from USAID, CDC or US embassies.

According to PEPFAR's 2004–2008 strategic document (2004), 15 billion USD were requested to the Congress for funding the plan, most of it directed to 15 focus countries. Apart from Botswana, Ethiopia and South Africa, the list was composed of Côte d'Ivoire, Guyana, Haiti, Kenya, Mozambique, Namibia, Nigeria, Rwanda, Tanzania, Uganda, Vietnam and Zambia. In 2009 these countries were given that status since they were 'home to approximately half of the world's estimated 33 million HIV-positive people and to almost 8 million children orphaned or made vulnerable by HIV/AIDS' (PEPFAR, 2009b). Still, funding was also extended to other countries, generally those where USAID was operating. However, in PEPFAR's second five-year period (2009–2013) strategy (PEPFAR, 2009a), the category of focus country virtually disappeared, later re-emerging under the auspices of GHI.

In addition to this division of labour, several PEPFAR-initiated projects have sought to include private companies in the host countries and, as such, accomplish an idea of country ownership described by a joint public and private collaboration. Two interviewees with different United States government agencies in Botswana gave two examples from the business sector from that country. One underlined the role of telecommunication companies in preventing actions against HIV/AIDS.

[Cell] phone technologies [in Botswana] are good. There is a deal in which Maskom [mobile communications provider] offers 100 Pula [Botswana currency] to its users when subscribing alert SMS for taking medications. This is a case of country ownership of the projects, in fact. Another stressed the structural relevance of Botswana diamonds public-private Debswana in the same efforts, which at the end of the day contribute to its success as a socially responsible organisation.

For us, country ownership is not government ownership, but ownership by the government, privates and civil society. This is why you want Debswana to be involved in this too.

Since the beginning, PEPFAR has attempted to constitute a change – if not a revolution – in two ways of organising and implementing international aid. One way had to do with augmenting levels of interagency collaboration among the various United States government agencies. Although two senior officials with USAID and DoD have claimed a prevailing view that historically both organisations have gone along very closely, PEPFAR's coordination has found it necessary to appeal for them to '"leave their uniforms at the door" and come together in the common cause of turning the tide against the HIV/AIDS pandemic' (PEPFAR, 2011b). To an extent, this setting constitutes an experiment of a larger hypothesis of reformulating US international development from a 'whole-of-government' (Herrling, 2009) perspective. For instance, the inclusion of the US African Growth and Opportunity Act (AGOA) in PEPFAR's division of labour is an example of that, especially in terms of the economic empowerment of people living with AIDS (PEPFAR, 2009c). Another way has concerned the character of relations between the US government and their counterparts in the country of implementation. According to the 2009 PEPFAR report to Congress, which focuses on partnerships, PEPFAR aims to change relations by turning an asymmetric relationship into one between equals.

The United States is changing the paradigm for development, rejecting the flawed 'donor-recipient' mentality and replacing it with an ethic of partnership that emphasises country ownership, good governance, and accountability. Partnership is rooted in hope for and faith in people. Partnership means honest relationships between equals based on mutual respect, understanding and trust, with obligations and responsibilities for each partner. Partnership is the foundation of PEPFAR's success and of what Secretary of State Condoleezza Rice has called 'transformational diplomacy'. (PEPFAR, 2009c: 18–19)

The constitution of 'partnership frameworks' signed between the United States of America and host countries' representatives include the principles of country ownership; sustainability; support for country coordination of resources; United States government interagency collaboration; engagement and participation; strategic framework; flexibility, progress towards policy reform and increased financial accountability; integration of HIV/AIDS into strengthened health systems and a broader health and development agenda; monitoring and evaluation; collaborative but not contractual; transparency; and 'do no harm' (PEPFAR, 2011c).[1]

Considering the book's basilar understanding of the international system as characterised by asymmetry, in international partnerships such as PEPFAR this is not just a question of one side possessing funds and exerting influence and the other side possessing very little at those levels. Commenting on research activities in Botswana, an interviewee with a Botswanan government ministry has called it 'scientific imperialism' the way US universities land in the country, request ethics approval, obtain blood samples, return to the United States of America and publish papers based on those samples, without being clear to what extent the 'blood-donor country' benefits from it. This asymmetry is further cemented on the security rationale attached to programmes like PEPFAR, which views the subjects of intervention as threats to the United States and international security, but also on bringing host countries' institutions, namely governments, to closer external scrutiny, ripping apart the porous border between the postcolonial state and the international community.

However, perhaps the greatest example of the asymmetry between the United States of America and recipient societies is the dependency created by the unlimited free provision of lifelong drugs by the former to the latter. This dependency corresponds to what Mead Over (2008) calls the 'ballooning entitlement' by recipient countries. This 'entitlement' is a result of a continuing public commitment to free provision of

ARVs by the United States leadership under PEPFAR in a context characterised by, on the one hand, growing financial difficulties to live up to that commitment, and, on the other, an increasing number of new infections. For Over, this uneasy system of dependency holds potential negative effects in the long run. Over emphasises the problem of 'entitlement' that recipient countries start to own with regard to receiving assistance from the United States of America, particularly in the case of antiretroviral drugs, which shall have to be handed to patients over the course of a lifetime so they have the desired lasting effect.

> To the extent that AIDS treatment is viewed as an entitlement by all parties to the transaction, the donor governments and their citizens on the one hand and the recipient governments and their patients on the other, the recipient governments and individuals might have diminished incentives to prevent HIV infection or to use efficiently the externally provided resources. Furthermore, it is human nature for people who are dependent on others to resent the dependency relationship. ... In the extreme, it is possible that a strong AIDS program in [PEPFAR focus] countries will create a kind of postmodern colonial relationship between the US and these countries – undermining the quality of these bilateral relationships. (Over, 2008: 19)

However, since this book is ultimately concerned with agency by national governments, and how it manifests itself, it is interesting to explore how interviewed implementers address this question of asymmetry. Here one verifies a clear difference of perspective between respondents with a United States government agency, and other respondents who, although part of the division of labour, have a critical view of the process. For instance, an interviewee with the United States government reiterated that imperialism is not a United States foreign policy aim. Yet, two rather emblematic positions could be found in one's inquiry. An African interviewee with a United States-based implementing NGO gave a rather pessimistic comment:

> Overall, before PEPFAR there were few ARVs available. Now there are more, and that means better health and less mortality, and thus less orphans. But now PEPFAR is changing priorities and countries in Africa are crying because they depend heavily on the ARV programme PEPFAR initiated. It is sad that we put our fate in the hands of the West.

Yet, another responded with the same characteristics put it in rather different terms: 'PEPFAR originates from early programmes for the military overseas and seeks to attain objectives of United States security. It is up to the Africans to do the most they can from it'. To an extent, Chapters 6, 7 and 8 respond to the latter's observation.

According to a 2009 GAO report, major fund-channelling US government agencies 'CDC and USAID [had] developed and implemented practices to provide accountability over PEPFAR awards, such as reviewing programmatic reports and financial data and providing technical assistance to partners' (GAO, 2009: 28). These practices included required reports; expenditure data and work plans; site visit checklists and reports; direct assistance; umbrella grant managers (for sub-partners); sub-awards; and third-party technical assistance providers (GAO, 2009: 28–30). Yet, the same report found difficulties in the area of compliance due to lack of USAID and CDC staff, overburden, and different reporting time frames (GAO, 2009: 32–35).

One of the main top-down disciplinary transmission belts is observed in the weight that bureaucratic compliance holds. While the implementation of surveillance practices is generally expectable to be pursued by funders and complied by recipients, several questions still arise. Focusing on the experience of non-United States government implementers, one such question has to do with how time consuming and even difficult it can be to collect the required information, especially when it is done by volunteers and in a context of scarcity of means of communication. An interviewee with a South African faith-based organisation (FBO) commented:

> The project relies vastly on lots of church volunteers, who nevertheless receive a small payment. It is difficult to get people to report, and thus match PEPFAR's requirements. Reporting is no less than monthly. What is required from field workers and volunteers is who has been reached, how were public gatherings. ... Field workers report to their supervisors, and they report to the main office in Cape Town. The main obstacles are found in the lowest levels. Reporting is a matter of copying and faxing, but it takes a lot of time.

Another interviewee with a sub-partner FBO, but in Botswana, lamented while pointing at piles of paper in his small office to be delivered to its prime partner: 'Funds come with conditions. It is difficult to be flexible. Look, this is the bureaucracy we have to go through!' Another NGO respondent, in South Africa, gave a different nuance:

Many organisations I have been working with have refused PEPFAR funding given the administrative overload and the reporting compulsiveness. This tendency has been augmenting. Besides, requirements are very stringent. We have to report every single month. We have to comply with the United States government. This is all about compliance or not. For PEPFAR it is more important to report than work in the field. Our office here is just to deal with bureaucracy.

Another South Africa respondent insisted on the stringent need to report.

How can I put it diplomatically?...Partners have to do lots of reporting, to pay a lot of attention to numbers. PEPFAR is very much centred in obtaining numbers, and that is difficult to pursue by implementing organisations. In fact many implementing people are constantly worried about gathering numbers and thus showing service (to PEPFAR coordination).

Another NGO interviewee in South Africa gave an interesting insight framed in terms of West versus non-West, and how apparently opposing institutions (funder and funded) 'ally' themselves:

We have deep links with the communities, and it is often difficult for them to comply with the reporting because it requires skills that people do not have, for example, deadlines. People in the ground are not like us in the Western world; they are not used to deadlines. Another thing has to do with the fact that we are preoccupied with quality, but PEPFAR is too demanding with numbers. If we do not get them the numbers, we do not get any funding or we have to return the money. USAID understands our position, but they are with their hands tied. Flexibility is something lacking. But this is not a criticism but a challenge.

Another NGO respondent in South Africa gave yet another insight, pointing at inter-implementing organisation level, which can be featured by competition and rivalry.

PEPFAR requirements are not in many instances relevant to the realities on the ground. For example, the way that PEPFAR demands that we count compromises on quality service provision and encourages competition among partners.

## United States foreign policy and security strategy for Africa

The real or constructed implications of HIV/AIDS, particularly in sub-Saharan Africa, where the epidemic was found proliferating extensively since the 1980s, too, have long become a subject of interest to the United States Department of State, namely its autonomous agency for international development, USAID. Addressed first as an issue of health and development, it increasingly became a topic in security discussions, even if asymmetrically, from the late 1980s through the 1990s. Congressional hearings and presidential documents across that time period demonstrate a security concern associated to the epidemic, both in its domestic (inside the United States of America) and international dimensions (Sheehan, 2008). After a sharp decline during most of the 1990s, it resurged in the late 1990s, yet with a larger emphasis on the link between AIDS and security than ever before (Sheehan, 2008: 163–164).

Richard Holbrooke, United States ambassador to the United Nations at the end of the 1990s, was arguably the key element in the US government to elaborate a security discourse about the epidemic that eventually led to the first United Nations Security Council meeting on HIV/AIDS on 10 January 2000. His discourse pointed at two interconnected aspects. One had to do with the impact on the military when operating overseas, in peacekeeping missions or else, and another on potential social disruptions in sites characterised by a hyper-epidemic. In an interview in May 2006, Holbrooke commented on both aspects.

> My first personal observation was in Cambodia in 1992 when I went there as a private citizen, and I saw the peacekeepers from the United Nations in Cambodia, and they were doing a good job. But at night I saw them wandering around the street drunk and going into whorehouses and so on and so forth, and I was quite upset about this. It was clear that they were spreading AIDS, and they were going to take AIDS back with them. (Holbrooke, 2006)

And after a visit paid to ten African countries in 1999 he observed:

> Watching kids sleep in the gutters in Lusaka [Zambia], knowing that they will become either prostitutes or rape victims, either getting or spreading the disease, because there's no shelter for them, and that the government is doing nothing about it, makes a powerful impression on you. ... I said: 'Look at the facts; it's not simply a humanitarian issue. If a country loses so many of its resources in fighting a disease

which takes down a third of its population, it's going to be destabilised, so it is a security issue.' ... Anyway, that was years ago. That issue is over. Everyone now accepts our definition of AIDS as a security issue – it's self-evident. (Holbrooke, 2006)

Also in January 2000, the United States Central Intelligence Agency (CIA) published a report which presented HIV/AIDS as a security threat to the United States (National Intelligence Council, 2000), followed by another in 2002 about the 'second wave' countries whose future experience with the epidemic will lead to disruptions with global consequences (Gordon, 2002). Following on these developments, Washington, DC-based think tank Center for Strategic and International Studies (CSIS) has also published along these lines. According to analysts Mark Schneider and Michael Moodie (2002), after Southern and Eastern Africa, strategically crucial countries such as Russia, India and China, together with very populous African countries such as Nigeria and Ethiopia, were emerging as the next regions severely affected by the epidemic.

In this regard, the topic of infectious diseases was thus framed in the 2002 Strategic Concept.

New flows of trade, investment, information, and technology are transforming national security. Globalisation has exposed us to new challenges and changed the way old challenges touch our interests and values, while also greatly enhancing our capacity to respond. Examples include: *Public health challenges like pandemics (HIV/AIDS, avian influenza) that recognize no borders.* The risks to social order are so great that traditional public health approaches may be inadequate, necessitating new strategies and responses. (The White House, 2006: 47, italics in the original)

A first and very influential narrative highlighted scenarios of socio-economic disruption, loss of state capability, violent conflict and terrorism within worst-affected societies in Southern and Eastern Africa (Elbe, 2003; Price-Smith, 2002; Altman, 2003). United States army official Charlene Jefferson summarises this complexity, where orphans and vulnerable children attract major attention:

Simply put, a disturbing new formula may be emerging; AIDS creates economic devastation. Economic devastation creates an atmosphere where stable governments cannot function. When stable governments cannot effectively function, terrorism thrives by exploiting the underlying conditions that promote the despair and the destructive visions of political change......... AIDS has created a steady stream of orphans who can be exploited and used for terrorist activities. (Jefferson, 2006: 6–7)

Princeton Lyman and J. Stephen Morrison (2006) have suggested that countries like Nigeria and South Africa offer safe havens for recruitment of children and youths for jihadist, anti-Western activities at home and abroad, exploiting on the epidemic effects. The question of international peacekeeping forces deployed in the developing world and their exposure to the virus through engagement with female sex workers was also explored by Stefan Elbe (2003), Matthew L. Lim (2004) and Martin Rupiya (2006). In Russia, AIDS proliferation within the army also became a matter of national security by the government, too, as a result of increasing incidence of the virus nationwide (Eberstadt, 2002; Sjösted, 2008). It should also be mentioned that AIDS has been likewise linked as a variable to other socially constructed threats, namely migrants and refugees and climate change (IRIN, 2006; AAP, 2008).

However, other authors, such as Laurie Garrett (2005) and Alex de Waal (de Waal, 2006), expressed scepticism about the propelled causality. The nexus is eminently speculative (McInnes, 2006) and based more on intuition than on evidence (Barnett and Prins, 2006). AIDS is a long-wave event, and hence it requires the careful analysis of three generations so one can draw peremptory conclusions about its real impact.

Put briefly, an infected person has children, these are orphaned and may grow up to be infected, but not before they have themselves had children – who are orphaned in turn. Hence a basic unit of social structure in most human societies, the three-generation bond linking grandparents, parents and children in a continuously reproduced pattern is rent asunder. (Barnett, 2006: 298)

De Waal has led a research team in recent years whose empirical evidence argues against the HIV-security framework as well (de Waal, 2010).

Notwithstanding, it is interesting to notice that at time of publication of the two CIA reports there was a change in United States administration (from Clinton to Bush), where Bush's first remarks on Africa were of little engagement with the continent. In 2000, George W. Bush stated that '[while] Africa may be important, it does not fit into the national interests, as far as I can see them' (Francis, 2010: 10), something that seems contradictory with the growing presentation of the epidemic as an existential threat. Nonetheless, after the 11 September 2001 attacks in New York City and Washington, DC, there was a resurgence of that rhetoric under a more comprehensive policy framework linking (failed) states, counter-insurgency, development and epidemics, too, with Africa broadly constituting an important site of analysis and implementation. At the end of his tenure (between 2006 and 2009), United States Global AIDS Coordinator Mark Dybul had used these terms:

> Our future is Africa's future and Africa's future is our future. So there's very much that long-term vision for a stable world in which we play a role and have a role. And it's in our self-interest. ... [These programs] have changed how people view America. ... people know what we stand for when we stand with them. And eight of ten of the countries in the world with the highest approval rating of the United States, sometimes higher than the United States itself, are in Africa. ... These programs touch lives. (Dybul, 2009)

However, the growing influence of China in Africa has also led to reinforced attention to the geopolitical implications (Osikena, 2010: 169–170). An interviewee with a US government agency in Botswana lamented that the United States of America does not get the same newspaper credit for the HIV/AIDS effort as Chinese building companies operating in the country do.

Nonetheless, the foreign policy and security argument is not by any means the only PEPFAR driver. As a large-scale humanitarian endeavour, humanitarianism and compassion for the sufferer are simultaneously at the core of PEPFAR since the very beginning. Still, the post-Bush administration has clearly downgraded the role of security as a driver. This is particularly visible in the latest *National Security Strategy* (The White House, 2010):

> The United States has a moral and strategic interest in promoting global health. When a child dies of a preventable disease, it offends our conscience; when a disease goes unchecked, it can endanger our own health; when children are sick, development is stalled. That is why we are continuing to invest in the fight against HIV/AIDS. Through the Global Health Initiative, we will strengthen health systems and invest in interventions to address areas where progress has lagged, including maternal and child health. And we are also pursuing the goal of reducing the burden of malaria and tuberculosis

and seeking the elimination of important neglected tropical diseases. (The White House, 2010,: 39)

While adopting new programmatic tools, that is, the Global Health Initiative (GHI), the focus has been on assisting with the provision of public health goods and services in a more encompassing way. This addresses the continuous civil society advocacy for development.

## Domestic constituencies

The United States of America has a large constituency implicated both in the policy making and practice of development-related issues, which can be seen as a product of the eminent rise as a military and economic superpower worldwide, particularly after the Second World War. Despite some resistance to allocating aid overseas by some advocates of a more inward, isolationist position, the majority of political leaders and their constituents, either for idealist or realist purposes (Ruttan, 1996: 2), are in favour of actively engaging in, and moreover leading, programmes that aim at improving human development indicators in the developing world (education, health), as well as economic growth, democracy and civil society. This tendency has been recently confirmed by a survey published by the Council on Foreign Relations that found that

> [there] is a widespread consensus in the United States that developed countries have a moral responsibility to work to reduce hunger and severe poverty and that helping poor countries develop serves the long-term interests of wealthy countries, including by developing trade partners and enhancing global stability. (Council on Foreign Relations, 2009)

It should be added that this 'consensus' is basically shared with other developed countries, therefore showing that this cannot be seen as a United States distinctive trace, as many policy makers and activists often seem to suggest in domestic settings when alluding to 'American values' (Goodwin, 2007: 49; Ziker, 2008: 10; Schaefer, 2009: 142). The same case is verified when respondents are enquired on whether or not they would be eager to pay more taxes in the name of international development, and they answer they would not. This response is arguably based on 'extremely exaggerated estimates' (Council on Foreign Relations, 2009) of the government's actual expenditure on foreign aid.

As large and comprehensive as it has been, PEPFAR has sought to attract the interest (and sometimes the criticism too) of the relevant constituency composed by universities and nongovernmental voluntary organisations. In his mid-1990s account of the domestic politics of governmental foreign assistance in the United States, Vernon W. Ruttan claimed that these two types of organisations were generally facing a rather unpredictable future as 'clients' of USAID (Ruttan, 1996: 203–251). The former's relationship with USAID had been declining since the early 1980s (Ruttan, 1996: 217) in an overall 'long history of frustration ... due in large part to the differing perceptions of administration and staff ... on the appropriate role of the two institutions [university and USAID]' (Ruttan, 1996: 220). The latter were generally appreciated over time for 'stimulating community development and empowerment [in the developing world]' (Ruttan, 1996: 235). However, the same author and former USAID official concluded in 1996 that they

> [unfortunately] ... have not been able to convince either the development professionals in the assistance agencies or the journalists who report on their activities in the field either that they have been very effective in providing relief in a manner that does not generate dependency or of their capacity to implement and manage development projects that achieve sustainability. (Ruttan, 1996: 235)

With PEPFAR these entities made a dramatic return, insisting publicly on their capacity to generate effective results.

A specific type of nongovernmental organisation involved in PEPFAR's division of labour that has been relatively distinctive is the faith-based organisation (FBO). Even though very significant funding has been allocated to non-faith-based organisations (for instance, in the areas of research and community development), FBOs were subject to 'positive discrimination' by the Bush administration, as one interviewee with a FBO-implementing agency admitted:

> As a faith-based organisation we benefited from the policy preference of the Bush administration. Now funding will be more dispersed among different organisations, secular and faith-based. Secular are more into distribution of condoms. We were discriminated positively.

This applied in terms of access to funding and given freedom to adopt their privileged policy of action, particularly as far as prevention is concerned, in turn, as will be discussed below, already legally trimmed to suit their preferences for messages of abstinence and marital fidelity at the expense of condoms and other 'liberal' approaches. Several authors associate this presence to the ascendancy of the Christian Right in the country, and the support it gave to Bush's consecutive elections (Dietrich, 2007; Buss and Herman, 2003; Marsden, 2008).

The Christian Right does not constitute, or agglomerate around, a single political entity in the United States political system. Therefore, several definitions have been advanced over time. For the purpose of this book, one builds on the conceptualisation by Lee Marsden, according to which

> [the] term 'Christian Right'...applies to conservative evangelicals and right-wing Catholics within the Republican Party whose religious persuasion determines their attitudes to political questions. This grouping consists of organisations, politicians, activists and supporters who are generally Protestant evangelicals, but also includes right-wing Catholics supportive of conservative moral and fiscal values on issues such as abortion, sexuality and free markets...united in their opposition to abortion, euthanasia, stem-cell research, homosexuality, same-sex marriage, promiscuity, secularism and big government. (Marsden, 2008: 3–4)

In addition to that, the Christian Right supports the war in Iraq and other military operations, and hence are, in principle, persuaded by the security rationales underlying development interventions, let alone their Christian sympathy for those in need of salvation, material and spiritual. As far as HIV/AIDS goes, Marsden refers to opinion polls that claim that 'between one-third and three-quarters considers AIDS to be a punishment from God' (Marsden, 2008: 75).

It should also be added that Christian Right's organisations have had their direct international relations with partners from all over the world, including sub-Saharan Africa, where Christianity has grown exponentially in the last decades, 'from 144 million in 1970 to 411 million by 2005' (Marsden, 2008: 76). Many African Catholics with connections to the United States of America have traditionally been associated with the Christian Right (Buss and Herman, 2003: 94), but the most recent 'renewalists' (that is, Pentecostals and Charismatics), 17 per cent of the total Christian population in sub-Saharan Africa, have stronger ties, and also have increased dramatically (Marsden, 2008: 76). As a result, they offer an ideological-institutional framework where the Christian

Right's influences can be disseminated, although, as Doris Buss and Didi Herman (2003: 95) have noted, it is not clear whether there is mutual share of world views between United States and African congregates. John W. Dietrich (2007: 290) points at Evangelical Janet Museveni, wife of Ugandan long-standing ruler Yoweri Museveni and head of Christian AIDS-funded Uganda Youth Forum, as an example of empathy between the United States Christian Right and Africa. However, Alex de Waal (2006: 99–100) has observed Janet Museveni's move as a collaborative effort of the ruling couple of maximising AIDS funding with several donors and their ideologies. Whereas the first lady works with absti-nence-backing United States partners, the president was turning to condoms-driven European donors.

With the change from Republican to Democrat administration, Christian Right-backed policies in PEPFAR, particularly the Mexico City Policy that forbids any federal funding for family planning activi-ties conducive to abortion, were reversed. This has given momentum to organisations on the opposite side of the spectrum, that is, liberal and supportive of sex education, condoms and consented abortion. However, that does not mean a retreat of the Christian Right, rather on the contrary. In fact, recent congressional debates on funding have reconsidered the reversal of that funding back to restriction.

## The presidency and bipartisanism

Considering the name of the programme, in which the president appears as the 'sponsor' of the programme, one ought to scrutinise the role of the presidency in the establishment and execution of PEPFAR. The same applies to the bipartisan character of this initiative, in which, since the beginning, it has been stressed by policy makers that it has been gath-ering both Republican and Democrat congressmen and senators in its endorsement, despite policy differences.

The figure of the president is regarded in itself as a cornerstone of foreign policy in the United States of America. As Glenn P. Hastedt claims in his in-depth study of United States foreign policy making, 'in the eyes of the public, it is the president who makes American foreign policy' (Hastedt, 2009: 184). Even though his advisors certainly play a role and hold their leverage on the defining decisions, examples throughout history demarcate the level of autonomy maintained by presidents (Hastedt, 2009: 184–186). In the case of PEPFAR, Bush has recognised the early advice he received from national security advisor Condoleezza Rice on establishing a HIV/AIDS programme with a humanitarian as well as security focus (McGreal, 2010). According to Hastedt, the nature of the president's personality has much to do with the decisions and initiatives that are pursued. One element of his personality that has been associated to PEPFAR concerns his world view, that is, the president's 'politically relevant beliefs' (Hastedt, 2009: 188). Moreover, in the case of PEPFAR promoter and leader George W. Bush, during most of the programme's history so far, Bush is regarded (following terminology by James David Barber cited by Hastedt) as an example of 'active-positive presidents [who] put a great deal of energy into being president and derive great satisfaction from doing so' (Hastedt, 2009: 188).

In the previous section, the important role of the Christian Right in the process of election and re-election of George W. Bush in 2000 and 2004 was highlighted. Some commentators have regarded the adoption of specific policies as part of a Christian Right-led political structure (Dietrich, 2007; Rosen, 2006). However, another opinion emphasises that Bush's decisions derive from his own (Christian) values. For instance, when asked what drove the establishment of PEPFAR, a long-standing official with a United States government PEPFAR-implementing agency has commented that 'in [her] personal opinion, it relied on the Bush person, a conservative, charitable individual who believed that this was the best thing to do'. Eventually, both elements do match one another.

Over the years, George W. Bush was constantly implicated by the media and commentators with the programme, often in a very personalised way, thus confirming the above claim of the president's centrality in (foreign) policy making. This intimate connection to the programme has been particularly emphasised in 2008 during the process that led to its reauthorisation and his personal visits to African countries, in which he insisted on the maintenance and reinforcement of the programme (Wolf and Page, 2008; Schaefer and Kim, 2008). After his retirement in early 2009, George W. Bush has acknowledged that PEPFAR was a major aspect of his foreign policy (McGreal, 2010), and his global AIDS coordinator Mark Dybul even suggested that a Nobel Peace Prize should be awarded to Bush.

> Dybul did say he believes that Bush deserves a Nobel Peace Prize for his work in Africa. 'There was literally no global response until President Bush came forward and said enough is enough,' he said. Dybul said that the global shift in the direction of development also warrants the prize. 'If you look at this objectively, no one can say that that is not the ring of a Nobel Peace Prize.' (Huseman, 2010)

However, other commentators in 2008 have argued that this engagement with PEPFAR and other presidential health initiatives, such as the President's Malaria Initiative, was a way to save face *vis-à-vis* the rising economic recession affecting the United States of America and the unresolved problems in the major foreign policy and military sites, Iraq and Afghanistan (Feffer, 2008).

Since its inception, PEPFAR has been characterised by bipartisanism, as both leading political forces in the United States Congress and Senate, Republicans and Democrats, have approved the plan in 2003 and reauthorised it in 2008. Despite the prominence of the figure of the president and the strong support by his Christian Right's constituency, more clearly visible in a number of policies, the almost simultaneous timings of reauthorisation and election of the next president proved the necessary political flexibility in order to not only continue but even expand the plan. Apart from questions of budgeting, which some Republican senators contested for sometime before the reauthorisation, the major dispute had to do with the notable requirement that one-third of the prevention money had to be spent on abstinence-only education (Feller, 2008).

As Barack Obama is elected in 2008 and inaugurates his mandate in early 2009, the presidential engagement in global health is upgraded toward the launch of the Global Health Initiative (GHI), which aims at strengthening health systems in countries with United States health and development assistance by building on the experience of previous initiatives, most notably PEPFAR (PEPFAR, 2010). GHI is implemented in 73 countries worldwide, eight of them, including Ethiopia, having 'GHI plus' status.[2] GHI plus countries receive additional technical and management assistance from the United States government and were selected according to 'criteria that include partner country interest, presence of the major GHI health programs, burden of disease, geographic diversity, and potential to leverage bilateral, multilateral, and foundation investments' (Kaiser, 2011: 7). The same applies to another development tool, the Millennium Challenge Corporation, which remains.

The importance of bipartisanism in US politics is also visible in another case. When starting his mandate in 2001, Bush maintained the African Growth and Opportunity Act (AGOA) (Schneidman, 2008), a relevant tool in the United States-Africa relationship. Established by the Clinton administration, AGOA was later articulated with the Leadership Against HIV/AIDS, Tuberculosis and Malaria Act of 2003, which established PEPFAR, and has been serving as a component of the plan's implementation since 2003.

## Between bilateralism and multilateralism

A remarkable feature of PEPFAR is its tendency to pursue a style of implementation mostly based on a bilateral relationship between US government implementing agencies and their counterparts and/ or recipient organisations in the host countries. Although important fund allocations to the Global Fund under PEPFAR have been occurring, the largest chunk of intervention has been done in a bilateral way.

The reason for this tendency has been explained as a need to secure autonomy with regard to policy decision, away from multilateral deliberation at the Global Fund and the United Nations system at large. A major reason for maintaining this bilateral orientation in global HIV/AIDS policy concerns the issues of abstinence-only and family planning, in which conflictive views between the Bush administration and the Western European and United Nations establishment persisted (Ingram, 2005). For instance, in 2002, funding to the United Nations Population Fund, in charge of family planning intervention worldwide, was suppressed by the Bush administration (Ingram, 2005: 391). As a whole, this trend was confirmed time and again in other instances, especially in the area of gas emissions control and climate change.

Another reason has to do with US policy makers and development practitioners' factual knowledge or only perception about the modus operandi of (multilateral) Global Fund staff *vis-à-vis* theirs, in terms of relations with the host countries' governments. An interviewee with a United States government agency commented that whereas Europeans (who work mostly through the Global Fund, apart from their own bilateral initiatives) have 'little problems' with transferring funds directly to African ministries, the United States of America is much less complacent in that regard. According to this interviewee, the chances of having money lost to corruption are higher when the tighter control of the United States system is not in place. The need to keep funding under control is so relevant that, if necessary, accountants are hired to work at the national ministries just to be sure that money is not stolen, that is, directed to the minister's extended family, as the interviewee explained. For this respondent, local 'theft' is still a fatality, yet one that can still be minimised if control is exerted directly by the donor country. Yet, the United States government is currently demonstrating more alignment and collaboration with other major stakeholders: country governments as well as other donors.

## Conclusion

Although the shift from emergency to sustainability mode suggests an apparent refrain from the exercise of deep-seated influence in the countries where it is implemented, the matter of fact is that PEPFAR stays as a project with very ambitious goals. Whether it is achieving it and how, that is another analysis; for the purpose of this book, it should be highlighted the flexible manner in which PEPFAR's leadership has been coping with constraints, particularly financial ones.

Indeed, while it is true that the PEPFAR cannot maintain the same levels of 'rushed' funding and needs to establish regional and policy priorities, it is equally valid to argue that the power project that it embodies has not changed qualitatively much. Inculcation of country ownership and 'shared responsibility' are solutions in the context of necessary adaptation. The same happens with regard to the combination of political rationales – between security concerns and humanitarian imperatives – and the involvement of domestic constituencies. Other governmental donors and international organisations are also increasingly part of the picture of United States global health policy, demonstrating further flexibility to manoeuvre this tremendous programme.

# 6
# Botswana: National Survival against HIV/AIDS

## Introduction

Botswana has long enjoyed an optimistic status in United States diplomacy as a 'model country' for Africa, that is, one where market economic systems and liberal democracy have been put into place consistently throughout the whole postcolonial age. Therefore, externally generated HIV/AIDS policies have been quite inclined to be successfully implemented, particularly when compared to other countries, notably South Africa and Ethiopia. As a 'model', the Botswanan experience is advanced as a subject of emulation by the rest of the developing world – in sub-Saharan Africa, to begin with.

This chapter explores the reasons why this has been the case, regardless of the effectiveness of those policies with regard to reducing the still very daunting epidemiological landscape. One argues that cooperative embracement of international HIV/AIDS policies by the Botswanan government is explained by a combination of relatively smooth transition from British Protectorate to independence and an utter historical need to achieve national survival in a very tense regional context. While prior, and after the independence, material development was deemed as the major solution to attain national integrity particularly in the face of South Africa, from the 1990s onwards the threat of HIV/AIDS has been the main driver of governmental action.

## Role of economic development in transition to independence

As a sovereign state, Botswana is the direct inheritor of the British Protectorate of Bechuanaland. This Protectorate was established in 1885 as a result of the necessity to prevent an alliance between the former Boer republic of Transvaal (now the Gauteng province of South Africa) and the former German South West Africa (now Namibia). Such alliance could undermine British access to former Southern Rhodesia (now Zimbabwe) from the former Cape Colony (Parsons, 1999).

Although it nominally formed a British domain, it was in the interest of the local Tswana rulers to maintain this alliance with the United Kingdom, given the record of conflict with Transvaal throughout the 19th century (Parsons, 1999). Five years after the constitution of the Protectorate, the British South Africa Company (BSAC) was established to proceed with the construction of a railway across Bechuanaland. The British government considered the allocation of the Protectorate to that company, which generated a worrying reaction by the local rulers. In 1895, the three Tswana kings, Bathoen, Khama III and Sebele, travelled to London and requested the British government not to proceed with that measure in exchange for the maintenance of Protectorate administration. After a lobbying campaign, the rulers were successful with that mission (Parsons, 1999). Nonetheless, the Tswana monarchs had to concede to the BSAC enterprise. But, all in all, it can be argued that the Tswana leaders benefited from the regime of Protectorate administered by the British. On the one hand, despite conceding to BSAC, they enjoyed a military protection from the Boer republic that they could hardly afford. Furthermore, the system of indirect rule allowed for the increase of their actual empowerment of their leadership. For instance, the local elite benefited from colonial capitalistic policies of cattle development, together with the British white farmers.

A reason why the United Kingdom was somehow easily persuaded to concede to the native rulers' request had to do with the fact that it always regarded Bechuanaland as a 'temporary expedient' (Parsons, 1999). Sooner or later, Botswana would be integrated either in former Southern Rhodesia or South Africa, since it was 'a mere appendage of South Africa, for which it provided migrant labour and the rail transit route to Rhodesia' (Parsons, 1999). Unlike the other two domains, subject to intense colonial rule and economic exploration, Botswana remained largely marginal in that process. In fact, no significant development was made in the country until the independence in 1966. For example, the construction of the capital city itself, Gaborone, only started in 1964. Until then the administrative centre was located in Mafikeng, on the South African side.

Transition to national sovereign rule was peaceful and never seriously contested British principles of political and economic organisation. The reason for such smoothness has been found in the fact that the dominating elite ante- and post-independence was one and the same, one of its great representatives consisting precisely on Seretse Khama (Varela, 2006: 266–267). A year before formal independence, in 1965, the first elections for self-government took place, and the moderate, liberal Bechuanaland Democratic Party was under the leadership of Seretse Khama, who became the first Prime Minister of Botswana and founding father of the modern state. With the independence, the Bechuanaland Democratic Party was renamed Botswana Democratic Party (BDP), and Khama became President of the Republic of Botswana. The BDP has won all multiparty elections until today, and Khama governed until his death in 1980. Ketumile Masire governed from 1980 to 1998 and Festus Mogae from 1998 to 2008. Seretse Khama Ian Khama, son of the first president, is the current president.

Transition to national sovereign rule was smooth, and the country never underwent internal, mass-scale, political violence, like its neighbours (Namibia, South Africa and Zimbabwe), which nevertheless affected Botswana at times. The national army itself was only established in 1977 as a consequence of a former Rhodesian army's incursion into Botswana in search for black insurgents. Later, in 1985 and 1986, bombings by the South African apartheid army took place in southern parts of the country (Kelebonye, 2010).

This transition was led by the same local and colonist elites, and the developmentalist framework based on market economy and liberal multiparty democracy was clearly aligned with the West. However, it should be stressed that, despite this configuration, Botswana's political leadership maintained a rather realist understanding of its political situation and the way the bipolar politics of the Cold War were having an impact on its survival as a country, particularly from the late 1970s until the end of apartheid, and more broadly the Cold War in the early 1990s. In one of the few political science articles on Botswana's foreign policy (already dating 20 years old), James J. Zaffiro argues that

> During the 1980s, Botswana was able to capitalise on friendly relations with both superpowers thus benefiting from their diplomatic support in times of crisis, such as in the aftermath of the 14 June 1985 South African Defence Force (SADF) raid in Gaborone. (Zaffiro, 1992: 59)

Although the domestic politics of the country were West-leaning, the reality of standing right in the core of numerous violent conflicts forced the Botswanan leadership to engage with all parties involved in difficult circumstances.

In 1966, at the time of independence, Botswana was one of the poorest countries in the world, and there was very limited power and communications infrastructure at the time. The country received large developmental support from the United Kingdom, and later from the United States, especially in the area of education and health. But two decades into independence, the country experienced massive growth rates. With the discovery and exploration of diamonds, it attained some of the highest growth rates in the world, achieving a 13 per cent annual growth in GDP between 1980 and 1989 (Hillbom, 2008: 191). This achievement was thanks to the discovery, exploration and trade of diamonds under the Debswana public-private partnership that put together the Botswana state and the mineral giant De Beers, founded by Cecil Rhodes, the early owner of the South African railway company.

Since 1966, year of the independence, Botswana became an Asian-style developmental state, whose initial goals consisted on developing basic infrastructure (roads, electricity, water) between the main towns.

> Four 'broad pillars' of Botswana's first national development plan included: (1) self-help; (2) assistance by other governments in major national undertakings beyond the resources of the country, such as the Shashi Dam and industrial development; (3) encouragement of private investment; and (4) education. (Zaffiro, 1992: 62)

The 'other governments' consisted mostly of the United Kingdom, provider of most of development funding; the United States of America, at a later stage and in a rather limited way (for instance, in the areas of education and training by the Peace Corps and some universities); the Soviet Union, even if indirectly (the Soviet anti-apartheid and pro-black liberation movements stances); and South Africa, the regional economic hegemony (Parsons, 1999).

> The planning and execution of economic development took off in 1967–1971 after the discovery of diamonds at Orapa. The essential precondition of this was renegotiation of the customs union with South Africa, so that state revenue would benefit from rising capital imports and mineral exports – rather than remaining a fixed percentage of total customs union income. This renegotiation was achieved in 1969. (Parsons, 1999)

In fact, relations with South Africa were thorny. On the one hand, South African trade cooperation was needed. On the other, being a black-led country, Botswana was not racially aligned with the apartheid in South Africa and Namibia, and (until 1980) the white minority-led former Rhodesia. Botswana was subject to air raids in 1985 and 1986 by South Africa since there was a suspicion that Botswana was hosting African National Congress (ANC) insurgents within its borders (Kelebonye, 2010; Parsons, 1999). The trade-off appeared to rely on both parties' commitment, if not to liberal, non-racial democracy, at least to capitalism. Botswana's foreign policy over time, from 1966 until today, has indeed been rather realist in terms of its formulation and execution.

As noted, Botswana started off its path of independence as one of the poorest countries in the world at the time of independence. Yet, with the exploration of diamonds, it attained remarkable growth rates which allowed the country to launch the necessary infrastructural development. At the same time, Botswana sought to maintain regular multiparty elections, presidential and parliamentary, even though they were always won by the same party, the BDP. But that did not seem to be highly problematic for analysts, since post-Second World War Sweden and Japan also exhibited the same characteristics.

> Some of the most impressive democratic developmental performers over the past half century, notably Sweden and Japan and more recently Botswana, have had one-party dominant systems, which, in their cases at least, seem to have combined the best of both developmental and democratic worlds. The dominant party was subject to regular democratic tests at the ballot box and constantly subject to the pressures of a free civil society, while at the same time maintaining the coherence, authority and capacity for long-term decision-making which is necessary for tackling the structural problems of development. (White, 2006: 66)

It should be added that this reversal of poverty was being obtained spectacularly and with 'good governance,' but also in a context of relative impoverishment of African postcolonial economies and defection to authoritarianism (Mkandawire, 2001; Schraeder, 1994; Acemoğlu et al., 2003: 80). The conditions that made Botswana so successful and turned it into an upper-middle income country after some decades are arguably intrinsic to Botswana's elites and the historical context of continuities from Protectorate's time. This 'initiator culture' consisted of a consecration of institutions of 'private property', which 'protect the property rights of actual and potential investors, provide political stability, and ensure that the political elites are constrained by the political system and the participating of a broad cross-section of society' (Acemoğlu et al., 2003: 84). It materialised into 'policies [that] served the interests of important coalition partners, the major cattlemen, and the foreign mineral extracting firms' (Froitzheim, 2009: 145). In sum, Acemoğlu and colleagues indicate the following factors explaining, apart from the availability of unskilled labour, which stopped migrating to South Africa for the mining industry, the success of Botswana:

> tribal institutions that encouraged broad-based participation and constraints on political leaders during the precolonial period; only limited effect of British colonisation on these precolonial institutions because of the peripheral nature of Botswana to the British Empire; the fact that upon independence, the most important rural interests, chiefs, and cattle owners, were politically powerful; the income from diamonds, which generated enough rents for the main political actors to increase the opportunity cost of further rent seeking; and, finally, a number of important and farsighted decisions by the post-independence leaders, in particular Seretse Khama and Quett Masire. (Acemoğlu et al., 2003: 84)

Apart from governmental stability and a propelled 'native initiator culture' (Maundeni, 2001), the marginalisation of nationalist, socialist movements and, increasingly, 'traditional' leadership allowed for the development of institutions and policies which facilitated backing from the Western powers, namely the United Kingdom (even if in decline) and their mining companies. Debswana, the public-private partnership for diamond exploration in Botswana, gathers the government and the South African mining giant De Beers, founded by Cecil Rhodes, the colonist millionaire who had established the British South African Company railways in the late 19th century (Froitzheim, 2009: 38). Yet, Botswana's 'right institutions' and 'good policies' can be replicated once 'individual actions' are put into place (Acemoğlu et al., 2003: 113). The focus on good foundational developmental structures is emphasised by Beaulier and Subrick, who added up the inexistence of an army in the first decade of independence that could drain resources like in the rest of Africa (Beaulier and Subrick, 2006).

However, Botswana's worldwide economic success occurred in a very specific context. Externally, it took place at a time when the general landscape of African countries was one of impoverishment and reversal to armed conflicts of different natures and autocracy. Internally, by the 1990s, Botswana was realising the minerals-driven ambition of the pre-independence political-economic elite. These were conditions unique to Botswana, as stressed above. As such, despite maintaining or even expanding domestic inequalities without major changes in levels of poverty and unemployment and features of liberal authoritarianism, as a later bibliography has started to suggest, Botswana easily stood out in the international arena as the 'miracle' of economic growth and stability in contemporary Africa.

As Botswana achieved upper-middle income status, by the mid-1990s, foreign agencies left the country, including USAID and the Peace Corps. This is an instance of the post-independence path of agency walked by the national elite, which sought to employ strategically available political and material resources in the construction of a country that at the time of independence was underdeveloped. From a point of colonialism (Protectorate) and neocolonialism (utter dependency on foreign resources for development), Botswana achieved an impressive degree of autonomy in the design and implementation of its own development policies that its integration in the global market of diamonds facilitated. Botswana emerged as one of the two developmental state stories (the other is Mauritius) in Africa in the 1990s.

## Botswana's renewed struggle for survival

However, in the early 2000s, foreign assistance resumed in full force due to the HIV/AIDS crisis. In the case of United States support, this followed a personal request by President Festus Mogae to the United States administration. HIV/AIDS emerged as one of the greatest threats to the country and its development prospects, together with the decreasing demand for diamonds. However, precisely because of the problem's magnitude, which undermines the survival of the nation, the government took an early decision of intervening actively in the epidemic. Assisting with the survival of a significant share of the population has evident consequences in terms of larger policies of development. Many studies about the social aspects of the epidemic have underlined over the years the severe impact on the development prospects of a country, since it primarily affects the most productive members of society, that is, young adults (Arndt and Lewis, 2000; Bauer, 2006; Fourie and Schönteich, 2001; Kim and Farmer, 2006; Whiteside and de Waal, 2004; Whiteside, 2004; 2009).

Post-independence's propelled success has come under jeopardy by the HIV/AIDS epidemic affecting the country and, as such, renewed Botswanan political leadership's concern for the country's survival after the end of the Cold War and the apartheid. Considering the very large size of the epidemic, HIV/AIDS intervention has constituted a question of survival for the country. Self-help is visible in the way the government decided to launch an antiretroviral programme – funded up to 80 per cent with public resources – and sought to obtain support from external sources, namely the Bill and Melinda Gates Foundation, the Global Fund and PEPFAR. Botswana's prevalence rate among adults aged 15 to 49 is 23 per cent (UNAIDS, 2013: 120). This accounts for the second biggest HIV/AIDS epidemic in the world after the small Southern African nation of Swaziland, whose rate is 26.5 per cent (UNAIDS, 2013: 121). Considering that the national population is only of 2 million (WHO, 2013: 156), one verifies how wide and serious is the magnitude of the epidemic. In 2013, an estimate of 340,000 people were living with AIDS (UNAIDS, 2013: 121).

When the first case was identified at Princess Marina Hospital in Gaborone in 1985 (AIDS Unit, 2007: 3), the government was quick to launch one of the first control programmes in the continent. After consulting with the international agencies, it established a one-year emergency plan in 1987 (Heald, 2005: 4–5), and then two medium-term plans, 1989–1997 and 1997–2002 (AIDS Unit, 2007: 3) and the national strategic framework for 2003–2009, which framed HIV/AIDS in the broader question of development. After the creation of the National AIDS Council (NAC) in 1995 under the Office of the President, the National AIDS Coordinating Agency (NACA) was set up in 1999 with the aim of implementing, coordinating, monitoring, evaluating and fundraising for HIV/AIDS, under the aegis of NAC (AIDS Unit, 2007: 9). In the late 1980s, the adopted approach was based on 'education and surveillance', in which condoms played a central role (Heald, 2005: 5). However, there was 'widespread disbelief' (Heald, 2005: 5) among the populace, since there was no mortality to demonstrate the severity of the disease. By the mid-1990s, that started to change because of the increasing number of deaths. Yet, it was still called 'the radio disease', since most of the mass HIV/AIDS awareness-raising used to be done through the radio, as it is still done today (Heald, 2005: 5).

Given the disappointing results of these waves of intervention, governmental leadership slowly disengaged from the response (Heald, 2005: 7). However, the publication of a number of reports in the early 2000s (Econsult, 2007: 121–123), especially one by the Botswana Institute for

Development Policy Analysis (BIDPA, 2000), became a game changer. Those reports presented grim demographic forecasts, whereby Botswana would dramatically lose its population in the case of absence of treatment programmes for those living with AIDS. An interviewed medical expatriate with a United States-implementing NGO who first worked in Botswana in the 1990s commented that by that time 'Botswana was faced with the fact that it had no choice. Ten years ago that was the burning issue. Survival was at stake. So, implementation had to start. ... There was a need for new thinking in the country'. Eventually, the country's economy would suffer dramatically with decreasing figures of growth, consumption and productivity. A 2007 published study on the labour force of Debswana, the diamond public-private partnership, concluded that 'among the 3558 participants [of the survey], annual HIV incidence was estimated to be 3.4 per cent, and HIV prevalence was 23.8 per cent' (Riviello et al., 2007). It would also scare foreign investors away. Eventually, the government launched a massive treatment programme in 2001 assisted by the African Comprehensive HIV/AIDS Partnership (ACHAP) of the Gates Foundation. In 2004, PEPFAR joined in, but only with purpose of 'filling the gaps', since the biggest chunk, reportedly 80 per cent of the expenditure, is taken up by the government (Froitzheim, 2009: 133). By 'filling the gaps', stakeholders mean priority intervention in the areas of management and capacity building of programmes and organisations, as it is further discussed in the next chapter. It largely corresponds to PEPFAR's second phase (2009–2013) purpose of sustaining 'country ownership' of actions carried out so far.

## Botswana's state leadership and pivotal role in PEPFAR programme

HIV/AIDS intervention in Botswana started in the mid-1980s, but it only became a matter of utmost importance for the national government in the beginning of the 2000s. The national antiretroviral programme was launched in 2001 primarily with domestic funds, complemented by other sources: the Bill and Melinda Gates Foundation's ACHAP, the Global Fund and, finally, PEPFAR. Responding to the epidemic was framed in terms of survival of the small national population of 2 million people, since the prevalence rate among adults corresponds to close to one-quarter of the total adult population. Arguably, due to the actual budgetary prioritisation of HIV/AIDS by the Botswanan government, HIV/AIDS became a topic associated with very much everything governance-related: a matter of public health, of course, but also of development and even national security (Molomo et al., 2007). For example, some programmes, assisted by the United States government, targeted directly the Botswana Defence Force.

PEPFAR was made part of a larger process ultimately aiming at the consolidation and expansion of an already developmental state in Botswana, while the perhaps more basic concern for survival is particularly salient. However, unlike the Ethiopian case, as one will show, PEPFAR is not a significant part in quantitative terms of the overall response. Often, interviewees referred to PEPFAR's role as one of only 'filling the gaps' of the national, government-led response. PEPFAR's funded activities mainly revolve around medical research, prevention and building organisational capacity. An interviewee with a US government-implementing agency stressed the 'invitee' character of her organisation's presence in the country's effort against the epidemic, after a short period in which the Botswanan government considered foreign assistance no longer necessary.

> Our organisation arrived in the country after the national independence and stayed until 1997....However, ten years ago, President Mogae asked the US government to return to the country to support the fight against AIDS.

To a large extent, PEPFAR's participation in the Botswanan effort corresponds to the main goal for the second five-year implementation phase (2009–2013): to assist national organisations (government and civil society) towards a country-owned, sustained response. Respondents with US government-implementing agencies are generally very glad about the process of PEPFAR's implementation *vis-à-vis* the final established goal. The country is generally regarded as a main leader of the overall process of implementation. One interviewee underscored PEPFAR's important role in terms of technical assistance and pointing at new policy directions (children and women). Yet, she stressed that the country – both the public and private sectors – engage strongly in the response, and thus 'own' it.

> In Botswana, PEPFAR had a significant impact in assisting the government. But the country was already way ahead comparing with other countries....In Botswana there are strong policies. Now the challenge is to roll out on gender and children. Our purpose is to fill gaps, and facilitate country ownership. For us, country ownership is not government ownership, but ownership by the government,

privates and civil society. That is why you want Debswana [diamonds company] to be involved in this too.

Another respondent reiterated the government's leadership in the process and place PEPFAR next to the other private (Gates Foundation) and public (the European Union through the Global Fund) donors.

Here the government has the lead. ACHAP is also leading. The EU [European Union] is also contributing, though more in education. And PEPFAR fills remaining gaps.

A third respondent with a US government-implementing agency gives the example of military aid to show the assimilation foreign aid received by the Botswanan government is subjected to in its strategic goals.

My personal view is that mostly everywhere…aid is given to the recipient militaries, and they just take it without much questioning. But that is not the case of Botswana. They only take the projects they want. They own the projects.

A fourth respondent underlines the national government's commitment and points at persisting difficulties of response.

The goal of country ownership is working well in Botswana, which depends on two things: political will and capacity. In Botswana there is good governance and the government shares the same core values with the US: caring for social welfare. There have not been obstacles, no major health system challenges. The only thing to be stressed is that there're very isolated rural populations, which is problematic in terms of prevention of transmission. That will require a lot of government commitment.

Confidence in Botswana's capability to maintain a steady response to the epidemic is also shared by PEPFAR's nongovernmental sector. Interestingly, one has found two professionals originally from two neighbouring countries among the supporters of the idea of national leadership and ownership in Botswana. One restates the idea of Botswana as an 'African model', this time around in the field of HIV/ AIDS: 'In Botswana the government is very committed. It has really been a model in Africa. It is not donor-dependent. Here PEPFAR only fulfilled gaps. The Botswana case should be repeated'. Another interviewee has comprehensively addressed a number of crucial implementation issues in which the government has been instrumental, from political involvement with public taboo matters to prevention to supply chain.

Facilitating conditions are the embracing political environment, featured by good governance. The health minister's recent statements on HIV/AIDS in prisons are another good example of the political elite's commitment to the struggle against AIDS, namely on the side of prevention. This is facilitating prevention work. Accountability is also to be mentioned. Concerning infrastructures, this country has good roads which help in the supply chain process.

The country's openness to the international community's recipes from the late 1980s through today has been a very important feature. Independent of the actual results of those recipes once implemented, which, as mentioned, were assessed very negatively, today's policies are generally embraced by the government and are regarded as proof of leadership in the struggle against AIDS, as interviewees state. An interviewee has commented that '[a] facilitating condition is the abundance of clear rules which trickle down from the international community to the government. Thanks to government's will many resources have been pooled together'.

From the national government's side, its leadership acknowledges the support given by external funders, including PEPFAR, in the struggle against the epidemic, namely in the social sphere.

PEPFAR supports OVCs [orphans and vulnerable children], and as such it helped to set up a network involving us plus the ministries of local government and health as well as civil society organisations. The government cannot do everything alone.... Without PEPFAR no CSOs [civil society organisations] would develop. It is assisting in building capacity for them. I worked at the district level, and what was working was peer-education by CSOs. They were important in mobilising people. One of them was TCM [Total Community Mobilisation], funded by ACHAP.[1] People adhered well and chiefs were collaborative.

Despite the recognisable engaged position of the government, most respondents, including one with a national ministry, have acknowledged the current worrisome economic situation. Considering the reliance on revenues associated with the diamonds trade, the decreasing global demand for that commodity sets out to undermine the costly effort. Despite decreases in drug prices, the programme will remain very expensive, in part as a result of more people surviving thanks to it. This will demand critical options and trade-offs by the government (Econsult, 2007: 118–120). Indeed, the pandemic in Botswana remains rampant, although consulting company Econsult in its report to the NACA refers to 'preliminary evidence of a fall in HIV prevalence rates amongst younger age groups suggests that these campaigns are effective, at least to a certain extent' (Econsult, 2007: 118). As a consequence, the struggling race to prevent the epidemic from reaching more catastrophic results in Botswana tightens and inserts crucial dilemmas for the national leadership.

In their article, Allen and Heald (2004) provided an explanation why preventive efforts were not improving the situation. They argued that the open acceptance of international intervention strategies, based on voluntary testing, condoms promotion and general human rights approaches, were facing enormous social constraints and eventually would be found counterproductive (Allen and Heald, 2004: 1152). As the epidemic's mortality was increasingly becoming visible to the public's eyes, 'more coercive measures [were] being advocated and even then in the face of intense opposition from outside agencies' (Allen and Heald, 2004: 1152). Since 2004, numerous projects – some of them funded under the auspices of PEPFAR – have been launched on several fronts, but there is a strong lack of certainty among interviewees of 'what works'. In other words, assuming that there are ongoing programmes which prevent transmission, one does not know exactly which actually work given the lack of impact measurement. Nonetheless, what is taken for certain is the central role of the state/government in this process today and in the coming future. This centrality is expressed not only in terms of funding largely interventions, such as the ARV programme, but also with regard to formulation and enforcement of policy, including 'draconian measures' (Allen and Heald, 2004: 1152) of surveillance that may undermine logics of human rights associated to HIV/AIDS, such as patients' volunteerism. Despite the external constraints that Allen and Heald allude to, the national government is the main institution in charge in this realm, thus reproducing the traditional understanding of public health politics as a realm of the national state.

## Pitfalls of state paternalism and HIV/AIDS implementation

The alignment with Western modes of political and economic organisation throughout the post-independence period is of particular relevance.

On the one hand, as mentioned previously, the transition to independence was a soft process led by the same elite – local and colonist – of the time of the British Protectorate of Bechuanaland. As such, in principle, and considering that the United Kingdom constituted the most important development donor for many years after 1966, the embracement of 'Western values' would be somewhat expectable. Furthermore, considering how the region surrounding the country was ridden by rather 'extremist' politics on both sides (from the 'leftist' movements of liberation around the Southern African region to the 'rightist' South African apartheid regime), it is interesting to observe that the Botswana regime retained those principles, no matter how weak and vulnerable it was, particularly until the formal end of apartheid. Botswana has basically remained a 'liberal country,' even if at times constrained by the necessities of assuring the country's self-help and pressures by traditional leaders and leftist parties such as the Botswana National Party. However, the adherence to and practice of political and institutional liberal and developmental values does not mean the disappearance of contradictions in that process. As such, this section deals with a body of literature that critically assesses the achievements of the 'Botswana miracle'.

Despite the adoption of representative democracy accompanied by impressive economic growth, structural social and political change has proved limited. According to Ellen Hillbom (2008), this framework is typical of 'pre-modern growth', in which a highly profit-making mining industry coexists with enduring forms of land tenure based on cattlemen and poor, subsistence agricultural practice. Employing Kuznet's model of modern economic growth (Hillbom, 2008: 193–195), Hillbom argues that Botswana only matches two out of six requirements for being a modern economy, that is, 'high rates of per capita and population growth, and high rate of productivity' (Hillbom, 2008: 194). From a technological point of view, Botswana has been stranded in low levels, especially in the agricultural sector, and with the exception of the mining industry (Hillbom, 2008: 195). At the level of the manufacturing sector, very little expansion has happened. Indeed, although supermarket and household lifestyle culture is booming in Gaborone, almost all products (except meat and milk) are imported from neighbouring South Africa. National production remains low, and Botswana remains a very subsistence-based society. This scenario is particularly bleak now, as the mining industry has peaked and has been tending to stagnate and decrease.

The registered high growth has not had the same repercussion in terms of decreases in poverty and unemployment. In fact, whereas the richest segment of society has grown richer, the poorest has grown even more poor (Hillbom, 2008: 206). Arguably, that is the outcome of ingrained historical socio-economic disparities deriving from pre-independence (Hillbom, 2008: 206). In addition to this, social change through the emergence of a challenging civil society is occurring fraily. Two explanations are concurrent. One, alluding to the experience of all neighbouring countries, Botswana did not undergo high levels of political-economic conflict to the point of generating struggle organisations of alternative ideological inspiration. Civil society 'is readily co-opted into state structures...and is prepared to work within the parameters deemed permissible by the state – and not beyond' (Molomo et al., 2007). This aspect is quite critical in the realm of HIV/AIDS implementation, including PEPFAR of course.

In fact, one of the reasons *inter alia* advanced to explain why prevention initiatives from the late 1980s through the 1990s did not deliver positive results had to do with the non-involvement of traditional doctors, churches and local communities (Heald, 2005; Allen and Heald, 2004). These reasons are reportedly present and remain very challenging as two interviewees with PEPFAR-implementing organisations emphasised. One, with a United States-based NGO, held that not only civil society, that is, non-state organisations, have to be incorporated but also need to be taught how to intervene as such.

> Skills are necessary to be given. We face the double challenge of having to implement and train people at the same time. People are used to receiving from the government, but they need to change their mindset. Civil society has to take its role.

PEPFAR has in fact been acting in terms of funding training activities, and the issue of civil society is also acknowledged by a respondent with a US government agency: 'Botswana is a middle-income country. It offers good facilities. People are trained. However, civil society is not part of the local culture.' Yet, an interviewee with a Botswanan governmental ministry also stressed the need for change in this area, and acknowledged PEPFAR's role in it: 'Without PEPFAR no CSOs [civil society organisations] would develop. It is assisting in building capacity for them. I worked at the district level, and what was working was peer-education by CSOs. They were important in mobilising people'.

Regarding the participation of outside-state organisations, nongovernmental organisations and networks dealing with youth, church attendants and other publics were allocated participative roles within PEPFAR's partnership framework's division of labour. Available scholarship tends to divide itself into positive and negative assertions, in turn depending on the overall appreciation of the outcomes of modernisation and development in the country. Whereas endorsers of the idea of Botswana as a 'model' enhance the striving and free character of civil society in the country (Holm et al., 1996), critical evaluations tend to emphasise its redundancy in the context of a dominating state (Taylor, 2003; Good and Taylor, 2008). But some other studies seem to diverge from these polarised perspectives too. Kiley and Hovorka's (2006) study of civil society organisations in the HIV/AIDS response underline their marginalisation by the state-led response for different reasons: 'geographical disparities, lack of financial and human resources and socio-cultural elements associated with HIV intervention strategies' (Kiley and Hovorka, 2006: 176). They argue that when better integrated and assisted they could improve the response. Attempting at finding reasons why prevention has been recurrently failing, Strain (2008) argues along the same lines. However, one's enquiry – which did not look for reasons why prevention is failing but how implementation happens – has identified a double pattern. On the one hand, civil society, notably the one funded by PEPFAR, is very collaborative with the state; with few exceptions, NGOs are not challengers of the norms imposed by the Botswanan government (and the United States government for the same reason). Yet, on the other, the international integration of local NGOs and similar entities with transnational, often United States-based institutions, offers learning experiences which allow them, at least on paper, to adopt the liberal approaches and ideas disseminated across the PEPFAR apparatus. As such, within the constraints of a pre-modern economic growth society, they become sites of globalisation and modernity. Also in this regard, civil society organisations in Botswana ought to be an exemplar model for others to follow.

Some NGO implementers have highlighted health indicators that emerge from a context of ongoing inequities and that PEPFAR-funded activities have helped to identify. One interviewee compared Botswana's health performance to neighbouring countries: 'Non-HIV indicators are poor. The infant mortality rate is very high. It is very similar to Lesotho and Swaziland, and yet Botswana is so much richer.' Another focused solely on the country: 'Here in Botswana mortality rate in general is still very serious.' However, a third implementer has shed light on a further health agenda: 'So many areas are in need such as non-communicable and mental diseases. Botswana has a very high rate of suicide, for example.' Yet, on state-society relations, the interviewees seem to confirm Molomo and colleagues' quotation above, as they generally find themselves aligned with the state-led framework. This also suggests the paternalistic character of this policy, in which the state drives an almost exclusive top-down biomedical approach (the treatment programme) without incorporating and empowering its citizens. Furthermore, the perceived unsustainable nature of this approach is fed by the propelled *'nouveau riche'* attitude of the state elites, whose recent wealth has allowed them to invest 'luxuriously' in facilities and technologies that end up being barely maximised by professionals and clients, while, at the same time, there are clear indications that the national income is severely at risk in the post-diamond future.

Particularly since 2008, after the direct nomination by former President Festus Mogae of the current President, Lieutenant-General Seretse Khama Ian Khama, a consolidating shift towards 'liberal authoritarianism' (Molomo et al., 2007) has been occurring through the introduction of senior military staff in the civil service. Apart from that, extra-judicial killings and increasing levels of corruption among the elite have been reported by the media (Direng, 2010; Mmegi, 2010; Bryson, 2010).

## Conclusion

Botswana has long been regarded as a model country in Africa in terms of representative democracy, economic development and, namely, adoption of major HIV/AIDS policies, in which the national government has played a very crucial role. In this regard, United States foreign policy is by no means an exception to such consensual perspective.

In order to understand such disposition to embrace foreign policies, it is important to bear in mind that the Botswanan government has historically been challenged with the difficult task of attaining national survival in the international system, given Botswana's particularly difficult regional circumstances. After achieving national integrity and economic viability, survival is now at stake in the age of the HIV/AIDS pandemic.

In the context of HIV/AIDS implementation, in which PEPFAR plays a complementing part of the national plan, the Botswanan government is leading and pivotal, as widely recognised by PEPFAR implementers and other HIV/AIDS stakeholders in the country. Such leadership constitutes the best proof of increasing prospects of country ownership, and thus sustainability of the struggle against the pandemic.

Nonetheless, it is also remarked that the paternalistic presence of the government in all aspects of HIV/AIDS implementation poses a problem with regard to the alleged fundamental involvement of the civil society (that is, out of state organisations) in this process. The need to open to civil society is also deemed a solution for a socio-political diagnostic which regards Botswana as incapable of solving historical problems of social stagnation and poverty.

# 7
# Ethiopia: Self-Help with External Support

## Introduction

In light of United States security policy, Ethiopia is a primary anchor state in the Horn of Africa region and Africa as a whole. In fact, in the context of difficult experiences with a number of neighbouring regions and countries (Somalia, Northern Kenya, Eritrea and South Sudan), Ethiopia emerges as the finest ally the United States government can, to some extent, rely on. However, in addition to international security, Ethiopia constitutes a great developmental and humanitarian challenge as well, in which a number of issues are pooled together, including malnutrition, refugee fluxes and overpopulation. With regard to HIV/AIDS, it should be remarked that the prevalence rate is relatively small when compared to parts of Eastern and, above all, Southern Africa. However, considering the large population, the estimated absolute number of people living with HIV/AIDS is close to one million, who, moreover, face other interrelated problems. In fact, as PEPFAR implementers demonstrate, HIV/AIDS intervention does not generally appear disentangled from the broader developmental landscape. As a whole, Ethiopia constitutes a fine example of an African country which gives breadth to a United States foreign policy that takes international security and humanitarian and development concerns as faces of the same coin.

From the Ethiopian government perspective, as discussed in the following pages, HIV/AIDS intervention is also part of a broader policy of state developmentalism for the 21st century which aims at legitimising not only the current government but also the regime. Founded in the aftermath of a long warfare against imperial order, and victorious against the Soviet-backed Dergue regime, the EPRDF regime of 'ethnic federalism' is confronted by internal and external threats. Furthermore, despite its grand design and strategy, this political plan is faced with limited capabilities to ensure human development independently, let alone a number of other contradictions that are discussed.

In fact, it should be signalled that in both United States and Ethiopian perspectives, which largely match, the scope of HIV/AIDS implementation cannot arguably be analysed in a meaningful way without duly considering the broader policy and empirical framework of security and development upon which it sits.

## Challenges of Ethiopian post-Dergue regime

The current ruling party in Ethiopia is the Ethiopian People's Revolutionary Democratic Front (EPRDF), an assemblage of regional parties[1] that, under the leadership of the Tigray People's Liberation Front (TPLF), combated and eventually ousted through guerrilla warfare the military regime of the Dergue in 1991.[2] Reasons motivating regime overthrow were the disastrous Soviet reforms, which imposed new cycles of famine and immiseration, as well as the so-called 'national question' (Vaughan, 2003: 40–80). In a historical context of internal colonisation led by the major Ethiopian ethnicity Amhara, over other ethnicities whose power stretched back to the emperorship rule, the Dergue regime was not eager to concede in its 'monolithic' (Berhe, 2004: 574) understanding of the Ethiopian nation and arguably rejected any alternative solution to the complex ethnic reality of the country.

As the Dergue's leader Mengistu Haile Mariam is driven out of power and forced into exile in Zimbabwe (where he still resides), the country's liberators proposed two fundamental policy frameworks for a new Ethiopia. The first is a political-administrative formula called 'ethnic federalism', in which the country is regionally divided along ethnic lines in order to respond to historical ethnic grievances. Nevertheless, the current political era has been considered by many analysts not far from continuities in terms of absolutist modes of rule, and persisting regional opposition to the leading post-conflict formula of 'ethnic federalism'. Often this has involved armed means against the central government in Addis Ababa. The second is economic development. The main inheritor of the TPLF, the EPRDF, has been in power uninterruptedly since 1991. Its consecutive governments have implemented several five-year development plans over the years. Considering the low base of development the country finds itself in, these plans have received large assistance from the main international donors and lenders. One of the latest relevant programmes of assistance was the World Bank's Poverty Reduction Strategy Programme of 2002/3 (Ministry of Finance, 2006).

The current, growth and transformation five-year plan was launched on 2 December 2010 and strives for the establishment of industry by 2020, building on double-digit growth rates in recent years (Hassen, 2010). Although the accuracy of those rates is highly disputed by the political opposition and even the International Monetary Fund (Teklehaimanot and Asfaw, 2010), they animate the government's latest endeavour: the construction of the Millennium Dam (since renamed Grand Ethiopian Renaissance Dam) on the Nile Basin entirely with national funds.[3] In addition to this developmental project, the government has been running a process of 'cheap' leasing of vast masses of land to foreign companies, mostly of Indian, Chinese, Pakistani and Saudi origin (Mariam, 2011). The Minister of Agricultural Development has claimed 'we [the government] hope that big commercial and intensive farms will solve the shortage of food in Ethiopia' (Mariam, 2011). This policy indeed happens in a context of continuous need of food assistance, which, despite the impressive growth, still affects sectors of the population and has led the government to repeatedly call for external assistance (IRIN, 2011).

The principles of social mobilisation of the masses of Leninist-Stalinist inspiration, acquired and developed by the TPLF during the armed struggle against the Dergue, are now being transferred to the developmental purposes by the EPRDF (Vaughan and Tronvoll, 2003). The party's symbol is a bee, and it serves to illustrate how the party wants the Ethiopian peoples to be: united, sovereign and very laborious. These ideas have seeped into Ethiopians' imaginary, shaping the vision they have of themselves. This was quite notable during the latest federal elections campaign in May 2010. When showing photographs depicting road improvements in the area and school children and adults attending HIV/AIDS awareness-raising events at a campaign booth in Arada, an Addis Ababa sub-city,[4] an EPRDF's youth league member argued

> Our government believes every Ethiopian is capable of working, no matter little skills he might have, as long he is not disabled. We took many jobless people away from the roads and put them working. First we give them training and then we pay them 200 birr [7.50 euro] per working day. The more a worker works the more he will earn. So if he is hard working he can get 2000 birr or more a month. These are all Ethiopians. We believe everyone is capable of earning their money

without assistance from anyone. We tell people not to give money to beggars.

Indeed, this is consistent with EPRDF leadership's goal of abolishing poverty as the ultimate target of the current developmental enterprises. The fight against poverty is an argument recurrently used to contend political opposition, as Redwan Hussien, then EPRDF secretariat head, claimed later in 2011 after the elections to the Ethiopian news agency Walta Information Centre.

The EPRDF has been underscoring the fact that poverty is the main enemy of the country and there is no worse enemy than poverty. Thus we have to beat poverty as quickly as possible and wage relentless battle against poverty since there is no lofty war than the war on poverty. Ethiopians should also benefit from every growth in proportion to the sacrifice they pay for growth and the yield obtained. The growth should therefore be rapid, sustainable and fair. By implementing these, we should quickly reduce poverty. [This] was the line of argument of the EPRDF which was countered by the opposition who could not understand the urgency of the call as poverty has been living with us since eternity. (Walta, 2011)

## Ethiopian use of international developmental and security framework

The Millennium Development Goals constituted a framework upon which programmes in several areas (health, education, gender, economic development) sit and set out to offer opportunities for those countries to ameliorate their records. However, this renewed policy and financial focus on development was accompanied by a growing concern of linking them to security and stabilisation concerns. To a large extent, development has become a question of containment and management of populations too. Despite improvements in recent years, Ethiopia is the 15th worst-positioned country in the latest edition of the United Nations Development Program's (UNDP) Human Development Report (UNDP, 2013: 146).

For the Ethiopian government, this development-security architecture has become a source of opportunities, despite some constraints. The major opportunity that it is being offered is the boost it gives to the current policy framework of state-led development and economic growth ('developmental state') assisted by the attraction of as much and diverse external funding as possible. Funding for Ethiopia traditionally originates from Western Europe, Northern America, Japan and Australia in addition to a range of donors and lenders, that is, so-called 'new partners', including Turkey, Saudi Arabia, United Arab Emirates, India and China. The current diversification of 'partners' can be observed in recent statements by charismatic late Ethiopian Prime Minister Meles Zenawi.

> We try to get help from every quarter ... This is because we need all the assistance we can get. It would be stupid for us to say to the Indians for example, that we prefer Chinese assistance. It would also be stupid for us to say to the Brits now that the Chinese are helping out with some infrastructure projects, keep your money. It doesn't make sense. We want to get as much assistance as we possibly can because on balance we get about half of the average assistance that other African countries get in per capita terms. It's not like we are overflowing with assistance. At this stage what we are trying to do is make the best use of every avenue we have. (Wallis, 2009)

It is hard to judge whether this diversification is the product of an intended governmental policy or just the result of a changing international environment, yet it is quite undeniable that it serves a government's clear purpose. Diversification of 'partners', especially non-Western ones, concerns the need to reduce dependency from the conditionalities attached to the provided funding. Those conditionalities refer to formalities around political and economic reform, as well as other sorts of pressure, such as statements by donor governments and embassies and reports by nongovernmental organisations with an impact on perceptions about the country and its government's ruling leadership inside the donor countries and around the international community.[5]

The question of perceptions nurtured by donor countries and the international community at large about the country's current development efforts and the Ethiopian People's Revolutionary Democratic Front (EPRDF) leadership is reportedly very important in the country's relations with the West. Ethiopian leaders are aware of the negative constructed image of the country, especially since the mid-1980s, due to large public events such as 1985 Live Aid, as an eminent site of hunger, poverty and underdevelopment. Therefore, they develop a foreign policy in order to show otherwise.

Throughout the last decade, Ethiopian leaders like Zenawi and former Minister of Health (currently Minister of Foreign Affairs) Tedros Adhanom Ghebreyesus have enjoyed a positive reputation as a new generation of

African leaders who present themselves as unequivocally committed to good governance and stability (Zimeta, 2010). Zenawi represented not just Ethiopia but the entire continent in international climate change summits, while Adhanom was the chair of the Global Fund until September 2011. Thus, while important international organisations and forums offer avenues of Ethiopian governmental promotion, it may also have an undermining effect. In effect, the Ethiopian government has been accused of manipulating international aid to reward supporters and punish opponents, legislating anti-democratic frameworks that impeded proper campaigning by the opposition in the latest governmental elections of May 2010, and violating the human rights of some ethnic groups. This also includes the jamming of the United States-based radio network Voice of America and the country expulsion of one journalist in 2010 (Catholic Information Service, 2010). This criticism has augmented after the elections' results were made public, in which the ruling government received 99 per cent of votes under allegations of not meeting international standards (Press TV, 2010). In the face of US government criticism, the Ethiopian leadership has nonetheless remained responsive.

Unlike many postcolonial African countries, whose subordination to former colonial masters is arguably persisting, the latter's consecutive regimes have been driven by a sense of equality among sovereigns (Furtado and Smith, 2007). As the host country of the African Union, an emblematic example concerns the tradition of granting free land to embassies worldwide, especially to African and donor countries, in order to attract further presence in the country. Addis Ababa has thus become one of the largest conglomerates of diplomatic representations in the world. In the case of relations with the United States of America, the country's biggest donor, the Ethiopian government has maintained a large ability to receive and manage assistance. This happened even in times of strong ideological differences that conduced to suspension of diplomatic relations, as it happened during the Soviet Union-backed military regime of the Dergue between 1974 and 1991, during the famines of the 1980s (Kissi, 1997). Despite the policy of not assisting regimes created by *coups d'état*, which led to the withdrawal of USAID from the country in those years, assistance was still facilitated. Even when formally suspended, the United States maintenance of support during the Haile Selassie and Dergue periods was primarily driven by humanitarian concerns.

Although geo-politics certainly played a role in United States relations with Ethiopia, some of the American proposals for the improvement of the conditions of Ethiopia's peasants were motivated by a concern for the sons and daughters of the soil. (Kissi, 1997: 432)

However, now the pendulum seems to swing more to the geopolitical side. Particularly after the failed military intervention in Somalia in 1994, but certainly after 11 September 2001 – and the subsequent War on Terror, which highlighted the problem of Islamic extremism in the Horn of Africa – United States policy for Ethiopia has become increasingly more power-driven (Gordon and Mazzetti, 2007: 14–16). In this context, Ethiopia emerges as the sole actor that the several post-Cold War US administrations can openly rely on. Yet, the same argument is applicable to the Ethiopian government. Its rationale for interacting, or 'partnering', with the United States government is based on national security goals and improving the social welfare of the population. Whereas for the United States of America what is at stake is the contention against suspected Al-Qaeda affiliated groups together with a favourable resolution of Somalia's state failure (both inland and at sea), for the Ethiopian government what concerns chiefly is the consolidation of territorial integrity and its control (Gordon and Mazzetti, 2007: 14–16). The purposes of the War on Terror in the Horn of Africa coincide quite explicitly with the EPRDF's own national policy of securing the borders and containing internal armed groups. As Zenawi once affirmed, 'we don't look at this as us joining the United States on the war on terrorism, we see it as the United States finally joining us because we've been victims for many years' (West, 2005: 4).

## HIV/AIDS implementation in Ethiopia

Unlike the cases of Botswana and South Africa, PEPFAR's implementation in Ethiopia is not justified for the scale of the HIV/AIDS epidemic alone, although in absolute terms it is a major health problem, since it affects 760,000 people (UNAIDS, 2013: 123). Given the size of the population of slightly over 84 million, HIV/AIDS sits alongside other pressing health concerns that have to do with all the direct and indirect consequences of urban and rural poverty, malnutrition, famine, population displacement and armed conflicts that affect the country. In addition to that, HIV/AIDS intervention often implicates activities around family planning, which moreover serves the goal of hampering population growth, considered a major obstacle to social development by policy makers, academics and general commentators (UK Commission for Africa, 2005: 105–106; Pausewang, 2009: 72; Dyer, 2009).[6]

HIV/AIDS as a distinct field of development/health intervention has represented an opportunity for the country to obtain resources from public and private donors, and simultaneously raise its international profile as the example of the Minister of Health Adhanom shows. Moreover, the history of the HIV/AIDS response in Ethiopia demonstrates a large deal of openness to the international community and eagerness to interact with it. After the discovery of the first HIV/AIDS case in the country in 1984 (Kloos and Mariam, 2000: 17), a national task force was established in 1985 with the aim of tackling the spread of the virus, followed by the first department of AIDS control in Ethiopia at the Ministry of Health in 1987 (Kitaw et al., 2006: 210). Together with the WHO, the then-leading international organisation in the field, two prevention and control programmes were launched for the 1987–1990 and 1992–1996 periods, but with 'little impact on the growth of the HIV epidemic in the country' (Kitaw et al., 2006: 210). Under another international institutional setting, as UNAIDS is launched in 1996, the Ethiopian health authorities designed with stakeholders National HIV/AIDS Strategic Plans for 2000–2004 and National AIDS Priority Strategies for 2001–2005. Finally, the HIV/AIDS Prevention and Control Office (HAPCO) was established in 2000 and has remained the leading HIV/AIDS authority for the country, headed by the president. However, according to interviews with senior professionals in the country, actual intervention remained very low, funded by the World Bank alone, until PEPFAR was established in the country in 2004. In 2009, activities funded by PEPFAR in the areas of HIV/AIDS prevention and treatment and correlated medical and developmental activities (other epidemics, family planning, education, evangelisation) were upgraded to 'Global Health Initiative (GHI) plus' status under that initiative. As discussed in the previous chapter, together with seven other countries, Ethiopia will receive further capacity and management support to pursue the efforts developed in the last seven years.

The plan accounts for improvements in terms of social development, including the health dimension (Hassen, 2010). Although the Ethiopian government is highly dependent on external funding in the area of health, the Ministry of Health's reports emphasise the centrality of a 'country-led' approach in policy making, management and implementation while simultaneously acknowledging and committing to such external frameworks like the Millennium Development Goals (Ministry of Health, 2008). This prospect of 'country ownership' is widely shared by the Tedros Adhanom Ghebreyesus (CGD, 2010).

For representatives with two major United States implementing agencies – one governmental and another nongovernmental – Ethiopian government's ownership is evident at the level of planning, yet faulty in terms of funding the efforts' consolidation. According to the former,

> The government has good policies and they have discipline to implement, something other governments of other countries do not have. ... They have a lot of ownership. They have a plan and know where to go. This is my understanding of ownership: having a plan. Other countries do not even have that. But they will hardly be able to fund by themselves. They cannot even pay salaries.

In turn, the latter respondent argued

> [In] terms of ownership, [national] government agencies are keen to lead the process and enjoy taking credit for it. 'We did this, we did that.' They rarely give partners credit for achievements. But when problems occur they call partners to fix them and do not do it themselves. We are often called to fix problems we are not obliged to, and when we refuse to do it, they just leave the, say, machine, road, and so on, abandoned. They always claim they ran out of funds.

On the same matter, an Ethiopian interviewee with an Ethiopian NGO gave a nuanced reaction, yet concurring with the latter two.

> We still need support from foreign governments because we are poor. Most of our activities are donor dependent. ... The idea is that Ethiopia will be independent from foreign aid in the future, but I do not know ... I am not a politician, and I do not want to talk about it.

According to the latest Health Sector Strategic Plan for 2005/6–2009/10, the ministry of health has ascertained clear policies in several areas: health service delivery and quality of care; health facilities construction and rehabilitation; human resource development; pharmaceutical services; information, education and communication; health management and management information system; monitoring and evaluation; and health care financing (Ministry of Health, 2005). The comprehensiveness of the Ethiopian health plan seems to match what the interviewee with a United States government agency quoted above has called PEPFAR's 'wrap-around' character in Ethiopia. PEPFAR has been funding activities in a multitude of areas: treatment, support to orphans and vulnerable children, family planning, training of health personnel, and even refugees and food aid (Ministry of Health, 2005). The launch of the Global Health Initiative (GHI) of the United States government has rendered Ethiopia, precisely for this comprehensive nature of implementation, a 'GHI plus' status together with seven other countries. As two interviewees with the United States government affirmed, this propensity has had to do with the very low base that current efforts build upon. After all, despite recent commendable improvements in the African context, Ethiopia is still the 15th least-developed country in the world according to the latest Human Development Report (UNDP, 2013).

Even during the Dergue, in which the politics of the Cold War put the United States of America and the Ethiopian regimes in adversarial camps, the Ethiopian government has seized opportunities deriving from US foreign policy agendas (humanitarian or geopolitical or both). Apart from the geopolitical situation of the Horn of Africa, it can be argued that one latest 'opportunity' has been precipitated by HIV/AIDS and its forecasted implications notably in terms of the linkage between HIV/AIDS and security. A decade ago, Ethiopia was considered a country belonging to the 'second wave of the HIV/AIDS epidemic' (Schneider and Moodie, 2002), after the 'first wave' of hyper-endemic Southern Africa. Ethiopia sat together with other countries with large populations with regional security status, such as Nigeria, India, China and Russia. However, the epidemic is of quite small proportions: just 1.3 per cent of prevalence rate among adults (UNAIDS, 2013: 120). Still, it represents an absolute number of 760,000 people. The opportunity seizure of international HIV/AIDS programmes has to be understood in a context of commitment to developmentalism as state ideology and practice, actual allocation of state resources to human development and articulation with different 'new partners' beyond the traditional Western European and Northern American donors. A manifestation of such commitment consisted on 'a record 117.8 billion birr annual budget for [2012], aiming to build infrastructure, health and education services' (IOL, 2011).

Apart from the question of financial sustainability, another constraint (and eventual consequence of that) concerns the limited presence of the state in the provision of services, especially in the rural areas where 82 per cent of the population lives (World Bank, 2011). Despite the investment in health extension programmes by the state, those who still have more influence in questions of health and disease are religious institutions, particularly the Ethiopian Orthodox Church and Islam, followed by other Christian denominations, such as the Catholic Church and a number of Protestant churches. Considering the policies around family planning in particular, the largest denominations and the Catholic Church pose obstacles to the dissemination of birth controlling services, namely those based on condoms. Family planning, which has been enhanced with the Obama administration, is seen by several PEPFAR stakeholders as a solution for what is perceived as a major impediment to Ethiopian development. Several implementers work in the vicinity of major religious churches with an aim to sensitise their positions. The quest for implementing family planning in Ethiopia has long been contemplated, but always failed to materialise, as an Ethiopian senior professional with a United States-based NGO has declared: 'Family planning started a long time ago, still in the time of Haile Selassie [1960s], but it did not go forward because of lack of resources, not political will'.

The problem of the limited presence of state institutions in the provision of goods and services in the area of health has to do with broader questions of the state assuring actual control across the vastness of the country and the persistence of regional movements struggling for further autonomy, if not independence from Addis Ababa. Anti-governmental armed opposition occurs in some parts of Oromia, the surrounding region of the federal capital city Addis Ababa, and the eastern region of Ogaden, neighbouring Somalia, suggesting that the provision of health services by the federal state to the local populations is very limited. As a result, this situation constrains the developmentalist ambition of the national government, but at the same time draws attention to the question of survival of the political regime, in which the broader foreign policies, discussed in the previous chapter, together with domestic developmentalist ones aim to ultimately serve.

The Ethiopian People's Revolutionary Democratic Front's (EPRDF) government in Ethiopia has been committed to the establishment of a state that is not only developmental but also democratic and inclusive of all Ethiopian peoples and nationalities. This was the promise made in 1991, when the alliance of movements that founded the EPRDF ousted the Dergue regime, accused of dictatorial and genocide policies between 1974 and 1991. After the change of regime, the new government in Addis Ababa has sought to obtain large amounts of funding from the international community with the goal of helping economic and political reform.

However, according to foreign observers and opposition politicians, this has found limited support in reality (HRW, 2010a; Aalen and Tronvoll, 2009; Epstein, 2010). The EPRDF has been ruling the country since 1991 without interruptions, often resorting to illiberal measures that stretch from police and army violence to subtle, sophisticated censorship mechanisms to keep its power unchallenged (HRW, 2010a). The Ethiopian regime is continuing the long tradition of Abyssinian absolutist power (Vaughan and Tronvoll, 2003), although this time around led by more ethnicities than the Amhara, especially the Tigrayan, and under a structure of democratic representation with regular elections.

Especially over the course of the last five years, the EPRDF has fostered increasing repressive laws that hamper opposition politics and raise limitations to nongovernmental participation (HRW, 2010a). This coincided with the aftermath of the electoral process of 2005, in which 200 people were killed by police forces during public protests denouncing abusive governmental interference in the electoral process, and the latest elections in 2010, in which the EPRDF has won all but three seats in the national parliament (Press TV, 2010). The leader of the main opposition party running in the 2005 elections, Birtukan Mideksa, was imprisoned for almost five years (Wadhams, 2010). In addition to this, a range of intelligence measures that involved jamming Voice of America radio broadcasts and censorship of Internet sites with content that criticise the ruling executive and party have been adopted (Catholic Information Service, 2010). The government has been accused of persecuting ethnic group members assembled around the Oromia and Ogaden Liberation Fronts, considered 'terrorist organisations' by Addis Ababa (Davison, 2011). Moreover, great development initiatives such as the Millennium Dam and the land leasing programmes affect the lifestyle and income of local subsistence peasants. It is not clear whether those projects and policies actually benefit the local populations or just contribute to their already marginalised socio-economic status. Finally, according to NGOs such as Human Rights Watch, or HRW (2010b), the massive volume of international aid, namely food and fertilisers for the agriculture, has been allegedly used as a tool for rewarding party loyalty and penalising dissent.

In 2009, the government issued new regulations on nongovernmental intervention with a potential constraining impact on PEPFAR-funded NGOs based in Ethiopia and abroad. The goal is twofold. One the one hand, it aims at ensuring accountability and transparency. On the other, it establishes that 'charities and civil societies should spend 70 per cent of the fund they solicit in the name of the public on activities to which they are established' (Ethiopian Weekly, 2009a). Accordingly, NGOs receiving 10 per cent or more funds from foreign sources are impeded to intervene in politically sensitive areas, such as:

the advancement of human and democratic rights; the promotion of equality between peoples, sexes or religions; campaigning for children's rights or the rights of the disabled; conflict resolution and reconciliation; work on criminal justice issues. (Ethiopian Weekly, 2009b)

Expectedly, this framework was subject to much criticism from the United States Embassy in Addis Ababa and the political opposition in Ethiopia. It was regarded as another attempt by the government to impede a larger participation in activities that inevitably implicate discussing the issues above.

However, independent of the polemic, only two interviewed implementers declared having conflicts with the regulation. One respondent is with a major United States government agency and the other is with a United States-based NGO. The latter had to resort to a strategy of circumvention of the law in order to maintain activities in the country. 'We do not speak about rights anymore. But we still do advocacy, although we do not speak in that way'. Yet, other respondents explicitly expressed an alignment with the national government's legal framework, as they see themselves as part of the government's developmental policies. One Ethiopian interviewee with a United States-based organisation has stated 'we always work in line with government policies, in which we assist them in implementing programmes'. Another interviewee with the same profile has emphasised the centrality of the government's policy: 'building capacity is an ideal. However, the government does not have capacity for it yet. Civil society still has to assist the government. Otherwise things can go backward'.

The EPRDF's stance seems to largely continue a trend initiated by former Emperor Haile Selassie in the 20th century. Although attempting to modernise social, economic and political structures through the constitution of a European type of state and some sort of capitalist exploration of the land, the maintenance of a regime of illiberal absolutism of self-rule remained and was further nurtured by the Dergue regime (Vaughan and Tronvoll, 2003). The personalisation of political life under the scenes of the façade of the modern state before, as cornerstone of the postcolonial African polity, is also found in contemporary Ethiopia at the very political elite level (Vaughan and Tronvoll, 2003). Every time forms of out-of-state contestation emerged they were faced with repression, as the leftist and ethno-nationalist movements of the 1960s, 1970s and 1980s – where the very EPRDF's origins are found – experienced. Writing about contemporary state-NGOs relations in the country, Sarah Vaughan and Kjetil Tronvoll argue that

National NGOs have often been the artificial product of the international need for tool to delivery of relief assistance and do not reflect the organic evolution and indigenous consolidation of civil society. ... Without the experience of a collective struggle to establish its own legitimate space outside the remit of the state, the voluntary sector has lacked cohesion and solidarity, and been overly expectant of the largesse of state or international bodies in facilitating its activities. (Vaughan and Tronvoll, 2003: 62–63)

The EPRDF itself has formed NGOs and development associations (Vaughan and Tronvoll, 2003: 65–66). In this context, it should be remarked the role of community-based credit and savings organisations, or *iddirs* (Mengesha, 2002).[7] However, it remains to be assessed to what extent *iddirs* do challenge political governance in Ethiopia.

Unlike countries like South Africa, the field of HIV/AIDS has not represented complex, tense and conflicting situations between the Ethiopian government, Ethiopian civil society and the broader international community. One main reason has to do with the relatively small impact of the epidemic in the country and the concurrent most pressing health issues. Another reason relates to the fact that HIV/AIDS, rather than a threat to the government's worldview and historical experience (as in the case of South Africa), represented an opportunity for the Ethiopian government to raise its international profile in the context of national difficulties and great necessity to secure and augment donor support for development (Wallis, 2009). As it happens with the PEPFAR implementers mentioned above, entities representing people living with AIDS are incorporated in the national, government-led response (HIV/AIDS Office, 2008: 22).

## Conclusion

Rather than a mere HIV/AIDS programme, PEPFAR in Ethiopia is another mosaic in the complex wall of security and development relations between the international community, notably the United States of America, and the host country. Although affecting close to one million people, HIV/AIDS cannot be said to constitute a particularly major threat to the Ethiopian population, as it does in Eastern and Southern Africa. Therefore, the epidemic and its programmes need to be related to other initiatives which respond to challenges posed by both military and human threats to the established regime in Addis Ababa. This is clearly the perspective of the ruling Ethiopian government, largely – yet not fully – matching with United States regional concerns.

The Ethiopian government is holding a widely acknowledged strategy of resorting to as much development and humanitarian assistance as possible, in order to consolidate a method of consolidating the political regime through state-led, or at least state-oriented, development. The government in Addis Ababa does engage in the international discourse around 'country ownership' and sustainability. However, it faces serious limitations to actually consummate such desire, as several PEPFAR implementers exemplified. Country ownership seems to rely mostly on 'political will', yet little on financial capacity. Moreover, from a policy perspective that reclaims larger involvement of civil society (minimally taken as 'out-of-state' organisations), the Ethiopian government is legally confining such alleged requisite.

# 8
# South Africa: Changing HIV/AIDS Policies

## Introduction

For the international community, particularly the Western world including the United States of America, South Africa constitutes a particular case of a country in which some of the best and the worst in contemporary African politics is witnessed. On the one hand, just like northern neighbour Botswana, it offers a relatively successful case of political transition to liberal representative democracy under the framework of a modern, globalised market economy. On the other hand, this country holds grave problems associated with economic inequality, insecurity and, interconnectedly, a ruinous public health situation, in which the HIV/AIDS pandemic is a very acute example. As a global health initiative with a focus on emergent HIV/AIDS implementation, PEPFAR was certainly conceived for a country such as this, as in the case of Botswana.

The problem of the HIV/AIDS pandemic holds a particular statute in the context of both domestic and international politics of South Africa. In fact, it has long served as realm of political struggle involving the government, South African civil society involved in HIV/AIDS advocacy, and the remainder of the major foreign governments and civil groups in the West. This was particularly intense during the presidency of Thabo Mbeki. Many authors on HIV/AIDS politics in South Africa have been holding positions that put policy implementation, its acceptance and rebuttal, including questions of epistemology around the HIV/AIDS science, at centre stage of the discussion. Debates tend to revolve around why it is that the South African government did not engage in HIV/AIDS best practices – that is, HIV/AIDS orthodoxy – to the point of standing unresponsive or even negating it and counterproposing another resolution.

Debates have also stressed the role of stakeholders, namely local and external civil societies, in the improvement of the policy responses, and other socio-political dynamics. Notwithstanding, this book shifts the analysis to the use the several post-apartheid governments have made of the pandemic politics with regard to its overall foreign policy *vis-à-vis* their constituencies and the African continent, particularly. As it will be discussed, this obviously has had consequences for the process of PEPFAR implementation in the country. PEPFAR largely – if not completely – mirrors the evolutive usage of the pandemic by succeeding governments. In its terms, South African governments have attempted to use the pandemic in order to garner international recognition, even if that might come as surprising to some readers.

## Post-apartheid politics of continental influence

South Africa is a continental power in Africa; actually a superpower in its immediate Southern African neighbourhood. Its hegemony is measured in very classical terms: very large, relative, gross domestic product (GDP) (roughly half of sub-Saharan Africa's total) and military capabilities. The recent invitation to join the group of emerging world economies with Brazil, Russia, India and China (the so-called 'BRICS') is symptomatic of the country's significance beyond its own neighbourhood and continent (IOL, 2010).

While South Africa's regional hegemony has long constituted a solid fact, the country's foreign policy practice over the last decades has exhibited different nuances. The apartheid period is characterized by the display of potent military might systematically inside and outside the country's borders in order to assure the political regime. However, in 1994, with the first multiracial elections and dismantlement of apartheid, a shift was under way, as Deon Geldenhuys describes:

> This reorientation flowed from a paradigm shift in South African foreign policy. The 'old' South Africa's realist thinking informed by the imperatives of survival in a hostile world, was replaced by a liberal idealist approach in which democratic South Africa would promote an ambitious reformist agenda abroad based on its internal experiences and values. (Geldenhuys, 2008: 2)

Unlike apartheid, the democratic era has rather been featured by the primacy of liberal idealism across the African continent and the world, as successive presidents (Nelson Mandela, Thabo Mbeki, Jacob Zuma) have been engaged in a new kind of pan-Africanist agenda with the aim of promoting representative democracy, good governance and economic development for the new millennium (Geldenhuys, 2010). Rhetoric of African Renaissance and establishment of the New Partnership for Africa's Development (NEPAD), constitute the cornerstones of this liberal-idealist agenda for the continent.

The discourse on African Renaissance stretches back to the immediate post-apartheid foreign policy of South Africa through Deputy President Thabo Mbeki. Mbeki formally introduced the idea of a renaissance in an address to an American audience in April 1997. Also in 1997, a document entitled *The African Renaissance: A Workable Dream* was released by the then-deputy president (Taylor, 2005: 33). Having generated a flourishing literature of debate and critique, African Renaissance essentially alludes to a 'third moment' of Africa's postcolonial existence, after decolonisation (1960s), followed by democratisation (1990s), and featured by 'social, political democratisation, economic regeneration and the improvement of Africa's geopolitical standing in world affairs' (Maloka, 2001). Although it was alluding to Africa as a whole, it became questionable to what extent this was a strategy of regional hegemony by the far most powerful economy in Africa to engage profitably with the rest of the continent in a new (post-apartheid) context. It backed the latest pan-African plan for development in the continent, NEPAD, set up as a result of collaborative efforts by a group of African countries (Algeria, Egypt, Nigeria, Senegal, South Africa), supported by the Organisation for African Unity and endorsed by a group of the eight most industrialised countries in the world (G8) (Maloka, 2001). Established in 2001, it promised a breakaway from the ineffective neoliberal policies imposed on African countries by structural adjustment policies and serious improvements in national governance through further democratisation, openness to civil society, transparency and accountability (Maloka, 2001).

Independent of the domestic regime – of separate development (apartheid) or liberal-democracy, with black majority – South Africa's relative capabilities *vis-à-vis* the regional neighbourhood and the rest of the continent render it hegemonic, at least unless other 'rivals' emerge. To a large extent, domestic regime change implied a change in international relations, particularly with Southern Africa, from an utterly isolationist position (apartheid) to friendly conviviality with neighbours, who moreover helped the leading political force, the ANC, to resist and eventually negotiate a regime transition (post-apartheid) (Schoeman, 2007). Indeed, while apartheid South Africa had vivid military incursions in Mozambique, Angola, Zimbabwe, and even Botswana, let alone

Namibia – which was part of South Africa until 1990 – the ANC was assisted by the leadership of those countries, or at least groups inside them (for example Botswana). It was also assisted by farther-away states, such as Zambia or Tanzania, not to mention political regimes and social movements around the world (Schoeman, 2007). Post-apartheid idealism is rooted on this mosaic of relations established during the anti-apartheid struggle, and resulted in the democratic will of sharing South Africa's relative wealth with the rest of the continent through aid, and prioritisation of the African continent and the Southern African subcontinent, in particular, in terms of international trade and foreign investment (Taylor, 2005). Eventually, South African companies, or multinationals with earlier strong presence in South Africa, increased their presence in key sectors like telecommunications, transport and distribution (Mutenheri, 2010).

This renewed hegemony of South Africa worked in diapason with the international framework of the United States of America and financial institutions, such as the International Monetary Fund and the World Bank, whose preponderance expanded with the retreat of the Soviet Union. Eventually, such hegemony proliferated to wider parts of Africa, whereby 'many African elites contribute to making neo-liberalism accepted as the "only" macro-economic framework and development strategy within which they (and by implication, all others) can work within' (Taylor, 2002: 21). Though not without some reservations, South Africa was accepted by the Southern African Development Community in 1994, a trade-facilitating organisation whose predominance until then rested on Zimbabwe, but that soon came under South African dominance (Schoeman, 2007). South Africa's post-apartheid liberal idealism constitutes a refoundation of the previous military power, yet with a benign tone. From a military point of view, the South African army is predicted to intervene merely in peacekeeping operations in the immediate and more distantly abroad (Baker and Lyman, 2008; Bond, 2006a: 152; Cilliers, 2008: 22). Furthermore, it has rolled back its nuclear armament programme and participates in international nuclear disarmament initiatives (Burgess and Purkitt, 2001).

The political-philosophical roots of post-apartheid South Africa, based on democracy, human rights and good governance, largely fits the United States of America's tenets indeed. Maintaining relations of alliance advances goals structured around regional/continental stabilisation *vis-à-vis* perceived armed conflicts, human security threats and Islamic terrorism. Expansion of markets and access to mineral reserves is of utmost importance too. As far as United States of America-South

Africa relations in particular go, they have shown a consistent pattern of proximity since the apartheid through today.[1] In this regard, the African Growth and Opportunity Act (AGOA) concurs towards that goal, as it aims at facilitating trade relations between South Africa (and Southern Africa as a whole) and the United States of America. This whole framework is frequently headed by United States leadership discourses around the need for anchor states such as South Africa to hold 'responsibility' both at home and in the region (Clinton, 2009). South Africa is induced as a hegemonic leader that should set the example towards the achievement of what, in the last analysis, are United States strategic goals, and which, after all, coincide with South African ones (Underwood, 2008). The resilience of liberal-democratic institutions and the primacy of the market posits South Africa as one of the very few countries in Africa not falling into any of the categories of 'failed states', 'critically weak states', 'weak states' and 'states to watch', according to the United States influential 'Index of State Weakness in the Developing World' (Rice and Patrick, 2008).

It should also be emphasised the contribution of United States-based and transnational solidarity groups, often composed of black diasporas, which campaigned to change foreign policy in favour of the end of apartheid (Gramby-Sobukwe, 2005). Some of those groups eventually have been playing eminent roles in the post-apartheid period under the auspices of United States-South Africa programmes of cooperation, namely the large mainstream Christian churches, that is, Catholics, Anglicans and other Christian denominations (Gramby-Sobukwe, 2005: 796). One major programme is certainly PEPFAR, in which implementers in South Africa have been the largest recipients (Bradbury and Kleinman, 2010).

PEPFAR's implementation in the country has been largely driven by a mixture of governmental and nongovernmental action. This is certainly another point of proximity between both countries, as demonstrated by strong involvement of both US-based and South African nongovernmental organisations. Nevertheless, both countries have disagreed on the issue of United States Africa Command (AFRICOM), a consequence of post-9/11 policy of surveillance in Africa (Ndlovu-Gatsheni and Ojakorotu, 2010). It has been repeatedly rejected by South Africa and other countries across the continent, though not by neighbouring Botswana (Burgess, 2009; Buchanan, 2008; McFate, 2008). Another point of contention between them referred to the politics of HIV/AIDS and, consequently, PEPFAR. This issue lasted for most of the Mbeki Presidency and is, at least partially, explained by the post-apartheid liberal idealism discussed so far.[2]

## Shifting politicisation of HIV/AIDS pandemic

The successive post-apartheid governments have not been indifferent to the nascent HIV/AIDS epidemic and its social meanings and consequences. This includes the first government, led by Nelson Mandela, which has been accused from apparently refusing to engage in a prompt response. It has been argued that this was driven by a relatively low HIV/AIDS prevalence. However, it has also been explained by the goal of building a democratic nation by excluding potential sources of interracial contention. Given the social aspects of the pandemic, in which the pandemic was soon subject to particular socio-anthropological framings, namely ethnic based, Mandela government has opted out for excluding the nascent epidemic from the major political arenas. Although perceived as 'unwilling', it has been argued that such governmental position is explained in light of the post-apartheid liberal idealism discussed in the previous section. Rather unfortunately, as stressed by HIV/AIDS advocates and scientists, this early government's option has contributed to the untameable expansion of the epidemic in the forthcoming years.

By the late 1990s, as the HIV/AIDS epidemic was becoming increasingly visible in view of several indicators (prevalence, mortality), the national government was under severe local and external pressure to respond more aggressively. However, not only Thabo Mbeki's government did not behave according to those expectations but also it even reduced and suspended programmes, namely drug-based treatment ones. This time round the question was not merely built on democratic, multiracial nation-building, as previously, but on specific scientific disputes. Again the government did not stand indifferent to the HIV/AIDS crisis; yet it framed its position in light of idealism rooted around the concept of African Renaissance. While it is true that the Mbeki administration did not enjoy much reputation in much of the international community, particularly in the West, it should be underlined that its position on the epidemic – its nature and response – aimed at building an influential discourse home and abroad, especially in Africa.

In the early 2000s, building on some unsettled scientific disputes on the nature of the human immunodeficiency virus (HIV), animated by natural scientists such as Peter Duesberg, Mbeki claimed that the biological causes of AIDS were unclear. For him, what was rather clear was a social cause: poverty (Schneider and Fassin, 2002: 49; Youde, 2007a: 5). Furthermore, for Mbeki the AIDS orthodoxy had become the West-led international community's new racist and colonialist mantra for showing to the world Africans' inferiority (Mackintosh, 2009: 33; Sitze,

2004: 770). In addition to that, he considered that this orthodoxy was paving the way for greedy pharmaceutical companies to sell highly toxic drugs to poor African countries (Mackintosh, 2009: 38). This argument was grounded on apartheid-time public health emergencies launched by the government which turned out to be particularly damaging for blacks. It also reflected cases of blacks' suspicion of public health measures (Youde, 2005: 424–426). However, as his biographer Mark Gevisser claimed in 2007, Mbeki did not mean to be 'denialist', yet a 'dissident', intellectually and politically (SABC News, 2007). In practice, many treatment programmes were suspended, and arguable 'African solutions for African problems' for the epidemic were put forward. His Minister of Health, the late Manto Tshabalala-Msimang, introduced a prescription based on garlic, olive oil, lemons and African potato (Kahn, 2009).

The politicisation of HIV/AIDS in that period occurred in the context of post-apartheid race relations but also the advancement, at home and across Africa, of the developmental rhetoric of African Renaissance. After the dismissal of Mbeki in 2008 after an ANC congressional meeting, Tshabalala-Msimang was also sacked by the transitional President Kgalema Motlanthe. And once President Jacob Zuma was elected party leader and later elected the country's president, an absolute reversal of policy took place. Before that, in 2002 and 2003, the Treatment Action Campaign (TAC) won court cases against the state that allowed provision of ARVs to infected pregnant women and to people with advanced AIDS (Oshry, 2007). The launch of PEPFAR in South Africa occurred precisely in the height of those disputes, and its first years of implementation (2003, 2004) were affected by the political context, which did not mean that PEPFAR was launched without endorsement of the national authorities. It was endorsed, even if under difficult conditions, as a former official with a United States government-implementing agency admitted: 'When it was to get the [PEPFAR] memorandum of understanding it was difficult for us to find the person [among the South African government] to sign. It was a massive job. But now it is changing in terms of getting contacts'.

Post-apartheid idealism of South African foreign policy can help to grasp Mbeki's position. Even though it was a mostly domestic event, this position reflects a will, eminently embodied in the figure of President Mbeki, of transmitting a set of values and ideas across Africa – and even the world – centred on the dignity of Africans and their resistance to prevailing racist and colonial images promoted by the West-led international community, as well as their 'affiliates', that is, activists, inside South Africa too. Although this presidential stance was observed as utterly unacceptable by the mainstream HIV/AIDS 'epistemic community' and irrational by the average international community, especially outside Africa, the idealist commitment to a set of values and ideas gave it meaning. It definitely was part of the project of African Renaissance – at home and around the continent – to fight back the historical constructed images around African (read: black) sexuality and even humanity.

Particularly since the end of 2009, the South African government, both at presidential and ministerial levels, has started to engage more seriously with the epidemic and its different domestic and foreign activist interlocutors. The launch of substantial testing and treatment programmes was so exciting that it led the head of UNAIDS, Michel Sidibé, to address President Zuma as an 'architect for AIDS strategy' on the 2009 World AIDS Day (SAPA, 2009). Relationship with funders like PEPFAR and its recipient organisations and the remaining HIV/AIDS community has improved to the point of Minister of Health Aaron Motsoaledi appearing as a guest speaker at the latest International AIDS Conference 2010 as a firm HIV/AIDS advocate. This was something almost unimaginable for a South African higher government official some years before. Yet, the permeating post-apartheid liberal idealism is found once again in the rhetoric. Minister Motsoaledi promises commitment at home and sensitivity for other African nations. He insisted that national governmental expenditure would be 80 per cent of the total cost, while at the same time liberating international resources for poorer countries with the same or higher burden (Bryson, 2010).

## PEPFAR's implementation: mirror of national policy change

Since the beginning, the process of PEPFAR's implementation in South Africa has reflected the shifting dynamics of the national governmental policy and the relationship between national governments and the mainstream HIV/AIDS epistemic community. Therefore, PEPFAR's early establishment was constrained by the context of opposition between the state/government and the nongovernmental arena, but the situation changed. Interviewees with different types of organisations – South African and United States-based governmental and nongovernmental – have converged on the idea of initial mistrust between the national government's leadership and PEPFAR's policies, which has evolved overtime. NGOs have been those who most insisted on that idea. One respondent has claimed that

> In the whole, in the beginning, there was a big problem. The government did not like [the offer of assistance] very much, because PEPFAR

partners and the government were doing the same thing at the same time. This generated big delays. Government officials were not sure if they wanted PEPFAR or not. Now there is more involvement of the government.

Another interviewee commented on the differences between the Mbeki and the current Zuma periods.

> Government attitudes have changed dramatically. Now it is easier with Zuma than with Mbeki. In Mbeki days, civil society and community-based organisations were fundamental in confronting the adversarial attitude of the government. The new government now admits they need help.... Before PEPFAR there was no money. PEPFAR put money in. However, PEPFAR had no framework for engaging with the government. They did not get along. Both were doing different things. NGOs were lying in between trying to do subterranean things, trying to escape government punishment. But now it is different.

Another respondent reiterated the previous idea: 'Collaboration with the government was a big obstacle in the beginning. But this issue has been addressed overtime'. A fourth interviewee conceded that 'In the beginning, it was not very well coordinated between the South African and the United States governments' yet, 'it got better over the last years'. At last, a fifth responded affirmed that, in its outset in South Africa, 'PEPFAR was much more about funding NGOs, namely American, and universities like Columbia. PEPFAR officials did not consult much the government. Back then, the government was holding a very strange position. Mbeki and the minister of health were negating the HIV and AIDS link and the whole AIDS ideology'.

Another commentator went even further in the critique of PEPFAR's implementation being primarily about biomedical intervention to the point of resonating historical grievances associated to the discriminating power of Western medicine in colonial Africa. In any case, PEPFAR's policy shift over time has also been noted.

> [More] recently PEPFAR people realised they have to work with the communities.... Support [in the beginning] was being given to the University of Natal, which was doing its stigmatising work in black townships. They just go to Umlazi to do their research and analysis. Why do not they do that work in Glenwood and other white areas as well, and just confine themselves to black areas?

The recent shift in the governmental policy for HIV/AIDS is also contemporary to a broader policy around development in the country. This is moreover coincident with a propelled left-leaning behaviour of the government after Mbeki's rather liberal approach to the issues of economic empowerment. Like Ethiopia, South Africa sets out to be a 'developmental state'. However, in South Africa, this orientation has not been so much a matter of enabling and feeding a process of economic growth and human development alone, but a question of conciliating that process with redistribution of wealth and social justice. Due to the regime of separate development instated by the National Party in 1948, which, drawn along ethnic lines, essentially strongly enhanced life opportunities (education, health, work) of a predominant minority (mostly of European descent) at the expense of a majority (mostly black). In practice, this system, which inherited many colonial elements, still finds continuities today, and generates diverging lifestyles of developed country-type for the upper-middle classes and developing country-type for the lower classes (Bond, 2004). Today, 17 years into the end of the apartheid regime after the first multiracial, democratic presidential elections in 1994, South Africa is one of the most unequal societies in the world, resembling countries with similar historical trajectories like Brazil or Mexico. As a result, the ideology of the developmental state has emerged with an aim to redistribute wealth across society, restore justice and generate opportunities for historically disadvantaged social groups, such as Black Economic Empowerment initiatives. Nevertheless, despite the current Zuma administration's endorsement of a more state-interventionist approach, on the ground, the latest years have been featured by notable riots and protests by residents in townships and informal settlements for the absence of service delivery leading to violent clashes with police forces, in a context of mounting unemployment, especially among the youth (Habib, 2005).

Several studies have linked the proliferation of HIV/AIDS to social determinants rooted in the apartheid regime and the current social condition of many South Africans and foreigners living in South Africa, notably the lack of medical assistance and forceful migrations (Hlongwane, 2003; Johnson, 2004; Marks, 2002). South Africa holds the fourth-highest prevalence rate among adults (15–49) in the world, with 17.9 per cent (UNAIDS, 2013: 121), after neighbouring Swaziland, Botswana and Lesotho. This means that a significant share of the population is not only infected but moreover affected by the pandemic. This includes adults and those dependent on them, notably children, as well as their own parents, who often have to be in charge of their grandchildren when parents fall ill and eventually die younger than expected (Bray, 2003; Tobin, 2010). Like in the case of Botswana, grim scenarios about the potential social, economic and even security consequences of the pandemic have been put forward, particularly from the late 1990s on.

Although the government funds up to 80 per cent of the overall response, PEPFAR has played a significant role in both quantitative and qualitative terms. South Africa has been the major PEPFAR focus country, and its focus areas have been very diverse: medical research, treatment and palliative services, orphans and vulnerable children, and prevention through the abstinence, be faithful and condoms policy (ABC) approach, among others. Whereas some organisations' work scope deals only with HIV/AIDS and correlative epidemics, like tuberculosis (for instance, medical research institutions and laboratories), many others have a wider developmental agenda upon which PEPFAR projects build. This was particularly visible among secular and faith-based development NGOs whose income-generation activities for populations (primarily HIV-affected) living in historically disadvantaged areas, such as townships and informal settlements, together with facilitating access to social grants, especially by children, aimed at addressing the lack of economic opportunities and social security.

However, the government faces the dilemma of having to sustain the response after PEPFAR and other big donors leave. Two types of reaction to that question are encountered, though. One type is eminently economistic and refers that sustainability is dependent on the economic recovery after the current recession. Along with Minister Motsoaledi (Bryson, 2010), it is argued that the government will not be able to take charge of the PEPFAR-initiated projects, due to the propelled economic downturn. For other stakeholders, yet another type of reaction is rather ethical/juridical: sustainability is a matter of the government complying with its 'constitutional' responsibility of providing care for the humans living within the countries' boundaries, and thus allocating resources accordingly. This perspective is observable in this comment about PEPFAR and the South African national response.

> PEPFAR has...filled gaps in the South African HIV policy providing ARVs to groups including illegal immigrants and refugees. However these groups should be able to receive treatment from the DoH [Department of Health] because constitutionally all people in South Africa are entitled to health care, not just citizens and residents.

For this observer, PEPFAR has addressed a matter that is an obligation of the South African government.

Nevertheless, prevention policies such as the so-called 'ABC (abstain, be faithful, condomise) strategy' and policies on family planning constitute a contested issue even today. The contestation relates to the propelled, unscientifically proven ability of abstinence/faithfulness activities really contributing to a decrease of infections (Gender Equity, 2004: 10–11) and its suitability to the domestic realities of intervention. One major problem with the efficacy of prevention based on abstinence/faithfulness is that it does not fit one of the most vulnerable groups to AIDS, namely women who engage in sex work or transactional sex. This group certainly cannot abstain from sex; therefore, prevention for them has to take another form. As for the Mexico City Policy, this policy inhibits the right of women to voluntarily access pregnancy interruption with United States funding, even if the country at stake has a favouring legislation. Answering to the question on the chief obstacles to implementation, an interviewee with a United States-based implementing NGO in South Africa said that 'the major limiting factor is the people who take decisions in Washington who do not understand South African reality'. Along the same lines, another interviewee, yet with a South African NGO, affirmed critically that 'we know better about the South African epidemic than United States politicians'. In fact, these comments are consistent with conclusions achieved by the United States Government Accountability Office (GAO) in a 2008 survey dedicated to that topic:

> although more than half of the 22 experts we interviewed acknowledged benefits of PEPFAR's overall prevention spending directive, the same number of experts expressed concern about the AB directive's effect on country-based and evidence-based programming.... However, 13 of 22 experts expressed concern that the AB directive has posed obstacles to country-based programming, and 13 experts said it has hindered development of integrated prevention programs. (GAO, 2008: 20)

Soon after the Obama election in 2008, the Mexico City Policy was reversed. This led to consequences, not only on family planning, which could be restored with larger choices, but even at the language level. Acknowledging Bush's role in the reauthorization, an interviewee with a South African NGO mentioned that 'with the new administration there are changes though. For instance, the GAG policy [that is, Mexico City Policy] has retreated. Now we can call prostitutes and not commercial sex workers'.

## Liberal economics, social inequalities, and HIV/AIDS implementation

South Africa accompanies Botswana in terms of the settlement of liberal values and institutions in function of domestic choices, although constraints associated to changes in the international system – end of the Cold War, demise of the Soviet Union and United States superpower hegemony – also played a role. The transition from apartheid to multi-racial democracy was the result of concessions on both sides (supporters and opponents of the apartheid). One concession consisted of the inflection of the 'revolutionary' economic policy agenda of the far-left sectors of the African National Congress (ANC), aiming at the nation-alisation of the major industries (namely mineral resources) and land reform. The ruling government of the ANC adopted social-democratic politics, with alignment with the Western European Socialist 'third-way' parties, who themselves were initiating agendas in their countries after the Cold War based on privatisations and other liberalising reforms (Bond, 2001). Comparing to Botswana, the South African experience of a much more technologically advanced capitalist system, developed during the decades of apartheid, has enhanced a more matured case of a liberal polity. Yet, this is a polity where the promises of social improve-ment in the post-apartheid era and the reality of social disparities often contradict each other very intensely.

The post-apartheid regime under the leadership of the ANC has embraced a liberal-idealist politics aimed at African empowerment through aid, economic opportunities and development, both at home and around the continent. Initiatives such as the Black Economic Empowerment (BEE), on the one hand, and the New Partnership for Africa's Development (NEPAD), on the other, materialise the idea of African Renaissance underneath governmental idealism. BEE favours the inclusion of black citizens in the business world through company creation and management of bigger companies. Through state inter-ventionism, BEE is a political tool that seeks '[the] construction of a procapitalist, interventionist state prepared to use its power, influence and divestment of assets to create a black bourgeoisie' (Southall, 2004: 326–327).

Although this model of economic governance is at the end not liberal in practice (Southall, 2004), the organisation and implementation of social welfare programmes really follows a liberal approach through the participation of public and private entities. The third-way social democ-racy of the ANC has maintained a commitment to liberal-capitalist economic policies including implementing social policy for the excluded populations based on a mixed system of governmental and nongovernmental intervention. Apart from income transfers to disadvantaged sectors of the population by the government (for example, social grants to children), an array of private institutions participate in poverty alleviation and economic empowerment: parastatal organisations, NGOs and for-profit private companies, such as insurance companies. As far as PEPFAR is concerned, this framework of social policy matches very neatly PEPFAR's own intervention rationales. It can be argued that the idealised profile for PEPFAR as grounded on liberally shared roles by the state and civil society is largely accomplished in South Africa, since the political-economic infrastructure intervention built upon resembles the United States model. This was particularly remarkable to observe especially during the Mbeki presidency and the concomitant context of policy struggle between the government and the domestic and international mainstream epistemic community on how to conceptualise and respond to the HIV/AIDS epidemic (Youde, 2007b). Even though, as noted by a NGO PEPFAR implementer, the South African and United States governments were, in the beginning, 'two parallel roads' – their policy frameworks did match.

The difficulty to respond to the growing socio-economic disparities expressed through constant demonstrations and strikes over salary and working conditions and regular riots on social delivery (power, water, jobs) across the country, especially in the most deprived areas, has generated a Marxist critique that argues that the current post-apartheid regime is a continuation of the previous exclusionary politics. Accordingly, racial apartheid became 'class apartheid' in a context of a 'global apartheid' essentially drawn along the lines of Global North and Global South (Bond, 2004). This issue of tremendous social disparities and the contradictions they produce has led to two political reactions. One has led to the engagement of 'progressive social movements' implicated in struggles around housing conditions, the environment and HIV/AIDS treatments, building on the anti-apartheid experience and affiliated with the World Social Forum (Bond, 2006b). Perhaps more visible and politically more consequential, another concerns 'nativist' resolutions for a future South Africa (Ndlovu-Gatsheni, 2009) such as those boosted by Julius Malema. Often inspired in the praxis of Zimbabwean President Robert Mugabe, the recently dismissed leader of the Youth League of the ANC has advocated the nationalisation of mines, land reform towards black ownership and the political guidance of blacks, accompanied by other ethnicities that, in his view, fought apartheid, such as coloureds and Asians. Malema advocates the exclusion of whites from political and economic power structures, because they neither are African nor supportive of an anticolonial political regime. Yet, for Sabelo J. Ndlovu-Gatsheni, the South African liberal tradition should prevail over nativism, even if under severe strain.

> The Zimbabwean version of nativism has very open racial connotations. In a multi-racial society like South Africa, nativism immediately locked horns with a very strong liberal tradition that continues to defend a liberal trajectory. But in both countries, the future of liberal democracy remains uncertain. (Ndlovu-Gatsheni, 2009: 75)

Within the formal structures of government, the ANC government has realised the social problems of the post-apartheid era too. Published in June 2011, the 'Diagnostic Overview' of the National Planning Commission of the Presidency of the Republic (2011) concludes that, despite 'relative success', 'eliminating poverty and inequality remain [the country's] main strategic challenges'. Among several specific 'challenges' (poor location and maintenance of infrastructure, spatial marginalisation of the poor, unsustainable growth path, uneven public service, corruption and societal divisions), the report stresses the 'massive disease burden' of the health system (Planning Commission, 2011: 20–22). The experts who elaborated the 'Diagnostic' remark the state's incapacity to address the HIV/AIDS issue.

> While the country's disease burden is rising, the health system is collapsing. This collapse is partly attributable to the nature of the disease burden; its breakdown lies also in institutional issues and implementation failures over a long period of time. (Planning Commission, 2011: 21)

However, apart from the issues around capacity, another aspect concerns the dimension of the economic empowerment of patients, particularly women and children living with AIDS who already find themselves at the margins of society. Several PEPFAR-funded programmes address this dimension, as remarked previously, in terms of policy rationale. Some assist in applications for social grants for children while others implement income-generation activities. But it is interesting to verify that, when asked about a propelled link between HIV/AIDS intervention and economic empowerment, many PEPFAR-implementing interviewees (not just in South Africa, but particularly in South Africa) do not establish any causality between one thing and the other. And when they do, they do not have evidence of that apart from the personal observation of their own projects. One interviewee with a South Africa-based implementing NGO gave a rather sceptical view. In fact, the potential economic impact of HIV/AIDS intervention is offset by the broader political-economic context of dire unemployment.

> The South African government, which now is very much engaged in HIV/AIDS, is anxious to give good news about the epidemic. In fact people are healthier and living longer; however, unemployment prevents people from those benefits. HIV/AIDS improvements are not having a direct contribution in labour productivity and economic development.

Yet, another respondent with the same profile went much further in stressing the defining role of unemployment by deconstructing the alleged causality between HIV/AIDS treatment and economic opportunities, especially among NGO implementers.

> PEPFAR's activities have nothing to do with social and economic development. That is the mantra they [the development industry] have to advance in order to justify themselves before the donors. In industrialised countries they could relate medical treatment to productiveness. However, we have 80 per cent of unemployment where we work, so it does not make much difference if they live longer and theoretically become more productive because they do not work. In fact, we could say that longer lives increases unemployment. I do not see a relation between AIDS treatment and higher GDP. To me AIDS work is a moral responsibility and nothing else.

However, according to the South African presidency's 'Diagnostic', the problem of unemployment lies at the core of the national socio-development strategy.

> South Africa has extremely high rates of unemployment and underemployment. A large proportion of out-of-school youth and adults are not working. Those in low income households that are working support many dependants and earn little relative to the cost of living. This is a central contributor to widespread poverty. Inactivity of broad sections of society reduces our potential for economic expansion. (Planning Commission, 2011: 9)

As such, it should not constitute a 'surprise' to what the previous two respondents have stated.

## Conclusion

Rather than engaging in the great debates on the HIV/AIDS policy twists and turns of the successive South African governments, the epistemological questions upon which they sit and the struggles between the government and civil society movements at home and abroad, this chapter has departed from the post-apartheid idealist politics that has driven action. Governments have framed their positions on the HIV/AIDS pandemic within the post-apartheid politics of projecting liberal idealism domestically and abroad, especially around sub-Saharan Africa. Shifting positions over time have reflected the management of such projection and have had a marked impact on the way PEPFAR has been implemented in the country since 2004.

Nonetheless, it should be remarked that both South Africa and the United States of America in the post-apartheid era share a commonality of political and economic frameworks that are visible in the way that the division of labour of PEPFAR's implementation has been organised. Implementation has proceeded in a combination of governmental and nongovernmental intervention. In the latter case, nongovernmental activity has been notably aggressive, demonstrating the weight of that sector in overall implementation. In turn, the alignment of economic agendas around liberal reform bares the grave issues of socio-economic inequality, eventually with a decisive impact on the social determinants of the HIV/AIDS pandemic.

# 9
# Conclusion: Recipient States Being Sovereign

## Introduction

Refocusing analysis in states and governments, namely recipient ones, away from leading contemporary scholarly approaches to individuals, populations and social forces has invited a reassessment of the structural realist contribution to International Politics. The basic concern for the role of states as essential units of the system is increasingly important not just for the study of global health governance as such, but also the understanding of broader phenomena in the developing world, in which the increasing diversity of foreign investment and aid assistance sources challenges the traditional postcolonial prevalence of Western countries. In this landscape, recipient states of major global health (and development, in general) programmes reinforce their capability to opt in and out for partnerships across the international system in order to accomplish their political agency. This certainly does not mean that any idea of absence of conditionality in a context of an enduring asymmetric system is completely or partially played out. Policy conditionality is taken theoretically and practically for granted regardless of aid being provided by the United States of America or China. The major difference is that currently smaller, weaker states operate in a framework in which the *possibility to choose* has enlarged significantly, in addition to crucial domestic variables that have to do with national developmentalist policy and practice aiming to attain fundamental political goals.

Nevertheless, the adoption of Waltzian concepts was not meant to be an open endorsement of his theory, since it is not fully applicable to the reality of relations of sub-Saharan African states with the West. This is because, first of all, structural realism proves too elitist for the reality of the postcolonial state in Africa. Waltz's theory was originally conceived to explain the behaviour of world powers, such as 19th century Europe or the Cold War. That is not applicable to a realm of states with different capabilities where propelled weaker states are expected not to have a strategy of their own beyond plain bandwagoning. Secondly, the methodological detachment of the external sphere of the state from the internal one does not help grasping the full set of interstate relations. Understood as a social relation, the state is sociologically and historically informed by the experience of the state which makes it distinct from others.

Indeed, despite the unequivocal asymmetry that features the international system, less powerful states in sub-Saharan Africa still act autonomously in that system, and, thus, pursue a strategic agenda of their own, even if under severe constraint. Each state/government analysed, and the characteristics of its agency *vis-à-vis* the international structure, reveals (and is revealed by) the historical experience of its construction and development. Considering the group of three countries under analysis here, different dynamics of agency are identified.

## Implementing PEPFAR: cross-country comparison of national agency

The pacific Botswanan post-independence settlement derives from the circumstances of British-Boer colonial relations in Southern Africa. In the late 19th century, in the face of pressures put by the Boer republics in the South, Tswana leaders sought to exchange with the United Kingdom military protection for concession of protectorate status and territory for the construction of a railway from the South African Cape colony to Southern Rhodesia (today's Zimbabwe). Although the settlement was inclined towards the adoption of Western political and economic institutions, the harsh reality lying at the core of Southern Africa, ridden by several high intensity armed conflicts, forced the Botswanan leadership to engage with all parties involved. This implied positive relations with the United Kingdom, the main postcolonial development funder; the two world rivals (United States of America and Soviet Union); former Rhodesia; and, most importantly, South Africa. The latter not only was the regional economic hegemony, but also the host of De Beers company, the partner in the public-private partnership (PPP) Debswana, in charge of exploring the diamond mines in the country. Relations with South Africa and former Rhodesia were particularly difficult, since the white supremacy regimes in both countries suspected of the existence of black insurgent bases in Botswana, actually raided and bombed some southern and northern parts of the country.

In the West, namely in the United States of America, in the context of sub-Saharan Africa, Botswana is regarded as a 'miracle' of good governance, economic growth and development. It is observed as a politically stable and peaceful country due not only to its smooth transition to independence, which occurred with almost no incidents, but also to the transparent process of exploration of its mineral resources, primarily diamonds, and employment of the wealth associated with it. In 1966, year of independence, Botswana was one of the poorest countries in the world, but after a few decades it climbed up to a middle-income position. The country has had regular elections, always won by the same party (Botswana Democratic Party), and adopted characteristics typical to the developmental state model visible in Eastern Asia at the time, since public expenditure was targeted at creating strategic infrastructures (roads, power stations). However, it should be understood that such reputation has not only been built around the policies and actions of Botswana's leaderships but, moreover, the comparative analysis that is done between Botswana and the average sub-Saharan African country. In fact, Botswana's political elites have been acting according to a strong logic of self-help. More recently, the major threat has shifted from aggressive behaviour of political regimes around it towards the HIV/ AIDS burden that affects a quarter of the adult population and, as such, constitutes a serious threat to the national survival.

The national government was fast persuaded by the international community (primarily WHO) about the necessity to intervene in order to prevent the disease. In the early 2000s, a number of studies on the economic impact of the epidemic convinced the political leadership to advance towards the funding of a massive treatment programme in order to contain the worrisome spread of the disease through the population. Initiated in 2001, this programme has been assisted by the Bill and Melinda Gates Foundation, the Global Fund and, finally, since 2004, PEPFAR. This highly debated measure, considering the high costs involved, was put forward in the name of national survival. As a result, the Botswanan government became the undisputed leader of the overall HIV/AIDS intervention in the country, given the public health, economic, social and even security implications. This happens especially in financial terms – as it funds 80 per cent of the effort – but also politically. In this regard, PEPFAR's financial participation is relatively marginal, yet in diapason with the envisaged policies of country ownership and sustainability. As several respondents commented, 'PEPFAR fills the gaps' of the overall response by addressing areas related to management and organisational capacity-building, something that should be replicated elsewhere. Currently, the HIV/AIDS epidemic poses an even more complex challenge to the state. Despite decreases on the cost of drugs, the recession of the global trade in diamonds poses an additional pressure on the relative prioritisation that the HIV/AIDS response has enjoyed throughout the last decade, apart from the general flattening on global HIV/AIDS initiatives funding. In any case, it remains clear that HIV/AIDS policy and implementation, for the existential threat it constitutes for the country's small population of 2 million people, shall remain a concern of the national government.

The case of Ethiopia is rather different from Botswana. The last decades have witnessed large-scale political violence across the country, together with serious problems of hunger, ill health and underdevelopment affecting several sectors of the country's large, and still growing, population. Inaugurated in 1991 with the ousting of the Dergue regime through guerrilla warfare, the current regime has been putting forward policies aimed at resolving long-lasting problems undermining the country's development. Led by the Ethiopian People's Revolutionary Democratic Front (EPRDF), those policies are structured around 'ethnic federalism' and state developmentalism with the goal of resolving domestic ethnic grievances and lifting the country from the bottom of the United Nations' Human Development Index. At the same time, and concomitantly, the new regime has been engaging in a policy, often through heavy military means, of securing territorial integrity and inviolability that have been threatened by domestic 'terrorist organisations' of ethnic/regional inspiration, as well as groups based in Somalia and allegedly affiliated with Al-Qaeda. As a result, the action of the national government in Addis Ababa is framed in terms of self-help, yet primarily concerned with the political regime's existence rather than, as in the case of Botswana, with the population as such.

As it was demonstrated in Chapter 7, the interaction with the international structure, particularly with the United States of America, reflects this concern for the regime's survival. Certainly, the issue of regime survival is something that, in principle, implicates all states, as Waltzian frameworks demonstrate. All regimes seek their self-help. Still, the interesting aspect about Ethiopia is that also the Dergue regime was driven by the same concern in its international action. Although officially assisted by the Soviet Union and the Warsaw Pact in light of Cold War politics, it received support, namely humanitarian, from the United States of America. Today, in the case of the EPRDF, assistance is sought from

Western countries but also from 'new partners', such as Turkey, Saudi Arabia, United Arab Emirates, India and China. In terms of international diplomacy, the country has been represented at the higher international level: former Prime Minister Meles Zenawi as African representative at summits on climate change and the United Kingdom Commission for Africa, and former Minister of Health (currently Minister of Foreign Affairs) Tedros Adhanom Ghebreyesus as chair of the Global Fund until September 2011.

Apart from basic geopolitical concerns, development indeed represents the major topic of foreign and domestic policy of the Ethiopian government. Since 1991 the government has been establishing five-year development plans that can be adapted to external assistance. The latest growth and transformation plan was launched in 2010 and looks forward to establish industry in 2020, based on the construction of the Millennium Dam on the Nile Basin and on leasing vast masses of agricultural land to foreign companies. Aimed at abolishing poverty in the long run, the plan underlines strongly a dimension of social development that includes improvement of health services under the guidance of the Ethiopian Ministry of Health. This is the part of the plan in which assistance through PEPFAR comes in, sitting alongside numerous other external (bilateral and multilateral) development initiatives, especially from North America, Western Europe and Japan.

Still, despite its small epidemic, it should be noticed that in the early 2000s, in the eve of PEPFAR's establishment, Ethiopia was presented as a country where the HIV/AIDS epidemic could reveal in the future a similar pattern of gravity as in Southern Africa, given its enlarging population. Independent of the empirical confirmation of such scenario, the emergence of large amounts of funds to tackle the epidemic was welcomed by the Ethiopian leadership in order to address the background problem of very deficient health care around the country. Moreover, such openness has been witnessed since the late 1980s when the first cases were identified in the country, and the international organisations in charge – first, WHO, then UNAIDS – came forth.

The committed character of the Ethiopian government has been regarded as an example of 'country ownership' by several players in the international aid arena in Ethiopia. However, the country's ability to fund large-scale interventions is still quite limited. In addition to this constraint, the state maintains a low capacity to reach to large sectors of the population, especially rural ones, where 82 per cent of the population live. From a broader perspective, considering the alluded security issues, the state has limited access to some regions of the country, especially the surrounding region of Addis Ababa, Oromia and the Eastern region of Ogaden. Yet, this is precisely revealing of those problems of security, and how the regime in Addis Ababa addresses them in order to safeguard its survival. Intentionally or unintentionally, this strategic goal is favoured by the current diversification of donors, which allows the government in Addis Ababa to act with less conditionalities in domains at stake in a context of securitisation, namely civil and media liberties.

In South Africa, since the transition to multiracial democracy in 1994, the country's governments have leaned from hard military power exertion during the apartheid towards transmission of liberal values (reconciliation, representative democracy, economic entrepreneurship) that can be seen in a number of instances and eventually held repercussions in the area of HIV/AIDS. This 'behaviour change' is not only the result of the relatively peaceful regime transition but also a reflection of the relations formed during the apartheid struggle with fellow African states that assisted logistically and ideologically the anti-apartheid movements, specially the ANC. Whereas Botswanan and Ethiopian dynamics point to self-help, South African behaviour emphasises the transmission of ideas, domestically and internationally, consonant with the transition from apartheid to multiracial democracy. Post-apartheid politics are visible from the inception of the democratic regime on former President Mandela's insistence on good governance and democracy in Africa. Later, it was continued by President Mbeki in discourses of African Renaissance and dignity of the black African. In policy terms, this new South African stance in African and world affairs was consolidated through the collective establishment of the New Partnership for African Development in 2001. At home this was represented by initiatives such as Black Economic Empowerment (BEE). The 'new' South Africa appeared very much aligned with the major world powers and international organisations through the committed adoption of liberal reforms. In terms of external policy, South Africa encouraged policies of human security, prevention of armed conflicts, or peacekeeping operations.

Relations between South Africa and the United States of America are very peculiar in light of the apartheid and democratic experiences. In fact, with a very short intermission in the late 1980s, when economic sanctions against apartheid rule were put into place, both countries collaborated very intensely. During apartheid, the United States of America was counting on apartheid's anticommunism to contain Soviet influence in the region. Afterwards, with the end of the Cold War and the apartheid, relations were maintained under a spirit of humanitarian cooperation, as PEPFAR shows, but with a security perspective too. Together with

Botswana, South Africa represents one of the few states which are not considered weak or failing in the African continent. Despite the coincidence of agendas, there have been issues of contention between both sides. One has to do with the establishment of the United States Africa Command (AFRICOM) on African soil, which South Africa has been barring determinately. Another regards HIV/AIDS and how it came to be addressed by the South African leadership under Mbeki, yet arguably still in light of the idealist politics of African Renaissance. Mbeki appeared as a self-proclaimed 'dissident' of the biomedical recipes promoted by the international community, since it was detrimental to the dignity of black Africans in his country and around the continent.

Although mainly a domestic event, Mbeki's 'rogue' position echoed across the African continent. Arguably it reflected a will of transmitting a set of values and ideas across Africa centred on the dignity of Africans and their resistance to prevailing racist and colonial images. However, particularly outside Africa, this position was observed as unacceptable and even irrational, and this was the issue between the United States of America and the South African government at the time. However, when higher level positions on HIV/AIDS changed dramatically with President Jacob Zuma and his Minister of Health Aaron Motsoaledi, it was in light of the same liberal-idealist framework. In international events, the South African leadership exhibits a pan-African position by calling for attention of donors to the difficulties of poorer African nations in the struggle against the disease.

PEPFAR's implementation in South Africa began in the middle of the controversy with President Mbeki. As a consequence, particularly during the first phase (2004–2008), PEPFAR's stakeholders were confronted with the need to conciliate actual implementation of projects with state's approvals. However, since the beginning of Zuma's presidency, and the 'burial of denialism', similarly to Ethiopia, interventions in several areas (medical research, treatment and palliative care, orphans and vulnerable children, prevention) under PEPFAR are incorporated in the state developmentalism that the ANC government is attempting to run with the purpose of overcoming the past of separate development and boosting economic empowerment. In fact, the government is now funding up 80 per cent of the overall response. However, like Botswana, the economic recession affecting the country, as well as donors, poses challenges of sustainability.

Table 9.1 below presents each country's demonstration of agency in function of the policy problems identified, strategies devised and goals

*Table 9.1*  State/government agency in light of PEPFAR experience

|  | Policy problem | Strategies | Political goals |
|---|---|---|---|
| **Botswana** | Very large HIV/AIDS epidemic | State-led response against HIV/AIDS, complemented by external assistance (PEPFAR, Gates Foundation, Global Fund) | National survival |
| **Ethiopia** | Very low human development | State-led developmentalism; diversification of international funders; international diplomacy (for example, UK Commission for Africa, climate change, global health) | Political regime survival |
| **South Africa** | Very large HIV/AIDS epidemic | Transmission of values on the dignity of Africans; public-private developmentalism | Liberal multiracial democracy; 'African Renaissance' |

aimed. It is observable that Botswana and South Africa share the same policy problem (very large HIV/AIDS epidemic); however, the strategies and political goals do not entirely coincide. The former seeks survival; the latter envisages the dissemination of liberal values. In turn, Botswana and Ethiopia attempt at similar goals (survival), even though the policy problem differs to an extent. For Botswana, the problem is eminently rooted in the epidemic; for Ethiopia, it lies generally on low human development. However, Botswana and Ethiopia share a strong state action. In the case of South Africa, despite a vivid governmental influence, the private sector's interference is remarkable too.

## Further questions on national agency

The acknowledgement that less powerful states, namely postcolonial and developing ones, hold agency *vis-à-vis* not only the international structure but the actual hegemonic powers within it paves the way to new questions regarding the nature of this agency and the role of the international system in this process. From the research conducted, the cases of Botswana and Ethiopia suggest a rationale of self-help and survival in the international system, rendering neorealist traditions a very suitable body to describe both past and present policies. In turn, South Africa is arguably driven by a liberal-idealist approach, yet only since 1994, following domestic regime change. As recurrently mentioned, the transmission of values on the dignity of Africans is part of a strategy that seeks the consolidation of liberal multilateral democracy and a transcending project of 'African Renaissance'. However, in the case of South Africa, the ante-1994 period requires a rather hard power-based approach, considering the previous politics of the apartheid regime as well as the far wealthier and military capabilities of the state. Eventually, a combination of both theories can help with the analysis of South Africa's behaviour, not only with regard to its broader relations with the region, the continent and the world, but also, and specifically, with PEPFAR and the politics of HIV/AIDS inside and beyond borders. As such, despite the idealism, a full understanding of the policy requires the maintenance of a neorealist 'analytical predisposition'. Studying the nature of the agency identified along these lines also confirms the need to address these dynamics in a domestic/international dialectic approach, since domestic regime change has clearly influenced South Africa's position internationally.

The analysis of PEPFAR's implementation has also drawn attention to various cross-cutting problems that point to local dynamics of social conflict. Often, this conflictuality refers to overarching issues on social inequalities, poverty and even armed violence, and contradicts major narratives about the states involved. This is particularly salient in the case of Botswana and South Africa, whose peaceful transitions to independence and multiracial democracy are generally considered remarkable through the adoption of Western institutions and values. In this regard, the question of adoption of liberal values and institutions, particularly in the Botswana case, is at stake.

Adoption of Western institutions and values such as representative democracy and market-based economy in Botswana arguably are not the result of reform determined by the international structure of international financial organisations and Western states since the 1980s, as discussed in Chapter 4. In Botswana, Western forms of political and economic organisation have been experienced since the independence, deriving from the post-independence settlement, in which the same colonial and postcolonial elite – colonist and local/native – prevailed. Maintaining an umbilical relationship with the United Kingdom, former protector and main development supporter after 1966, the adoption of liberal tenets of political representation and economic organisation is mostly due to the continuation of British influence in the process of statebuilding in Botswana. However, it is also explained by the position of the Botswanan governments throughout the Cold War and, more importantly, the apartheid regime in South Africa. Located in the heart of a region struggling with several highly intense ideological conflicts (leftist and black nationalist movements, on the one hand; rightist and white supremacist, on the other hand), the acceptance of liberal institutions consisted of the 'centrist' position that the country's survival and development depended on.

Although the combination of representative democracy and market-based economy with state developmentalism has consolidated the view of Botswana as an 'African miracle', critical literature on national achievements started to question the validity of underlying liberal values in contemporary Botswana. In spite of the fantastic economic growth in the 1980s, social disparities increased, as many Botswanan citizens remained stranded in subsistence agriculture and poverty. In addition to that, as the response to HIV/AIDS has shown, and several interviewed PEPFAR implementers confirmed, civil society, a critical bastion of liberalism, has not been significantly enhanced in terms of its participation in the country's main challenges. Moreover, in recent years, the country has witnessed a rising 'liberal authoritarianism', materialised in the introduction of senior military staff in the civil service, extra-judicial murders and severe corruption. It seems ironic that a country with an arguable tradition of holding liberal values seems to be receding in political liberties at a time external actors, including programmes such as PEPFAR that enhance civic participation, aim at diffusing those very values.

In South Africa, the adoption of Western values was the result of the post-apartheid compromise between the different political forces involved. To an extent, it implicated the retreat of revolutionary agenda of some sectors of the ANC and left-wing parties. The ANC-led government became a social-democratic party, akin to the European Socialist 'third way', with an aim of conciliating liberalisation of the economy with reduction of the deep-seated disparities inherited from apartheid. Major initiatives in this regard were the Black Economic Empowerment at home and NEPAD overseas. Additionally, it should be underlined the long-lasting integration of the South African economy, specially the mineral industries, in the global circuits of capital as a contributor for the relatively easy incorporation of liberalism in governance.

Social policy has clearly followed a liberal approach, in which a range of state and parastatal institutions, NGOs and private companies, including those funded under PEPFAR, intervened in the realm of marginalised populations. Nevertheless, social inequalities have not shrunk but rather increased, as frequent demonstrations, strikes and riots on service delivery confirm. The Diagnostic of the National Planning Commission has also reiterated the central problem that growing poverty and inequality poses in strategic terms. Eventually, dissatisfaction with the state of affairs has led to two political responses to the problems of liberal in the country. One is a critique promoted by social movements building on the anti-apartheid struggle that rally around problems such as housing or HIV/AIDS. Another emulates Zimbabwean President Robert Mugabe's 'nativist' proposals, which call for an absolute exoneration of white cadres in state and corporate structures, and nationalisation of the nation's strategic industries. Independent of the success of forces contesting liberalism, South Africa is clearly undergoing challenges to its post-apartheid settlement rooted around liberal premises.

Although committed to a democratic and all-inclusive state, the EPRDF government in Ethiopia has been severely criticised for its record so far. According to opposition politicians, human rights NGOs, academics and foreign diplomats, the government has consecutively implemented constraining measures that stretch from police and army violence to subtle sophisticated mechanisms of censorship. These measures have been accompanied by legislation that limits opposition politics and nongovernmental activities, for example, the Charities Law of 2009. This legislation has been mentioned by PEPFAR implementers, although not always receiving criticism. As discussed in the case of Botswana, this political tightening takes place under severe exposure to Western aid conditionality demanding political and civil society, thus questioning the actual efficacy – if purpose – of those conditionalities in the face of a propelled national regime's sovereignty to rule with a large degree of self-determination.

The EPRDF is found reproducing a political pattern that comes from the time of Haile Selassie, in which, parallel to a modernising ambition of political and social life, out-of-state forces are regarded with suspicion. This has implications for what can be taken as civil society, since the tendency, once foreign development assistance is assured, is for the state to create its own apparatus of nongovernmental organisations to apply for and administer the funding. Nonetheless, and despite occasional criticism at the diplomatic level, international funding is not suspended. The Ethiopian political arena is still highly featured by political conflict, namely opposition exerted by regionalist armed groups against the sovereignty of Addis Ababa over their regions (particularly Oromia and Ogaden) whose demands stretch from decentralisation to actual secession. More recently, the projects on land leasing and the Millennium Dam pose serious issues to the survival of resident communities, whose benefit from these initiatives is unclear. These dynamics suggest that more or less conflictual domestic dynamics may also influence the level and nature of agency the country holds both nationally and internationally.

## Donor diversification and post-2015 development goals

As 2015 approaches the Millennium Development Goals-based framework, which has laid ground for the major global developmental and health interventions, is coming to a close. At the same time, discussions on the post-2015 development agenda naturally heat on, and upcoming strategies and plans of intervention are being elaborated with the purpose of making sense of the unachievements so far and the need to renew the agenda of attaining sustainable development worldwide. In this regard, it is relevant for this book the positioning of recipient states in upcoming plans of action, particularly the idea of country ownership, which captures the policy view of such role. Country ownership emerged in 2005 in the Paris Declaration on Aid Effectiveness, in which it is presented as completely cornerstone to any idea of achieving sustainable, committed development goals by the developing world.

It is clear in several reports on the post-Millennium Development Goals that some idea of country ownership needs to be pursued in order to be effective in development practice (Task Team, 2013). Moreover, its prior absence is observed as an actual cause for failure to attain them (Task Team, 2012). However, it is questionable to what extent that country ownership as a commonly accepted technical concept that frames and drives policy generates outcomes that not only are expected but also satisfying for all stakeholders involved.

Considering PEPFAR's second phase of implementation, country ownership has been echoed as a programmatic goal to be pursed with flexibility in the aftermath of the previous emergency period, in the context of increasing difficulties to keep up with expansive moves by the United States government. While generally endorsed – even if with differing elaborations, as admitted by Eric Goosby – the actual practice of country ownership as a measure of how a project or activity is actually shared by both donor and recipient sides is influenced by factors which render this technicality at times redundant. Even if possibly not as influential today as in the early 2000s, the problem of 'owning' the delivery of goods and services in the area of health is linked to broader questions of how the developing, traditionally recipient world is governed. Considering the state failure literature of the 1990s and 2000s, in which poor and corrupted states in the developing world demonstrate incapability, if not unwillingness, to provide goods and services that enhance health care and education opportunities among their populations, country ownership does eventually appear as a renewed pressure to stimulate developing countries to provide goods and services, while simultaneously avoiding their own failure. However, this stimulus per se might just not be sufficient to render those targeted countries prone to basically take ownership of programmes and policies generally initiated externally.

In fact, in light of the comparative analysis carried out here, the capacity of a country to appropriate an externally initiated project – by financing it totally or in part and/or complying with implementation agenda – depends widely on the extent to which this *is* meaningful within the triad of political goals; strategies; and underlying policy problems. Assuming the validity and relevance of a concept of country ownership in development practice, research demonstrates that recipient states' policies and political goals really need to be thoroughly understood in order to comprehend whether and how such project is really owned by the national and local elites. Otherwise, country ownership will basically remain an unfulfilled inducement of the international community, particularly the United Nations system and the major development agencies.

Again, assuming the validity of country ownership as meaningful driving principle, a conclusion one comes to has to do with the primary reasons why a country decides not only to host an external project but also to engage in it, even to the point of paying totally or partially for it. In light of research, those reasons are not necessarily those that drive donors' behaviour. They may really be miles away from the original purposes; they might even be conflicting with those purposes at the end of the day. In this regard, the case of Ethiopia is arguably the best from this comparative study, in which, aside from general concerns for low human development, the attraction of external projects, namely from the United States of America, serves a broader goal of consolidating support against deemed terrorist action against the central state. In other words, external support for health and thus general well-being is obtained at the expense of expanding military capabilities. In the realm of HIV/AIDS intervention, considering the relatively low prevalence of the epidemic, this argument is further consolidated, even though one is quite aware of the absolute figures which certainly are of concern.

A recent relative fall in foreign development expenditure by traditional Western donors combined with a relative increase of influence by non-Western donors, such as Brazil, China, India and some Arab states, are gradually changing the landscape of global health governance and allowing recipient countries to diversify their choice of partnerships. Indeed, both in policy and implementation terms, Western donors face reducing capability to support multilateral and bilateral initiatives, at least the way they used to throughout the last decade. Even if this reduced capability arguably constitutes an undesired reaction to contextual events (financial-economic crisis), in the case of PEPFAR, for instance, the focus on country ownership as a means to achieve sustainability reflects an interest in steadily stepping back from the initial effort. As traditional, large-scale donors reduce their capabilities, recipient countries as a whole are challenged externally and internally to engage in health, and more expansively, social policy. Empirical evidence from Ethiopia, Botswana and South Africa, demonstrates the inclusion of such policies in larger state-developmentalist agendas.

With regard to non-traditional players in the developing, recipient world (at least in comparative terms), countries such as Brazil, China or India, have been dramatically evolving from a situation in which they appear as objects of external policy (for example, as recipients of global health programmes) towards subjects of foreign policy. In the case of 'emerging' actors, particularly Brazil, research shows the relevance of their own domestic experience with the epidemic, and how it contributed to larger concerns around nationbuilding but also an improvement of their international standing, the case of HIV/AIDS being a case in point (Lieberman, 2009). If one takes the case of South Africa as another such case of 'emergence', then this dual standing as recipient and putative donor becomes really puzzling. This demand for further research to understand emerging countries' complexity is necessarily with regard to how such potential is organised, spoken and eventually practiced.

It has been recurrently insisted throughout the book that the exercise of agency by recipient countries is very much constrained by the international structure, yet not impossible. This autonomy is hypothetically enhanced through the gradual diversification of donors and partners, and their disparate policy conditionalities, in the international scene in recent years. However, it is unclear whether an increase in the quantity of partners leads to qualitative change in 'business-as-usual' in development aid (and trade) relations. As also increasingly witnessed in United States of America, Europe and the Western world at large, these new players tend to refuse the donor-recipient language by insisting on perspectives of South-South cooperation in the bilateral and multilateral schemes. In their case, they aim at breaking through the spectres of neocolonial relations that current development assistance systems maintain by emphasising a shared developing past. Encompassing political and business ties between themselves and the developing world provide substance to these agendas.

# Notes

## 1 Introduction: Agency in Global Health

1. The 15 focus countries were Botswana, Côte d'Ivoire, Ethiopia, French Guiana, Haiti, Kenya, Mozambique, Namibia, Nigeria, Rwanda, South Africa, Tanzania, Uganda, Vietnam and Zambia.
2. Countries are Bangladesh, Ethiopia, Guatemala, Kenya, Malawi, Mali, Nepal, and Rwanda.
3. As a qualitative study, the whole claims made by interviewees are merely as informative pieces for the broader discussions, and never as scientifically conclusive arguments. It is not one's concern to question the validity of such claims, but solely to build on the social, political and professional experiences that come attached to those claims, and the way they are put forward.

## 2 Global Health Governance and Role of States

1. Outside Africa, a striking case of 'rogueness' in global health governance corresponds to the invocation of sovereign rights by the Indonesian government over the decision of not sharing A/H5N1 flu virus samples with the World Health Organisation. This position was adopted under the belief that, once disbursed for research and development of a vaccine, Indonesia would hardly benefit from it, since it would prove too costly to be purchased with the major Western pharmaceutical companies.

## 3 Recipient States in an Asymmetric System

1. Initiated by Waltz, the agenda in International Relations on system, structure and agency was later enhanced by Alexander Wendt (1999) and Colin Wight (2006), among others. However, for the purpose of this book one is confined to Waltz's propositions.
2. Though not explicitly Marxist, Foucault shared an agenda deriving from Marxian analysis of society and economy born out of the Frankfurt School. Hence, Marxism lays the foundations for Foucauldian application to International Relations, which, according to Jan Selby (2007), has not been properly acknowledged by the scholarly community. Explaining liberal practices, Foucault sheds precious light on how power works, or is meant to work, within capitalist societies, but, according to Selby (2007: 340–341), not why it works the way it does. For him, it is explained by Marxism: 'the ceaseless accumulation of capital, and attendant conflicts amongst capitalists, classes and states' (Selby, 2007: 340). Hence, both traditions – Foucauldian and Marxist – are 'mutually enriching' (Selby, 2007) and, moreover, reiterate the conclusion of Foucault himself (Macdonald, 2002).

3. In his article, Ayoob (2002) refers to the Washington Consensus, since his earlier developments of the 'subaltern realism' perspective started in the early 1990s, as the liberal developmental proposal based on market dominance and state structure reduction emerged victorious under the name of Washington Consensus. One could hypothesise that an example of 'strong state' suggested by Ayoob corresponds to the revival of the 'developmental state', as it will be discussed in this book, particularly with regard to Ethiopia and Botswana.

## 4   International Developments of States in Africa

1. Parastatals are organisations that belong to the state apparatus and whose budgets come, fully or partially, from external sources.

## 5   PEPFAR: Project of Global Transformation

1. At the time of this writing, 21 partnership frameworks had been signed, including with Botswana (December 2010), Ethiopia (October 2010) and South Africa (December 2010).
2. The other countries are Kenya, Malawi, Mali, Rwanda, Bangladesh, Nepal and Guatemala.

## 6   Botswana: National Survival against HIV/AIDS

1. TCM was described in these terms by Allen and Heald (2004: 1147): 'One of the ... strategies to complement the ARV programme was called "total community mobilisation". This, as with so much else in Botswana, was designed as a top down intervention. An army of field-officers were to undertake door-to-door visits, and to talk at various community gatherings and hold workshops.'

## 7   Ethiopia: Self-Help with External Support

1. In the aftermath of the Dergue's deposition these included, apart from the TPLF, Afar Liberation Front, Benishangul People's Liberation Movement, Islamic Front for the Liberation of Oromia, Issa and Gurgura Liberation Front, Ogaden Liberation Front (Horiale), Oromo Abo Liberation Front, Ogaden National Liberation Front, Sidama Liberation Movement, United Oromo People's Liberation Front, and Western Somali Liberation Front (Vaughan, 2003: 28).
2. The Dergue was a regime established in 1974 in the aftermath of the overthrow of Emperor Haile Selassie. The process of overthrow began after civic protests against his absolutist rule, rising capitalist exploitation of the land, and incapacity to address several famines affecting the country.
3. The strategic importance of the gigantic Millennium Dam is threefold. First, it responds to the demands of power supply that national development plans

require. Ethiopia, notably its capital city, is often affected by power cuts during the day and night that undermine business life, particularly for those without electricity generators. Second, it serves as an example of national commitment to a great cause, since the dam is aimed to be primarily funded by domestic resources, despite the fear of a dramatic inflationary pressure (Giorgis, 2011). And finally, it challenges a historical geopolitical complex of inferiority with regard to Egypt, whose potential forceful intervention in Ethiopia in case of modification of the Nile water's regime has long constituted a source of fear for Addis Ababa's leadership.

4. Sub-city is an administrative division within a city in Ethiopia.
5. However, this is not to suggest that non-Western partners do not impose conditions on the Ethiopian government, since they hypothetically do. The focus on Western aid relations with Ethiopia has to do with the book's case study, which is precisely an aid programme by the leading Western power.
6. However, Berhanu Abegaz (2004: 321–322) emphasises that population growth should not be regarded as a primary cause of underdevelopment in Ethiopia.
7. Some *iddirs* have been involved in PEPFAR-funded intervention through Save the Children United States in terms of counselling, food donations and financial assistance (Kurata, 2008).

# 8 South Africa: Changing HIV/AIDS Policies

1. In fact, the United States of America backed the apartheid regime for a long time, at different levels (Underwood, 2008: 9; Campbell, 2008). The main reason for that concerns the Cold War geopolitical game at stake in Southern Africa. Given the military and diplomatic assistance that the Soviet Union was providing to the regimes in Tanzania, Mozambique, Angola and Zimbabwe, in turn hosting the ANC and other anti-apartheid movements, the United States of America assisted the South African regime as it was containing communism (Burgess and Purkitt, 2001: 85; Ndlovu-Gatsheni and Ojakorotu, 2010: 95). The CIA was active in the counterterrorist domain (Hutton, 2010). At the same time, protecting South Africa meant protecting the capitalist political economy South Africa was grounded upon, namely United States companies working on South African soil (Bond, 2008).
2. This governmental 'denialism', as put by pro-treatment civil society groups, has been alternatively explained in terms of an ethnic boundary that cuts across the South African society, which, in turn, leads to an absence of 'collective shared risk', if not a collective state of denial between the different ethnic groups (Lieberman, 2009). Since government policy making and implementation in such complex area as HIV/AIDS prevention and treatment requires a sense of collective risk among different ethnic groups in order to engender 'compliance and consent' (Lieberman, 2009: 7) by the public, Lieberman concludes that the more ethnically stratified the national polity finds itself, the less the national community is inclined to accept the underlying idea of a shared collective risk and thus support policies of response. The author argues that the ethnic boundaries cutting across South African societies – broadly, between whites and blacks – led to a lack of 'collective shared risk'. Both ethnic groups were in a 'state of denial'. While whites would see the

epidemic as blacks' problem, and blacks would vision it as whites' problem, the government did not step in aggressively, in a context of post-apartheid fragile national/ethnic relations. The opposite case in Lieberman's study was Brazil, whose efficiency of the government's response relied on the tenuous ethnic boundary existing across Brazilian society.

# References

Aalen, L. and Tronvoll, K. (2009) 'The End of Democracy? Curtailing Political and Civil Rights in Ethiopia', *Review of African Political Economy*, 36(120), 193–207.

Abegaz, B. (2004) 'Escaping Ethiopia's Poverty Trap: The Case for a Second Agrarian Reform', *The Journal of Modern African Studies*, 42(3), 313–342.

Acemoğlu, D. et al. (2003) 'An African Success Story: Botswana' in Rodrik, D. (ed.) *in Search of Prosperity: Analytic Narratives on Economic Growth* (Princeton, NJ and Oxford: Princeton University Press).

Adelman, C.C. and Eberstadt, N. (2008) *Foreign Aid: What Works and What Doesn't* (Washington, DC: American Enterprise Institute for Public Policy Research).

AIDS and Human Rights Research Unit (2007) 'HIV, AIDS and the Law in Botswana' in AIDS and Human Rights Research Unit (ed.) *Human Rights Protected? Nine Southern African Country Reports on HIV, Law, AIDS and the Law* (Pretoria: Pretoria University Law Press).

Allen, T. and Heald, S. (2004) 'HIV/AIDS Policy in Africa: What Has Worked in Uganda and What Has Failed in Botswana?', *Journal of International Development*, 16, 1141–1154.

Altman, D. (2003) 'AIDS and Security', *International Relations*, 17(4), 417–427.

APP (2008) 'Global Warming Set to Fan the HIV Fire', http://news.theage.com.au/national/global-warming-set-to-fan-the-hiv-fire-20080430–29eh.html, date accessed 29 April 2008.

Armitage, R. L. and Nye, J. S. (2007) *CSIS Commission on Smart Power. a Smarter, More Secure America* (Washington, DC: Center for Strategic & International Studies).

Arndt, C. and Lewis, J. (2000) *The Macro Implications of HIV/AIDS in South Africa: A Preliminary Assessment* (Washington, DC: Purdue University).

Arnold, D. (1997) 'The Place of 'the Tropics' in Western Medical Ideas Since 1750', *Tropical Medicine and International Health*, 2(4), 303–313.

Ayoob, M. (2002) 'Inequality and Theorizing in International Relations: The Case for Subaltern Realism', *International Studies Review*, 4(3), 27–48.

Baker, P.H. and Lyman, P.N. (2008) 'South Africa: From Beacon of Hope to Rogue Democracy', http://www.cfr.org/content/thinktank/South_Africa_Paper_Dec_2008.pdf, date accessed 3 May 2014.

Ban, J. (2003), 'Health as a Global Security Challenge', *The Whitehead Journal of Diplomacy and International Relations* 4(2), 19–28.

Barnett, T. (2006) 'A Long-Wave Event. HIV/AIDS, Politics, Governance and "Security": Sundering the Intergenerational Bond?', *International Affairs*, 82(2), 291–313.

Barnett, T. and Prins, G. (2006) 'HIV/AIDS and Security: Fact, Fiction and Evidence – A Report to UNAIDS', *International Affairs*, 82(2), 931–952.

Bar-On, A. (2002) 'Going against World Trends: Social Protection in Botswana', *Social Policy Journal*, 1(4), 23–41.

Bashford, A. (1999) 'Epidemic and Governmentality: Smallpox in Sydney, 1881', *Critical Public Health*, 9(4), 301–316.

Bashford, A. (2006) 'Global Biopolitics and the History of World Health', *History of Human Sciences*, 19(67), 67–88.

Bauer, H. (2006) 'Demographic Characteristics of HIV: II. What Determines the Frequency of Positive HIV Tests?', *Journal of Scientific Exploration*, 20(1), 69–94.

Bayart, J.–F. (2009) *The State in Africa. The Politics of the Belly* (London: Polity Press).

Beaulier, S.A. and Subrick, J.R. (2006) 'The Political Foundations of Development: The Case of Botswana', *Constitutional Political Economy*, 17, 103–115.

Beck, U. (1992) *Risk Society: Towards a New Modernity* (London: Sage Publications).

Beck, U. (1995) 'A Reinvenção da Política: Rumo a Uma Teoria da Modernização Reflexiva' in Beck, U., Giddens, A. and Lash, S. (eds) *Modernização Reflexiva. Política, Tradição e Estética na Ordem Social Moderna* (São Paulo: UNESP).

Beck, U. (2006) 'Living in the World Risk Society', *Economy and Society*, 35(3), 329–345.

Behringer, R.M. (2005) 'Middle Power Leadership on the Human Security Agenda' *Cooperation and Conflict: Journal of the Nordic International Studies Association*, 40(3), 305–342.

Berhe, A. (2004) 'The Origins of the Tibray's People Liberation Front', *African Affairs*, 103(413), 569–592.

Bickerton, C. (2007) 'State-building. Exporting State Failure' in Bickerton, C. et al. (eds) *Politics Without Sovereignty. A Critique of Contemporary International Relations* (London: University College London Press).

Bickerton, C. et al. (eds) (2007) *Politics Without Sovereignty. A Critique of Contemporary International Relations* (London: University College London Press).

BIDPA (2000) *The Macroeconomic Impacts of the HIV/AIDS Epidemic in Botswana* (Gaborone: BIDPA).

Bond, P. (2001) 'Pretoria's Perspective on Globalization: A Critique', *Politikon*, 28(1), 81–94.

Bond, P. (2004) 'From Racial to Class Apartheid. South Africa's Frustrating Decade of Freedom', *Monthly Review: An Independent Socialist Review*, 55(10), 45–59.

Bond, P. (2006a) 'Reconciliation and Economic Reaction: Flaw's in South Africa's Elite Transition', *Journal of International Affairs*, 60(1), 141–156.

Bond, P. (2006b) 'Global Governance Campaigning and MDGs: From Top-Down to Bottom-Up Anti-poverty Work', *Third World Quarterly*, 27(2), 339–354.

Bond, P. (2008) 'Emerging African Resistance to Economic Crisis, Global Finance, Free Trade and Corporate Profit-Taking…and Why Barack Obama's Advisors Could Hurt Africa (Again)', http://ccs.ukzn.ac.za/files/Bond%20Osisa%20 14%20November%202008.pdf, date accessed 3 May 2014.

Bowen, G.S. et al. (1992) 'First Year of AIDS Services Delivery Under Title I of the Ryan White CARE Act', *Public Health Reports*, 107(5), 491–499.

Bradbury, M. and Kleinman, M. (2010) *Winning Hearts and Minds? Examining the Relationship Between Aid and Security in Kenya* (Medford, MA: Feinstein International Center, Tufts University).

Bray, R. (2003) *Predicting the Social Consequences of Orphanhood in South Africa* (Cape Town: University of Cape Town).

Brigg, M. (2002) 'Post-Development, Foucault and the Colonisation Metaphor', *Third World Quarterly*, 23(3), 421–436.

Brinkerhoff, D.W. and Brinkerhoff, J.M. (2004) 'Partnerships between international donors and non-governmental development organizations: opportunities and constraints', *International Review of Administrative Sciences*, 70(2), 253–270.

Brower, J and Chalk, P. (2003) *The Global Threat of New and Reemerging Infectious Diseases: Reconciling U.S. National Security and Public Health Policy* (Santa Monica, CA: Rand Corporation).

Brown, W. (2006) 'Africa and International Relations: A Comment on IR Theory, Anarchy and Statehood', *Review of International Studies*, 32, 119–143.

Bryson, D. (2010a) 'Critics Express Fears for Botswana's Lauded Democracy, But President Says He's No Dictator', http://www.brandonsun.com/world/breaking-news/critics-express-fears-for-botswanas-lauded-democracy-but-president-says-hes-nodictator-92511899.html, date accessed 13 May 2010.

Bryson, D. (2010b) 'AP Interview: South African Health Minister Concerned at Costs of Coping with AIDS', http://news.therecord.com/printArticle/822825, date accessed 1 December 2010.

Buchanan, R.B. (2008) *USAFRICOM: Operational Considerations Are Paramount in Selecting a Headquarters Location* (Newport, RI: Naval War College).

Burgess, S. and Purkitt, H. (2001) *The Rollback of South Africa's Chemical and Biological Warfare Program* (Maxwell Air Force Base, Montgomery, AL: Air War College and Air University).

Buss, D. and Herman, D. (2003) *Globalizing Family Values. The Christian Right in International Politics* (Minneapolis, London: University of Minnesota Press).

Cameron-Smith, A. (2007) *Strange Bodies and Familiar Spaces: W. J. R. Simpson and the Threat of Disease in Calcutta and the Tropical City, 1880–1910* (Sydney: University of Sydney).

Campbell, H. (2008) 'Remilitarisation of African Societies: Analysis of the Planning Behind Proposed US Africa Command', *International Journal of African Renaissance Studies*, 3(1), 6–34.

Carr, E.H. (1939) *The Twenty Years' Crisis, 1919–1939: An Introduction to the Study of International Relations* (Basingstoke: Palgrave Macmillan Press).

Carroll, P.E. (2002) 'Medical Police and the History of Public Health', *Medical History*, 46, 461–494.

Catholic Information Service (2010) 'Voice of America Journalist Expelled', http://allafrica.com/stories/printable/201006221196.html, date accessed 22 June 2010.

Center for Global Development: CGD (2010) 'Country Ownership and Rethinking Global Health Partnerships from Dependence to Symbiosis', http://blogs.cgdev.org/globalhealth/2010/06/country-ownership-and-rethinking-global-health-partners, date accessed 25 June 2010.

Center for Health and Gender Equity (2004) *Debunking the Myths in the U.S. Global AIDS Strategy: An Evidence-Based Analysis* (Takoma Park, MD: Center for Health and Gender Equity).

Chabal, P. and Deloz, J.-P. (1999) *Africa Works: Disorder as Political Instrument* (Oxford: International African Institute in Association with James Currey and Indiana University Press).

Chandler, D. (2006) *Empire in Denial: The Politics of State-Building* (London: Pluto).

Chandler, D. (2009a) 'Critiquing Liberal Cosmopolitanism? The Limits of the Biopolitical Approach', *International Political Sociology*, 3, 53–70.

Chandler, D. (2009b) *Hollow Hegemony. Rethinking Global Politics, Power and Resistance* (London: Pluto).

Cheek, R.B. (2001) 'Playing God with HIV. HIV Treatment in Southern Africa', http://www.issafrica.org/pubs/ASR/10No4/Cheek.html, date accessed 27 June 2008.

Cheru, F. (2002) *African Renaissance* (London and New York: Zed Books).

Cilliers, J. (2008) *Africa in the New World. How Global and Domestic Developments Will Impact by 2025* (Pretoria: Institute for Security Studies).

Clapham, C. (1996) *African and the International System. The Politics of State Survival* (Cambridge: Cambridge University Press).

Clinton, H.R. (2009) 'Remarks at the Corporate Council on Africa's Seventh Biennial U.S.-Africa Business Summit', http://angola.usembassy.gov/remarks_ at_the_corporate_council_on_africas_seventh_biennial_u.s.-africa_business_ summit, date accessed 1 October 2009.

Cooke, B. (2003) 'A New Continuity with Colonial Administration: Participation in Development Management', *Third World Quarterly*, 24(1), 47–61.

Cooper, R. (2004) *The Breaking of Nations. Order and Chaos in the Twenty-First Century* (London: Atlantic Books).

Council on Foreign Relations (2009) 'U.S. Opinion on Development and Humanitarian Aid' in Council on Foreign Relations (ed.) *Public Opinion on Global Issues* (New York: Council on Foreign Relations).

Cox, R.W. (1981) 'Social Forces, States and World Orders: Beyond International Relations', *Millennium – Journal of International Studies*, 10(2), 126–155.

Cox, R.W. (2005) 'Global Perestroika' in Wilkinson, R. (ed.) *The Global Governance Reader* (London and New York: Routledge).

Dar, S. and Cooke, B. (ed.) (2008) *The New Development Management* (London: Zed Books).

Davison, W. (2011) 'Ethiopian Denies Arrest of Opposition Party Activists', http://www.bloomberg.com/news/print/2011–03–29/ethiopian-governmen, date accessed 30 March 2011.

Debiel, T. and Werthes, S. (2006) *Human Security on Foreign Policy Agendas. Changes, Concepts and Cases* (Duisburg-Essen: Institute for Development and Peace).

De Goede, M.J. (2010) 'Postcolonial Critique and the Production of Local Modernity: Bringing in Agency and Subjectivity in the Study of Post-war State Building', http://www.durkheim.sciencespobordeaux.fr/Cahiers%20de%20SPIRIT_4/ Cahiers%20de%20Spirit_4_DeGoede.pdf, date accessed 3 May 2014.

De Waal, A. (2006) *AIDS and Power. Why There Is No Political Crisis – Yet* (London: Zed Books).

De Waal, A. (2010) 'Reframing Governance, Security and Conflict in the Light of HIV/AIDS: A Synthesis of Findings from the AIDS, Security and Conflict Initiative', *Social Science & Medicine*, 70, 114–120.

Direng, N. (2010) 'Botswana Loses Billions to Corruption – Magistrate', http:// www.mmegi.bw/index.php?sid=31&sid2=1&aid=3223&dir=2010/June/ Thursday24, date accessed 25 June 2010.

Douzinas, C. (2007) *Human Rights and Empire: The Political Philosophy of Cosmopolitanism* (London: Routledge Cavendish).

Drezner, D.W. (2007) 'Should Celebrities Set the Global Agenda?', http:// www.cgdev.org/files/15091_file_Should_celebrities_set_the_global_agenda_ LATIMES.12.30.07.pdf, date accessed 3 May 2014.

Duber, H.C. et al. (2010) 'Is There an Association Between PEPFAR Funding and Improvement in National Health Indicators in Africa? A Retrospective Study', *Journal of the International AIDS Society*, 13(21), 1–9.

DuBois, M. (1991) 'The Governance of the Third World: A Foucauldian Perspective on Power Relations in Development', *Alternatives*, 16(1), 1–30.

Duffield, M. (2002) 'Social Reconstruction and the Radicalization of Development: Aid as a Relation of Global Liberal Governance', *Development and Change*, 33(5), 1049–1071.

Duffield, M. (2005) 'Governing the Borderlands: Decoding the Power of Aid' in Wilkinson, R. (ed.) *The Global Governance Reader* (London and New York: Routledge).

Duffield, M. (2007) *Development, Security and Unending War* (Cambridge; Malden: Polity).

Duffield, M. (2010) 'The Liberal Way of Development and the Development-Security Impasse: Exploring the Global Life-Chance Divide', *Security Dialogue*, 41(1), 53–76.

Dunn, K.C. and Shaw, T.M. (eds) (2001) *Africa's Challenges to International Relations Theory* (Basingstoke: Palgrave Macmillan).

Dybul, M. (2009) 'The Global Fight Against HIV/AIDS', http://www.state.gov/r/pa/ei/coffee/113121.htm, date accessed 8 January 2009.

Dyer, G. (2009) 'Ethiopia: Population, Famine and Fate', http://www.mmorning.com/ArticleC.asp?Article=7158&CategoryID=5, date accessed 14 September 2009.

Eberstadt, N. (2002) 'The Future of AIDS', http://www.foreignaffairs.org/20021101faessay9990/nicholas-eberstadt/the-future-of-aids, date accessed 7 October 2007.

Economic Commission for Africa (2011) *Economic Report on Africa 2011. Governing Development in Africa – The Role of the State in Economic Transformation* (Addis Ababa: Economic Commission for Africa).

Econsult (2007) *Macroeconomic Impact of HIV/AIDS* (Gaborone: United Nations Development Programme and National AIDS Coordinating Agency).

Elbe, S. (2003) 'Diseases, AIDS and Other Pandemics' in Missiroli, A. (ed.) *Disasters, Diseases, Disruptions: A New D-drive for the EU* (Paris: Institute for Security Studies).

Elbe, S. (2006) 'Should HIV/AIDS Be Securitized? The Ethical Dilemmas of Linking HIV/AIDS and Security', *International Studies Quarterly*, 50, 119–144.

Elbe, S. (2010) *Security and Global Health: Toward the Medicalization of Insecurity* (Cambridge: Polity).

Engberg-Petersen, P. et al. (eds) (1996) *Limits of Adjustment in Africa* (Portsmouth, NH: Heinemann).

Epstein, H. (2010) 'Cruel Ethiopia', http://www.nybooks.com/articles/archives/2010/apr/20/cruel-ethiopia/?pagination=false, date accessed 29 April 2010.

Escobar, A. (1984/1985) 'Discourse and Power in Development: Michel Foucault and the Relevance of his Work to the Third World', *Alternatives*, 10(3), 377–400.

Esquire (2008) 'The Americans Have Landed', http://www.esquire.com/print-this/features/africacommand0707, date accessed 21 March 2008.

Ethiopian Weekly (2009a) 'Parliament Passes Bill Governing NGOs, Civil Societies', *Ethiopian Weekly Press Digest*, XVI, 15 January 2009.

Ethiopian Weekly (2009b) 'Ethiopia Imposes Aid Agency Curbs', *Ethiopian Weekly Press Digest*, XVI, 15 January 2009.

Fage, J.D. (1988) *A History of Africa* (London: Hutchinson).

Federal HIV/AIDS Prevention and Control Office (2008) *Report on Progress Towards Implementation of the UN Declaration of Commitment on HIV/AIDS* (Addis Ababa: Federal HIV/AIDS Prevention and Control Office).

Federal Ministry of Health (2005) *Health Sector Strategic Plan (HSDP–III) 2005/6–2009/10* (Addis Ababa: Federal Ministry of Health).

Federal Ministry of Health (2008) 'Compact between the Government of the Federal Democratic Republic of Ethiopia and the Development Partners on Scaling Up For Reaching the Health MDGs through the Health Sector Development Programme in the Framework of the International Health Partnership', http://www.internationalhealthpartnership.net/CMS_files/documents/ihp_Ethiopia_compact_EN.pdf, date accessed 3 May 2014.

Fee, E. and Parry, M. (2008) 'Jonathan Mann, HIV/AIDS, and Human Rights', *Journal of Public Health Policy*, 29, 54–71.

Feffer, J. (2008) *Desperately Looking for Legacy*, http://www.fpif.org/fpifzines/wb/4960, date accessed 14 December 2008.

Ferguson, J. (1994) *The Anti-Politics Machine. Development, Depoliticization, and Bureaucratic Power in Lesotho* (Minneapolis and London: University of Minnesota Press).

Fidler, D. (1999) *International Law and Infectious Diseases* (Oxford: Clarendon Press).

Fidler, D. (2004) 'Constitutional Outlines of Public Health's "New World Order"', *Temple Law Review*, 77.

Fidler, D. (2005) 'Health as Foreign Policy: Between Principle and Power', *Whitehead Journal of Diplomacy and International Relations*, 6(2), 179–194.

Fidler, D. (2008) 'After the Revolution: Global Health Politics in a Time of Economic Crisis and Threatening Future Trends', *Global Health Governance*, 2(2), 1–21.

Fidler, D. and Gostin, L.O. (2006) 'The New International Health Regulations: An Historic Development for International Law and Public Health', *Journal of Law, Medicine & Ethics*, 33(4), 85–94.

Foucault, M. (1978) *The History of Sexuality. Vol. 1: An Introduction* (New York: Random House, Inc.).

Foucault, M. (1980) 'The Confessions of the Flesh' in Gordon, C. (ed.) *Power/Knowledge. Selected Interviews and Other Writings. 1972–1977* (New York: Pantheon Books).

Foucault, M. (1984) 'Bio-Power' in Rabinow, P. (ed.) *The Foucault Reader* (New York: Pantheon Books).

Foucault, M. (1994) *The Birth of the Clinic: An Archeology of Medical Perception* (New York: Vintage Books).

Foucault, M. (2006) *É Preciso Defender a Sociedade!* (Lisboa: Livros do Brasil).

Fourie, P. and Schönteich, M. (2001) *Africa's New Security Threat. HIV/AIDS and Human Security in Southern Africa*, http://www.issafrica.org/pubs/ASR/10No4/Fourie.html, date accessed 28 May 2008.

Francis, D.J. (2010) 'Introduction: AFRICOM – US Strategic Interests and African Security' in Francis, D.J. (ed.) *US Strategy in Africa. AFRICOM, Terrorism and Security Challenges* (Oxon, UK and New York: Routledge).

Fritz, V. and Rocha Menocal, A. (2007) 'Developmental States in the New Millennium: Concepts and Challenges for a New Aid Agenda', *Development Policy Review*, 25(5), 531–552.

Froitzheim, J.L. (2009) *Escaping Africa's Predatory Trap: The Social Origins of Development and Democracy in Botswana and Mauritius* (Charlottesville, VA: University of Virginia).

Furtado, X. and Smith, W.J. (2007) *Ethiopia: Aid, Ownership, and Sovereignty* (Oxford: University College Oxford).

GAO: Government Accountability Office (2004) *U.S. AIDS Coordinator Addressing Some Key Challenges to Expanding Treatment, But Others Remain* (Washington, DC: U.S. Government Accountability Office).

GAO: Government Accountability Office (2005) *Selection of Antiretroviral Medications Provided under U.S. Emergency Plan Is Limited* (Washington, DC: U.S. Government Accountability Office).

GAO: Government Accountability Office (2008) *Global HIV/AIDS. A More Country-Based Approach Could Improve Allocation of PEPFAR Funding* (Washington, DC: U.S. Government Accountability Office).

GAO: Government Accountability Office (2009) *President's Emergency Plan for AIDS Relief. Partner Selection and Oversight Follow Accepted Practices But Would Benefit from Enhanced Planning and Accountability* (Washington, DC: U.S. Government Accountability Office).

GAO: Government Accountability Office (2010) *President's Emergency Plan for AIDS Relief. Efforts to Align Programs with Partner Countries' HIV/AIDS Strategies and Promote Partner Country Ownership* (Washington, DC: U.S. Government Accountability Office).

Garrett, L. (2005) *HIV and National Security: Where Are the Links?* (New York: Council on Foreign Relations).

Geldenhuys, D. (2008) *The Idea-Driven Foreign Policy of a Regional Power: The Case of South Africa* (Hamburg: Regional Powers Network (RPN) Conference).

Ghani, A. and Lockhart, C. (2008) *Fixing Failed States: A Framework for Rebuilding a Fractured World* (Oxford: Oxford University Press).

Giddens, A. (1990) *The Consequences of Modernity* (Cambridge: Polity).

Gilchrist, H.E. (2003) *Haile Selassie and American Missionaries: Inadvertent Agents of Oromo Identity in Ethiopia* (Chapel Hill, NC: North Carolina State University).

Gilpin, R. (1987) *The Political Economy of International Relations* (Princeton, NJ and Oxford: Princeton University Press).

Ginty, R.M. (2010) 'Hybrid Peace: The Interaction Between Top-Down and Bottom-Up Peace', *Security Dialogue*, 41(4), 391–412.

Giorgis, T.G. (2011) *A Nation Rallies Behind a Cause*, http://allafrica.com/stories/printable/201104121065.html, date accessed 12 April 2011.

Good, K. and Taylor, I. (2008) 'Botswana: A Minimalist Democracy', *Democratization*, 15(4), 750–765.

Goodwin, D.L. (2007) *USAID and Economic Growth Thesis. A Critical Assessment of USAID Foreign Aid Policies Post-9/11* (Lawrence, KS: University of Kansas).

Goosby, E. et al. (2012) 'Raising the Bar: PEPFAR and New Paradigms for Global Health', *Journal of Acquired Immune Deficiency Syndrome*, 60(3), 158–162.

Gordon, D.F. (2002) 'The Next Wave of HIV/AIDS: Nigeria, Ethiopia, Russia, India and China', www.fas.org/nic/hiv-aids.html, date accessed 26 February 2008.

Gordon, M.R. and Mazzetti, M. (2007) 'U.S. Used Base in Ethiopia to Hunt Al-Qaeda', http://www.nytimes.com/2007/02/23/world/africa/23somalia.html?ei=5088&en=acdfb04, date accessed 21 March 2008.

Gossett, C.W. (2010) 'The Impact of AIDS on the Botswana Civil Service: A Case Study of the Police and Prison Services', *International Journal of Public Administration*, 33(5), 240–250.

Gramby-Sobukwe, S. (2005) 'Africa and U.S. Foreign Policy: Contributions of the Diaspora to Democratic African Leadership', *Journal of Black Studies*, 35(6), 779–801.

Haas, P.M. (1992) 'Introduction: Epistemic Communities and International Policy Coordination', *International Organization*, 46(1), 1–35.

Habib, A. (2005) 'State-Civil Society Relations in Post-Apartheid South Africa', *Social Research*, 72(3), 671–692.

Hardt, M. and Negri, A. (2004) *Multitude. War and Democracy in the Age of Empire* (London: Penguin Books).

Hassen, A. (2010) 'The Growth and Transformation Plan: A Long Time Coming!', http://www.waltainfo.com/index2.php?option=com_content&task=view&id= 23355&pop=1&page=0..., date accessed 17 September 2010.

Hastedt, G.P. (2009) *American Foreign Policy. Past, Present, Future* (Upper Saddle River, NJ: Pearson Prentice Hall).

Heald, S. (2005) 'Abstain or Die: The Development of HIV/AIDS Policy in Botswana', *Journal of Biosocial Science*, 1–13.

Heinecken, L. (2003) 'Facing a Merciless Enemy: HIV/AIDS and the South African Armed Forces', *Armed Forces & Society*, 29(2), 281–300.

Herrling, S. (2009) 'Obama Launches Whole-of-Government Review of U.S. Global Development Policy', http://blogs.cgdev.org/mca-monitor/2009/09/ obama-launches-whole-of-government-review-of-u-s-global-development- policy.php, date accessed 18 July 2011.

Hillbom, E. (2008) 'Diamonds or Development? A Structural Assessment of Botswana's Forty Years of Success', *Journal of Modern African Studies*, 46(2), 191–214.

Hlongwane, C.N. (2003) *How Apartheid Predisposed Blacks to HIV Infection and AIDS in South Africa* (Dekalb, IL: Northern Illinois University).

Holbrooke, R. (2006) 'The Age of Aids', http://www.pbs.org/wgbh/pages/front- line/aids/interviews/holbrooke.html, date accessed 21 February 2008.

HRW: Human Rights Watch (2010a) *One Hundred Ways of Putting Pressure. Violations of Freedom of Expression and Association in Ethiopia* (New York: Human Rights Watch).

HRW: Human Rights Watch (2010b) *Development without Freedom. How Aid Underwrites Repression in Ethiopia* (New York: Human Rights Watch).

Huseman, J. (2010) 'Bush Recounts Global AIDS Initiative, PEPFAR', http://www. smudailycampus.com/news/bush-recounts-global-aids-initiati, date accessed 21 January 2010.

Hutton, L. (2010) 'Siege, Survival and Alliance: South African-Israeli Relations in the 1970s', http://www.issafrica.org/iss_today.php?ID=960, date accessed 3 June 2010.

Hwenda, L. et al. (2011) 'Why African Countries Need to Participate in Global Health Security Discourse', *Global Health Governance*, 4(2), 1–24.

Ingram, A. (2005) 'Global Leadership and Global Health: Contending Meta-narratives, Divergent Responses, Fatal Consequences', *International Relations*, 19(4), 381–402.

IOL (2010) 'SA Invited to Join BRIC Nations', http://www.thestar.co.za/sa-invit- ed-to-join-bric-nations-1.1005107?ot=inmsa.ArticlePrintPageLayout.ot,   date accessed 25 December 2010.

IOL (2011) 'Ethiopia budget to expand to fight poverty', http://www.pretorianews. co.za/ethiopia-budget-to-expand-to-fight-povert, date accessed 21 June 2011.

IRIN (2006) 'Global HIV/AIDS News and Analysis', http://www.plusnews.org/ MediaTools.aspx, date accessed 26 June 2008.

IRIN (2011) 'Ethiopia: Help "Trickling In" for Millions Needing Food Aid', http:// allafrica.com/stories/printable/201105070056.html, date accessed 7 May 2011.

Jabri, V. (2007) *War and the Transformation of Global Politics* (Basingstoke: Palgrave Macmillan).

Jefferson, C.D. (2006) *The Bush African Policy: Fighting the Global War on Terrorism* (Carlisle, PA: U.S. Army War College).

Jessop, B. (2003) *The Dynamics of Partnership and Governance Failure* (Lancaster: Lancaster University).

Johnson, K. (2004) 'The Politics of AIDS Policy Development and Implementation in Post-Apartheid South Africa', *Africa Today*, 51(2), 107–128.

Kahn, T. (2009) *Legacy on Aids Overshadows High Ideals* (Johannesburg: Business Day).

Kaiser Network (2010) 'Is AIDS Activism Dead?', http://kff.org/global-health-policy/event/aids-2010-is-aids-activism-dead/, date accessed 19 June 2010.

Kaiser Network (2011) *The U.S. Global Health Initiative: A Country Analysis* (Menlo Park, CA: Henry J. Kaiser Family Foundation).

Kaldor, M. (1999) *New and Old Wars: Organised Violence in a Global Era* (Cambridge: Polity).

Kaufmann, D. (2011) *On Africa's New Dawn: From Premature Exuberance to Tempered Optimism*, http://www.brookings.edu/opinions/2011/0607_africa_new_dawn_kaufm...., date accessed 9 June 2011.

Kay, A. and Williams, O. (2008) *The International Political Economy of Global Health Governance* (San Francisco: International Studies Association Annual Conference).

Kelebonye, G. (2010) 'The Day the SADF Bombed My Village,' *Mmegi*, 18 June 2010.

Keohane, R. (1984) *After Hegemony: Cooperation and Discord in the World Political Economy* (Princeton, NJ: Princeton University Press).

Kettl, D.F. (2008) 'The Key to Networks Government' in Kettl, D.F. and Goldsmith, S. (eds) *Unlocking the Power of Networks. Keys to High-Performance Government* (Washington, DC: Brookings Institution Press).

Kiley, E.E. and Hovorka, A.J. (2006) 'Civil Society Organisations and the National HIV/AIDS Response in Botswana', *African Journal of AIDS Research*, 5(2), 167–178.

Kim, J.Y. and Farmer, P. (2006) 'AIDS in 2006 – Moving Toward One World, One Hope?', *New England Journal of Medicine*, 355(7), 645–647.

Kissi, E. (1997) *Famine and the Politics of Food Relief in the United States Relations with Ethiopia: 1950–1991* (Montreal: Concordia University).

Kitaw, Y. et al. (2006) 'Ethiopia' in Beck, E.J. et al. (eds) *The HIV Pandemic* (Oxford: Oxford University Press).

Klingebiel, S. (ed.) (2006) *New Interfaces Between Security and Development: Changing Concepts and Approaches* (Bonn: Deutsches Institut für Entwicklungspolitik).

Kloos, H. and Mariam, H.D. (2000) 'HIV/AIDS in Ethiopia: An Overview', *Northeast African Studies*, 7(1), 13–40.

Kragelund, P. (2011) 'Back to BASICs? The Rejuvenation of Non–traditional Donors' Development Cooperation with Africa', *Development and Change*, 42(2), 585–607.

Krasner, S. and Pascual, C. (2005) 'Addressing State Failure', *Foreign Affairs*, 84(4), 153–163.

Kurata, P. (2008) 'Ethiopian Burial Societies Join Fight Against HIV/Aids', http://allafrica.com/stories/printable/200811240361.html, date accessed 21 November 2008.

Lancaster, C. (2007) *The Chinese Aid System* (Washington, DC: Center for Global Development).

Lemke, T. (2000) *Foucault, Governmentality, and Critique* (Amherst, MA: Rethinking Marxism Conference).

Lemke, T. (2001) 'The Birth of Bio-Politics – Michel Foucault's Lecture at the Collège de France on Neo-Liberal Governmentality', *Economy & Society*, 30(2), 190–207.

Lesufi, I. (2004) 'South Africa and the Rest of the Continent: Towards a Critique of the Political Economy of NEPAD', *Current Sociology*, 52(5), 809–829.

Lieberman, E. (2009) *Boundaries of Contagion. How Ethnic Politics Have Shaped Government Responses to AIDS* (Princeton, NJ: Princeton University Press).

Lim, M.L. (2004) 'Combating AIDS', http://usinfo.state.gov/journals/itps/1104/ijpe/lim.htm, date accessed 25 June 2008.

Lyman, P.N. and Morrison, J.S. (2006) *More than Humanitarianism: A Strategic U.S. Approach Toward Africa* (New York: Council on Foreign Relations).

Lyons, T. (2006) *Avoiding Conflict in the Horn of Africa. U.S. Policy Toward Ethiopia and Eritrea* (New York: Council on Foreign Relations).

Macdonald, B.J. (2002) 'Marx, Foucault, Genealogy. (Influence of Karl Marx on Philosophy of Michel Foucault)', http://www.highbeam.com/DocPrint.aspx?DocId=1G1:90464720, date accessed 7 January 2008.

Mackintosh, D. (2009) *The Politicisation of HIV/AIDS in South Africa: Responses of the Treatment Action Campaign and South African Government, 1994–2004 – A Literature Review* (Cape Town: Centre for Social Science Research).

Maloka, E.T. (2001) 'The South African "African Renaissance Debate" – A Critique', *Polis*, 8.

Mann, M. (2003) *Incoherent Empire* (London, UK and New York, NY: Verso).

Mariam, A.G. (2011) 'Ethiopia – A Country for Sale', http://allafrica.com/stories/printable/201104020086.html, date accessed 2 April 2011.

Marks, S. (2002) 'An Epidemic Waiting to Happen? The Spread of HIV/AIDS in South Africa in Social and Historical Perspective', *African Studies*, 61(1), 13–26.

Marsden, L. (2008) *For God's Sake. The Christian Right and US Foreign Policy* (London and New York: Zed Books).

Maundeni, Z. (2001) 'State Culture and Development in Botswana and Zimbabwe', *Journal of Modern African Studies*, 40(1), 105–132.

Mbabazi, P. et al. (2002) 'Governance for Reconstruction in Africa: Challenges for Policy Communities and Coalitions', *Global Networks*, 2(1), 31–47.

McFate, S. (2008) 'U.S. Africa Command: A New Strategic Paradigm?', *Military Review*, January-February, 10–21.

McGreal, C. (2010) 'Bush's Memoirs: Confronting Aids "A Key Element of My Foreign Policy"', http://www.guardian.co.uk/world/2010/nov/08/bush-memoirs-aids-foreign-policy/print, date accessed 12 November 2010.

McInnes, C. (2006) 'HIV/AIDS and Security', *International Affairs*, 82(2), 315–326.

McInnes, C. and Lee, K. (2006) 'Health, Security and Foreign Policy', *Review of International Studies*, 32, 5–23.

Mearsheimer, J. (2001) *The Tragedy of Great Power Politics* (New York: Norton).

Medical News Today (2009) 'FDA Marks 100th HIV/AIDS Drug Authorized For Purchase Under PEPFAR', http://www.medicalnewstoday.com/printerfriend-lynews.php?newsid=166412, date accessed 13 October 2009.

Meisenhelder, T. (1997) 'The Developmental State in Mauritius', *Journal of Modern African Studies*, 35(2), 279–297.

Mengesha, S.T. (2002) *The Role of Civil Society Organizations in Poverty Alleviation, Sustainable Development and Change: The Cases of Iddirs in Akaki, Nazreth and Addis Ababa* (Addis Ababa: Addis Ababa University).

Milward, H.B. and Provan, K.G. (2000) 'Governing the Hollow State', *Journal of Public Administration Research and Theory*, 10(2), 359–379.

Ministry of Finance and Economic Development (2006) *Ethiopia: Building on Progress. A Plan for Accelerated and Sustained Development to End Poverty (PASDEP)* (Addis Ababa: Ministry of Finance and Economic Development).

Mkandawire, T. (2001) 'Thinking about Developmental States in Africa', *Cambridge Journal of Economics*, 25(3), 289–313.

Mmegi (2010) 'Botswana Spends Big on Soldiers', *Mmegi*, 27, 18 June 2010.

Mogae, F. (2006) 'Diamonds for Development', http://www.cfr.org/publication/11729/diamonds_for_development_rush_transcript_federal_news_service.html, date accessed 22 October 2008.

Mohamed, J. (1999) 'Epidemics and Public Health in Late Colonial Somaliland', http://storm.prohosting.com/~mbali/doc147.htm, date accessed 2 September 2008.

Morgenthau, H. (1948) *Politics Among Nations: The Struggle for Power and Peace* (New York: Alfred A. Knopf).

MSF: Médecins sans Frontières (2008) *Running in a Place: Too Many Patients Still in Need of HIV/AIDS Treatment*, http://www.msf.org.uk/sites/uk/files/2008_Running_in_Place__Too_Many_Patients_Still_in_Urgent_Need_of_HIVAIDS_Treatment_201103180708.pdf, date accessed 3 May 2014.

Mutenheri, F. (2010) 'South-South Co-operation or Sub-Imperialism? South African 'Quiet Diplomacy', SADC Docility, and the Underdevelopment of Zimbabwe', *OSSREA Bulletin*, 7(1), 32–41.

National Intelligence Council (2000) *The Global Infectious Disease Threat and Its Implications for the United States* (Washington, DC: Central Intelligence Agency).

Ncube, M. et al. (2011) *The Middle of the Pyramid: Dynamics of the Middle Class in Africa* (Tunis: African Development Bank Group).

Ndlovu-Gatsheni, S.J. (2009) 'Africa for Africans or Africa for 'Natives' Only? 'New Nationalism' and Nativism in Zimbabwe and South Africa', *Africa Spectrum*, 44(1), 61–78.

Ndlovu-Gatsheni, S.J. and Ojakorotu, V. (2010) 'Surveillance over a Zone of Conflict: Africom and the Politics of Securitisation of Africa', *Journal of Pan African Studies*, 3(6), 94–110.

Nguyen, V.-K. (2010) *The Republic of Therapy: Triage and Sovereignty in West Africa's Time of AIDS* (Durham, NC: Duke University Press Books).

Noorbaksh, M. (2008) 'Politics, Economy, and the Threats of AIDS in Africa: The Case of Botswana', *Comparative Studies of South Asia, Africa and the Middle East*, 28(2), 351.

Office of the United States President's Spokesman (2010) *U.S. Government Support for Global Health Efforts* (Washington, DC: The White House).

Office of the United States Trade Representative (2008) *2008 Comprehensive Report on U.S. Trade and Investment Policy Toward Sub-Saharan Africa and Implementation of the African Growth and Opportunity Act* (Washington, DC: Office of the United States Trade Representative).

Osei-Hwedie, B.Z. (2001) 'HIV/AIDS and the Politics of Domestic Response: The Case of Botswana', *International Relations*, 15(6), 55–68.

Oshry, N. (2007) *Is the Treatment Action Campaign Effective? A Literature Review* (Cape Town: Centre for Social Science Research).

Osikena, J. (2010) 'Geo-Politics beyond Washington: Africa's Alternative Security and Development Partnerships' in Francis, D.J. (ed.) *US Strategy in Africa. AFRICOM, Terrorism and Security Challenges* (Oxon, UK and New York: Routledge).

Over, M. (2008) *Prevention Failure: The Ballooning Entitlement Burden of U.S. Global AIDS Treatment Spending and What to Do About It* (Washington, DC: Center for Global Development).

Over, M. (2009) 'PEPFAR Might Be Saving Millions of Lives – But We Don't Have Evidence Yet', http://blogs.cgdev.org/globalhealth/2009/04/pepfar-might-be-saving-millions-of-lives-%e2%80%93-but-we-don%e2%80%99t-have-evidence-yet.php, date accessed 30 April 2009.

Owen, J.W. and Roberts, O. (2005) 'Globalisation, Health and Foreign Policy: Emerging Linkages and Interests', *Globalization and Health*, 1(12), 1–5.

Owusu, F. (2006) 'Discourses on Development from Dependency to Neoliberalism' in Smith, M.S. (ed.) *Beyond the 'African Tragedy'. Discourses on Development and the Global Economy* (Hampshire, UK and Burlington, VT: Ashgate).

Parsons, N. (1999) 'A Brief History of Botswana', http://www.thuto.org/ubh/bw/bhp1.htm, date accessed 19 August 2010.

Patrick, S. (2008) 'U.S. Policy toward Fragile States: An Integrated Approach to Security and Development' in Birdsall, N. (ed.) *The White House and the World: A Global Development Agenda for the Next U.S. President* (Washington, DC: Center for Global Development).

Pausewang, S. (2009) 'Ethiopia: A Political View from Below', *South African Journal of International Affairs*, 16(1), 69–85.

PEPFAR (2004) *The President's Emergency Plan for AIDS Relief: U.S. Five Year Global HIV/AIDS Strategy*, http://2001–2009.state.gov/s/gac/plan/29712.htm, date accessed 16 July 2011.

PEPFAR (2009a) *Celebrating Life: The U.S. President's Emergency Plan for AIDS Relief* (Washington, DC: Office of the U.S. Global AIDS Coordinator).

PEPFAR (2009b) *The U.S. President's Emergency Plan for AIDS Relief. Five–Year Strategy* (Washington, DC: Office of the Global AIDS Coordinator).

PEPFAR (2009c) 'Focus Countries', http://2006–2009.pepfar.gov/countries/c19418.htm, date accessed 17 December 2011.

PEPFAR (2010) *Implementation of the Global Health Initiative: Consultation Document* (Washington, DC: Office of the Global AIDS Coordinator).

PEPFAR (2011a) 'Partnership Frameworks', http://www.pepfar.gov/frameworks/index.htm, date accessed 18 July 2011.

PEPFAR (2011b) *The U.S. President's Emergency Plan for AIDS Relief Seventh Annual Report to Congress* (Washington, DC: Office of the Global AIDS Coordinator).

PEPFAR (2011c) 'Implementing Agencies', http://www.pepfar.gov/agencies/index.htm, date accessed 18 July 2011.

PEPFAR (2011d) 'DRAFT Guidance for PEPFAR Partnership Frameworks and Partnership Framework Implementation Plans – Version 1', http://www.pepfar. gov/guidance/framework/120513.htm, date accessed 18 July 2011.

PEPFAR (2012) *PEPFAR FY2013 Country Operational Plan (COP) Guidance* (Washington, DC: PEPFAR).

Pereira, R. (2008) 'Processes of Securitization of Infectious Diseases and Western Hegemonic Power: A Historical-Political Analysis', *Global Health Governance*, 2(1).

Pereira, R. (2009) 'PEPFAR Project Implementation and the Pursuit of the United States National Interest' in Pape, U. and Bartelink, B. (eds) *Negotiating World Views, Facing Practical Challenges. Political, Social and Religious Dimensions in the Fight Against HIV/AIDS* (Groningen: University of Groningen).

Permanent Mission of Ethiopia to the United Nations (2007) 'Permanent Mission of Ethiopia to the United Nations', http://www.un.int/wcm/content/site/ethiopia, date accessed 27 June 2008.

Press TV (2010) 'EPRDF Landslide Confirmed in Ethiopia', http://www.presstv.ir/pop/Print/?id=131434, date accessed 21 June 2010.

Price-Smith, A. (2002) *The Health of Nations. Infectious Disease, Environmental Change and Their Effects on National Security and Development* (Cambridge, MA: Massachusetts Institute of Technology).

Radelet, S. (2010) *Emerging Africa: How 17 Countries Are Leading the Way* (Baltimore, MD: Brookings Institution Press).

Rankin, L. (2009) *A Policy Analysis of the Ryan White Comprehensive AIDS Resources Emergency Act of 1990* (Long Beach: California State University).

Reno, W. (1995) *Corruption and State Politics in Sierra Leone* (New York: Cambridge University Press).

Renzio, P. et al. (2008) *Reforming Foreign Aid Practices: What Country Ownership Is and What Donors Can Do to Support It.* (Oxford: University College Oxford).

Ricci, J. (2009) 'Global Health Governance and the State: Premature Claims of A Post–International Framework', *Global Health Governance*, 3(1), 1–18.

Rice, S.E. and Patrick, S. (2008) *Index of State Weakness in the Developing World* (Washington, DC: The Brookings Institution).

Richmond, O. (2010) 'Resistance and the Post-liberal Peace', *Millennium: Journal of International Studies*, 38(3), 1–28.

Riviello, E.D. et al. (2007) 'HIV in the Workplace in Botswana: Incidence, Prevalence, and Disease Severity', *AIDS Research and Human Retroviruses*, 23(12), 1453–1459.

Roelofs, J. (2009) 'Networks and Democracy. It Ain't Necessarily So', *American Behavioral Scientist*, 52(7), 990–1005.

Rosen, D. (2006) 'Bush's Foreign Sex Policy', http://www.counterpunch.org/rosen12222006.html, date accessed 16 November 2009.

Rosenberg, J. (1990) 'A Non-Realist Theory of Sovereignty? Giddens' *The Nation State and Violence*', *Millennium – Journal of International Studies*, 19(2), 249–259.

Rosenberg, J. (1994) 'The International Imagination: IR Theory and "Classic Social Analysis"', *Millennium – Journal of International Studies*, 23(1), 85–108.

Rotberg, R.I. (2004) 'The Failure and Collapse of Nation-States: Breakdom, Prevention, and Repair' in Rotberg, R.I. (ed.) (2004) *When States Fail. Causes and Consequences* (Princeton, NJ: Princeton University Press).

Rupiya, M. (2006) *The Enemy Within: Southern African Militaries' Quarter-Century Battle with HIV and AIDS* (Pretoria: Institute for Security Studies).

Ruttan, V.W. (1996) *United States Development Assistance Policy. The Domestic Politics of Foreign Aid* (Baltimore, MD and London: The Johns Hopkins University Press).

SABC News (2007) 'Mbeki Not an Aids Denialist: Author' http://www.sabcnews.com/Article/PrintWholeStory/0,2160,159145,00.html, date accessed 13 November 2007.

Saker, L. et al. (2004) *Globalization and Infectious Diseases: A Review of the Linkages* (Geneva: World Health Organisation).

SAPA (2009) 'Zuma "Architect for Aids Strategy"', http://www.news24.com/printArticle.aspx?iframe&aid=b8f4126c-9997–418e-b540–013b..., date accessed 21 December 2009.

Schaefer, B.D. and Kim, A.B. (2008) 'President Bush's Trip to Africa: Solidifying U.S. Partnerships with the Region', http://edgeweb.heritage.org/Research/Africa/wm1817.cfm?renderforprint=1, date accessed 6 May 2009.

Schaefer, D.D.A. (2009) 'US Foreign Policy and Aid to the Peace Corps', *Journal of Social Sciences*, 5(2), 139–145.

Schneider, H. and Fassin, D. (2002) 'Denial and Defiance: A Socio–political Analysis of AIDS in South Africa', *AIDS*, 16(4), 45–51.

Schneider, M. and Moodie, M. (2002) *The Destabilizing Impacts of HIV/AIDS. First Wave Hits Eastern and Southern Africa; Second Wave Threatens India, China, Russia, Ethiopia, Nigeria* (Washington, DC: Center for Strategic and International Studies).

Schneidman, W.W. (2008) *Obama's Three Objectives for Continent*, http://allafrica.com/stories/printable/200809291346.html, date accessed 17 October 2008.

Schoeman, M. (2007) 'South Africa' in Cawthra, G. et al. (eds) *Security and Democracy in Southern Africa* (Johannesburg: Wits University Press).

Schönteich, M. (1999) 'Age and Aids: South Africa's Crime Time Bomb?', http://www.issafrica.org/pubs/ASR/8No4/SchOnteich.html, date accessed 25 June 2008.

Schraeder, P.J. (1994) 'Elites as Facilitators or Impediments to Political Development? Some Lessons from the 'Third Wave' of Democratization in Africa', *Journal of Developing Areas*, 29(1), 69–90.

Schrecker, T. (2009) 'The G8, Globalization, and the Need for a Global Health Ethic' in Maclean, S.L. et al. (eds) *Health for Some. The Political Economy of Global Health Governance* (Basingstoke and New York: Palgrave Macmillan).

Selby, J. (2007) 'Engaging Foucault: Discourse, Liberal Governance and the Limits of Foucauldian IR', *International Relations*, 21(3), 324–345.

Sheehan, C. (2008) *Securitizing the HIV/AIDS Pandemic in U.S. Foreign Policy* (Washington, DC: American University).

Shillinger, K. (2006) *From Hegemon to Champion: South Africa and Strategic Balance* (IV Conferência Internacional FLAD/IPRI-UNL Estratégia e segurança na África Austral, FLAD).

Sitze, A. (2004) 'Denialism', *The South Atlantic Quarterly*, 103(4), 769–811.

Sjösted, R. (2008) 'Exploring the Construction of Threats: The Securitization of HIV/AIDS in Russia', *Security Dialogue*, 39(7), 7–29.

South African National Planning Commission (2011) *Diagnostic Overview* (Pretoria: The Presidency of the Republic of South Africa).

Southall, R. (2004) 'The ANC & Black Capitalism in South Africa', *Review of African Political Economy*, 31(100), 313–328.

Spicer, N. et al. (2010) 'National and Subnational HIV/AIDS Coordination: Are Global Health Initiatives Closing the Gap Between Intent and Practice?', *Globalization and Health*, 6(3), 1–16.

Stein, H. (2000) *The Development of the Developmental State in Africa: A Theoretical Inquiry* (Copenhagen: Centre of African Studies, University of Copenhagen).

Strain, R.M. (2008) *Battle from the Bottom: The Role of Indigenous AIDS NGOs in Botswana* (Philadelphia: University of Pennsylvania).

Swidler, A. (2007) 'Syncretism and Subversion in AIDS Governance: How Locals Cope with Global Demands' in Poku, N.K. et al. (eds) *AIDS and Governance* (Hampshire: Ashgate).

Taylor, I. (2002) *The New Partnership for Africa's Development and the Global Political Economy: Towards the African Century or Another False Start?* (Accra: CODESRIA/TWN-Africa conference).

Taylor, I. (2003) 'As Good as It Gets? Botswana's "Democratic Development"', in Melber, H. (ed.) *Limits to Liberation in Southern Africa* (Cape Town: Human Sciences Research Council).

Taylor, I. (2005) *NEPAD: Towards Africa's Development or Another False Start?* (Boulder, CO and London: Lynne Rienner Publishers).

Teklehaimanot, H. and Asfaw, A. (2010) 'Defiant Meles Snubs Criticism', http://allafrica.com/stories/printable/201012070740.html, date accessed 20 January 2010.

Thompson, H. (2007) 'PEPFAR MythBusters: Episode Two', http://rhrealitycheck.org/article/2007/03/22/pepfar-mythbusters–episode–two/, date accessed 3 May 2014.

Tobin, L. (2010) 'South Africa's Children Caring for Parents with Aids', http://www.guardian.co.uk/education/2010/jun/22/hiv-aids-child-carers-south-africa/print, date accessed 22 June 2010.

UK Commission for Africa (2005) *Our Common Interest. Report of the Commission for Africa* (London: Commission for Africa).

UNAIDS: United Nations Joint Programme on HIV/AIDS (2013) *UNAIDS Global Report* (Geneva: UNAIDS).

Underwood, T.L. (2008) 'United States Relations with South Africa: Why Now Is a Critical Time to Strengthen Them', *Africa Security Review*, 17(1), 6–19.

UNDP: United Nations Development Programme (1994) *Human Development Report* (New York: United Nations Development Programme).

UNDP: United Nations Development Programme (2013) *Human Development Report 2013* (New York: United Nations Development Programme).

United Nations System Task Team on the Post-2015 UN Development Agenda (2012) *Realizing the Future We Want for All. Report to the Secretary-General* (New York: United Nations).

United Nations System Task Team on the Post-2015 UN Development Agenda (2013) *A Renewed Global Partnership for Development* (New York: United Nations).

Van de Walle, N. (2001) *African Economies and the Politics of Permanent Crisis, 1979–1999* (Cambridge: Cambridge University Press).

Varela, H. (2006) 'Botswana: entre el autoritarismo liberal y la democracia' in Cornejo, R. (ed.) *En los intersticios de la democracia y el autoritarismo. Algunos casos de Asia, África y América Latina* (Buenos Aires: Consejo Latinoamericano de Ciencias Sociales).

Vaughan, S. (2003) *Ethnicity and Power in Ethiopia* (Edinburgh: University of Edinburgh).

Vaughan, S. and Tronvoll, K. (2003) *The Culture of Power in Contemporary Ethiopian Political Life* (Stockholm: Swedish International Development Cooperation Agency).

Dietrich, J.W. (2007) 'The Politics of PEPFAR: The President's Emergency Plan for AIDS Relief', *Ethics & International Affairs*, 23(3), 277–292.

Wadhams, N. (2010) 'Ethiopian Opposition Leader's Release: For Show?', http://www.time.com/time/world/article/0,8599,2024273,00.html, date accessed 10 October 2010.

Wallis, W. (2009) 'FT Interview with Ethiopia's Prime Minister', http://www.ft.com/cms/s/0/dc04c378-5f62-11de-93d1-00144feabdc0.html, date accessed 2 July 2009.

Walta Information Center (2011) 'Interview with Ato Redwan Hussien, EPRDF Secretariat Head', http://www.waltainfo.com, date accessed 17 January 2011.

Waltz, K.N. (1979) *Theory of International Politics* (New York: McGraw-Hill).

Welle, K. (2001) *Contending Discourses on 'Partnership'. A Comparative Analysis of the Rural Water and Sanitation Sector in Ghana* (London: School of Oriental and African Studies, University of London).

West, D.L. (2005) *Combating Terrorism in the Horn of Africa and Yemen* (Cambridge, MA: John F. Kennedy School of Government, Harvard University).

White, G. (2006) 'Towards a Democratic Developmental State', *IDS Bulletin*, 37(4), 60–70.

White House (2006) *The National Security Strategy of the United States of America* (Washington, DC: The White House).

White House (2010) *The National Security Strategy of the United States of America* (Washington, DC: The White House).

Whiteside, A. (2004) 'Health, Economic Growth, and Competitiveness in Africa' in Hernández-Catá, E. et al. (eds) *The Africa Competitiveness Report 2004* (Geneva: World Economic Forum).

Whiteside, A. (2009) 'Is AIDS Exceptional?', http://www.aids2031.org/pdfs/aids%20exceptionalism_paper25.pdf, date accessed 10 November 2009.

Whiteside, A. and De Waal, A. (2004) '"That's Resources You See!": Political Economy, Ethics and the HIV/AIDS Epidemic', *New Political Economy*, 9(4), 581–594.

Whitfield, L. and Maipose, G. (2008) *Managing Aid Dependence: How African Governments Lost Ownership and How They Can Regain It* (University of Oxford).

WHO: World Health Organisation (2007) *International Health Regulations (2005): Areas of Work for Implementation* (Geneva: WHO).

WHO: World Health Organisation (2008) *WHO in 60 Years: A Chronology of Public Health Milestones* (Geneva: WHO).

WHO: World Health Organisation (2013) *World Health Statistics 2013* (Geneva: WHO).

Wilkinson, L. and Power, H. (1998) 'The London and Liverpool Schools of Tropical Medicine 1898–1998', *British Medical Bulletin*, 54(2), 281–292.

Williams, O. and Rushton, S. (2009) *Global Health Governance as a Contested Space: Competing Discourses, Interests and Actors* (New York: 50th International Studies Association Annual Convention).

Wolf, R. and Page, S. (2008) 'Bush Wants Twice the Funding for AIDS', http://www. usatoday.com/news/washington/2008–01–24-bushinside_N.htm?csp=34, date accessed 30 January 2008.

World Bank (2011) Rural Population (% of Total Population), http://data.worldbank.org/indicator/SP.RUR.TOTL.ZS, date accessed 20 December 2011.

Youde, J. (2005) 'The Development of a Counter-Epistemic Community: AIDS, South Africa, and International Regimes', *International Relations*, 19(4), 421–439.

Youde, J. (2007a) 'Ideology's Role in AIDS Policies in Uganda and South Africa', http://diplomacy.shu.edu/academics/global_health/journal/PDF/Prescott-article.pdf, date accessed 27 June 2008.

Youde, J. (2007b) *AIDS, South Africa, and the Politics of Knowledge* (Hampshire: Ashgate).

Zaffiro, J. (1992) 'U.S. Relations with Botswana: 1966–1989', *TransAfrica Forum*, 9(3), 57–74.

Zartman, W. (1995) *Collapsed States: The Disintegration and Restoration of Legitimate Authority* (Boulder, CO: Lynne Rienner).

Zenawi, M. (2006) 'African Development: Dead Ends and New Beginnings' http:// www.africanidea.org/m_zenawI_aug_9_2006.pdf, date accessed 29 December 2011.

Ziker, A.K. (2008) *Race, Conservative Politics, and U.S. Foreign Policy in the Postcolonial World, 1948–1968* (Houston, TX: Rice University).

Zimeta, M.G. (2010) 'Ethiopia's Election Results and the Myths of African Politics', http://www.theatlantic.com/international/archive/2010/06/ethiopias-election-results-and-the-myths-of-african-politics/58623/, date accessed 26 June 2010.

# Index

11 September 2001 terrorist attacks, 5, 19, 55–56, 83, 116

abstinence, be faithful and condoms policy, 86, 135, 136
  abstinence support, 87
  abstinence-only education, 89–90, 136
  condoms distribution, 85–87, 99
  condoms promotion, 104
  access to health, 17
accountability, 8, 57, 59, 76, 77, 103
  financial, 76
  transparency and, 121, 127
ACHAP (African Comprehensive HIV/AIDS Partnership), 100, 102–103
Addis Ababa
  central government in, 111, 123–124, 145
  diplomatic conglomerate, 115
  struggling against, 120, 152
*African Development, Dead Ends and New Beginnings*, 63
  *see* Zenawi, Meles (1955–2012)
African Renaissance, 58, 130, 149
  idea of, 137
  politics of, 148
  project of, 132, 150
  rhetoric of, 127, 131, 147
African Union, 62, 115
  *see* Organisation for African Unity
Africanist critique of International Relations, 11, 34, 39, 43–45
Afro-pessimism, 60
agency, 39, 77
  absence of, 3, 11
  agency/resistance, 38
  concept of 4
  cross-country comparison of, 143–149
  degree of, 4, 31

further question on, 149–153
  human, 3, 40–41
  national, 14
  political, 142
  research of, 2, 11, 38
  state, 31–32, 40–41, 143
  states characteristic, 3
  structure/agency, 42–45, 157
AGOA (African Growth and Opportunity Act), 75, 89, 129
Aid conditionality, 53–54, 64, 114, 142, 147, 152, 155
AIDS denialism, 159
  burial of, 148
  HIV/AIDS orthodoxy, 125, 130–131
  HIV/AIDS science, 125
Algeria, 48, 59, 127
'American values', 84
Amerithrax, 19
Amharas, 63, 111, 121
anarchy, 34, 39, 45
  cooperation under, 42
  hierarchy v anarchy, 32–33
  taming of, 34
ANC (African National Congress), 27, 64, 139
  anti-apartheid struggle, 159
  congressional meeting (2008), 131
  far-left sectors, 137
  insurgents, 96
  post-apartheid transition, 127–128, 147, 151
  third-way, 137
  Youth League, 138
Anglican Church, 129
Angola, 48, 127, 159
antiretrovirals, 25, 68, 77
  acquisition of, 68
  Botswanan national programmes, 99–100
  suspension of treatment with, 27
  treatment with, 6

apartheid, 13, 105, 131
  anti-apartheid struggle, 95, 147,
    152
  army, 94, 150
  dismantlement of, 64
  National Party, 134
  technological developments, 137
  United States backing of, 159
  *see* separate development
Arab states, 65, 155
  *see also* Saudi Arabia
  *see also* United Arab Emirates
armed conflicts, 9, 67, 98, 116, 128,
  143
  prevention of, 147
Asian growth models, 61
asymmetry
  in Africa relations
    agency and, 42–45
  between powerful and weaker
    states, 4
  interstate, 2
Australia, 22, 54, 114
Ayoob, Mohammed (1942), 42–44

ballooning entitlement, 76–77
Bayart, Jean-François (1950), 47
Bechuanaland, 93
  Bechuanaland Democratic Party,
    94
  Protectorate of, 92, 105
Beck, Ulrich (1944), 18
Big Pharma, 7
  *see* pharmaceutical companies
Bill and Melinda Gates Foundation,
    24, 26, 99, 100, 102, 144, 149
biopolitics, 21
  concept of, 35–36
  framework of, 2, 55
  rationalisation of, 21
biopower, 21
  concept of 35
  essentialisation of, 41
  framework of, 2, 55
birth control, 23, 120
Birx, Deborah, 72
black diasporas, 129
black ownership, 138
Board of Health of, 22

Botswana
  Botswana Defence Force, 101
  Botswana Democratic Party, 94,
    144
  'Botswana miracle', 98, 105, 144,
    151
  Botswana as a model, 9, 62–63, 92,
    102–103, 107–108, 146
  Botswana National AIDS
    Coordinating Agency, 99
  Botswana National AIDS Council, 99
  Botswana National Party, 105
  'initiator culture', 96–97
  liberal authoritarianism, 98, 108, 151
  'nouveau riche' attitude, 108
  political transition, 125
  population's survival, 13
  role of economic development,
    92–98
Brazil
  as emerging country 54, 126, 155
BRICs, 126
British Colony of New South Wales,
    22 British-Boer relations, 143
BSAC (British South Africa
    Company), 93, 97
Bush, George W. (1946), 5–7, 82
  active-positive presidency, 88
  Bush administration (2001–2009),
    5, 85–90, 136
  post-Bush administration, 83

Cape Colony, 93, 143
CARE Act (1990), 67–68
Carr, Edward H. (1892–1982), 1
Catholic Church, 119–120, 129
CDC (Centers for Disease Control
    and Prevention), 72, 74, 78
Chandler, David, 3, 40–41
  *see Empire in Denial* (2006)
  *see Hollow Hegemony* (2009)
China
  as emerging country, 54, 126, 155
  as HIV/AIDS epidemic second-wave
    country, 81, 155
  HIV/AIDS in, 17
  influence in Africa, 61–62, 65, 83
  partnering with Ethiopia, 114, 146
  regional prominence of, 24, 119

cholera, 19, 22
Christian Right, 6, 86–89
  *see* right-wing Catholics
civil war, 17
Clapham, Christopher, 40
  idea of state, 63
  politics of state survival, 52
Clausewitz, Carl von (1780–1831), 35
Clinton, Hillary (1947), 66
Clinton Initiative, 24
Clinton, William 'Bill' (1946), 5, 82
  administration, 89 (1993–2001)
Cold War, 1, 94
  during the Derg, 137
  end of, 33, 54, 99
  late, 67
Columbia University, 133
corruption, 27
  increasing levels of, 139
  money lost to, 90
  public, 73
  severe, 151
country ownership, 7–10, 14
  case of, 75–76, 100–107
  definition of, 72, 153–155
  empowerment and, 37
  policies of, 144–146
  shared responsibility and, 91
Cox, Robert W. (1926), 24
critical theory, 2–3, 11, 33–42

De Beers, 62, 95, 97, 147
de Waal, Alex (1963), 82
Debswana, 62, 75, 95, 97, 100, 102,
  143
  diamonds exploration, 95–97,
    143–145
  post-diamond future, 108
decolonisation, 39, 55, 58
  after, 127
democratisation, 17, 127
  in the 1990s, 59
dependency, 49, 52, 64, 68, 85, 98
  reduction of, 114
  system of, 76–77
Dergue,
  regime, 119–120, 122, 145
developmental state, 13, 53–62
  in Africa, 98

Asian-style, 95
  in Botswana, 101
  cross-country comparison,
    145–151
  democratic, 62, 96
  in Ethiopia, 113–123
  in South Africa, 134
dignity of Africans
  transmission of values on,
    131–132, 147–149
donor diversification, 61, 64
  in Ethiopia, 114, 147–149
drugs
  generic, 7, 69, 70
  injectors, 17
  trafficking in, 16, 54
Duesberg, Peter (1936), 130
Duffield, Mark, 36–37, 40–41
  development through security, 36
  governance at a distance, 37, 55
  security-development nexus, 36
Dybul, Mark (1963), 6, 83, 88

East Asian Tigers, 59
  economic growth success stories
    of, 59
  economic inequality, 125, 141
Econsult, 104
Egypt, 31, 59, 127
  Ethiopian relations with, 159
*Empire in Denial* (2006), 57, 62
  *see* Chandler, David
energy resources
  scarcity of, 18
environmental damage, 16
epidemic surveillance, 21
EPRDF (Ethiopian People's
  Revolutionary Democratic
  Front), 13, 110–114, 116,
    120–123, 145
  Youth league, 112
Eritrea, 9, 110, 111
Escobar, Arturo (1952), 37
Ethiopia
  Charities Law of 2009, 152
  ethnic federalism, 110–111, 145
  ethnic grievances, 111, 145
  *Health Sector Strategic Plan* (2005),
    118

Ethiopia – (*Continued*)
  HIV/AIDS Prevention and Control
    Office, 117
  National AIDS Priority Strategies
    for 2001–2005, 117
  National HIV/AIDS Strategic Plans
    for 2000–2004, 117
  national question, 111
  population displacement, 116
  population growth, 116, 159
  post-2005 elections protests, 178
Ethiopian Orthodox Church, 119
European defence and foreign
    security policy, 16
European Union, 102
Evangelical Churches, 86
external v internal detachment,
    42–45

facilitator state v 'rogue' state,
    26–28
Fage, J. D. (1921–2002), 49–50
family planning, 71, 74, 87, 90,
    116–117, 119–120, 136
famine, 67, 111, 115–116, 158
female sex workers, 82, 136
Ferguson, James (1959), 18, 37
Fidler, David, 11, 16, 19–26
foreign investment
  in Africa, 61, 142
  in Botswana, 128
Foucault, Michel (1926–1984), 24,
    35–36
Frankfurt School, 36, 157

Gaborone, 93–94, 105
  Princess Marina Hospital, 99
Garrett, Laurie, 82
Gauteng, 93
  *see also* Transvaal
Geldenhuys, Deon, 126–127
German South West Africa, 93
  *see* Namibia
Gevisser, Mark, 131
Ghebreyesus, Tedros Adhanom
    (1965), 26, 114, 117, 131, 146
Giddens, Anthony (1938), 4
  Ontological security, 18
Glenwood, Durban, 133

Global Fund, 8, 18–19, 24–27,
    90–102, 144–149
global health
  construction of, 16–18
  governance
    constitutionalism, 19–24
    contradictions of, 25–26
    role of states, 26–28
global warming, 18
globalisation of trade, 17
  new threats provoked by, 28
good governance, 11
  commitment to, 9
  partnership as a means to, 38
Goosby, Eric (1953), 68, 72, 153
governmentalities, 64–65
governmentality
  concept of, 21–22, 35
  Western v African, 52–53
Grand Ethiopian Renaissance Dam,
    112

hegemony-based approaches, 33
  discussion of, 39–42
Hillbom, Ellen, 105
*The History of Sexuality* (1978), 35–36
HIV/AIDS epidemic
  effects, 82
  implications of, 80–84
  scepticism of, 82
  social aspects of, 128–130
  social determinants of, 134
Holbrooke, Richard (1941–2010),
    80–81
*Hollow Hegemony* (2009), 41–42
  *see* Chandler, David
Hollywood celebrities, 20–21
Horn of Africa, 9, 13, 110, 119
  extremism in the, 116
  war on terror in the, 116
Human Development Index, 53, 145
human rights regimes, 36
  Human Rights Watch, 121
human security
  foreign policy based on, 28
  links to global health, 16–18
  policy paradigm, 1, 11, 15
  humanitarianism, 83
Hussien, Redwan, 113

Ian Khama, Seretse Khama (1953), 94, 108
*iddirs*, 123, 159
import deficits, 49
Index of State Weakness in the Developing World, 129
India
  drug companies, 70
  as emerging country, 54
  as Ethiopia partner, 114, 126, 146
  land leasing, 112
  as regional power, 24
  second wave country, 17, 81, 119
infant mortality rate, 107
infectious diseases
  securitisation of, 23
inflation control, 51
international aid, 48, 75, 115
  role in Ethiopia, 121, 146
International AIDS Conference (2010), 132
international development, 2, 30
international hygienist conferences (1830s), 19, 21–22
International Monetary Fund, 19, 37, 128
  Structural adjustment programmes, 51
International Relations v Public Health, 17
international stability
  threats to, 59–60
international structure 143–155
  African states entrenched in, 31
  structure/agency, 42–45, 157
  West-hegemonic, 11
international trade, 20, 33, 128
Islam, 119
  Islamic extremism, 9, 116, 128

Japan, 1, 4, 33, 42, 54, 96, 114, 146
juridical-territorial sovereignty, 64

Khama, Seretse (1921–1980), 93, 94
Krasner, Stephen (1942), 56
Kuznet's model of modern economic growth, 105

labour productivity, 140

League of Nations, 23
  Economics Office, 19
  Health Office, 22
Lesotho, 107, 134
liberal cosmopolitans, 41
liberal power
  transmitted medically, 11
  unprecendented wave of, 54
liberalism, 40–41, 58
  civil society as bastion of, 151–152
Live Aid concerts (1985), 114
loan giving, 48, 61
Lusaka, 80
  *see* Zambia

Mafikeng, 93
Malema, Julius (1981), 138, 139
malnutrition, 110, 116
Mandela, Nelson (1918–2013), 13, 126, 130, 147
Mariam, Mengistu Haile (1937), 111
Masire, Quett Ketumile (1925), 94, 97
Mauritius, 59, 62, 67, 98
Mbeki, Thabo (1942)
  accusation of AIDS denialism, 27, 131
  administration (1999–2008), 13–14, 27, 60, 125–126, 138
  African Renaissance, 58, 127, 147
  economic policy, 134
  views on AIDS, 24, 129–131, 148
Mbeki v Zuma policies on AIDS, 133
medical police, 22–23
Mexico City Policy, 87, 136
middle class indicator of growth, 61
Middle Powers Initiative, 1
migration, 2, 16–18, 54, 82, 135
Mogae, Festus (1939), 94, 98, 101, 108
'Monterrey Consensus' (2002), 72
  *see also* United Nations, International Conference on Development's Financing
Morgenthau, Hans (1904–1980), 1
Motlanthe, Kgalema (1949), 131
Motsoaledi, Aaron (1958), 132, 148
Mozambique, 48, 74, 127, 157, 159
Mugabe, Robert (1924), 138, 152

multiracial democracy, 137, 147–149
Museveni
  Jane (1948), 87
  Yoweri (1944), 87

Namibia, 48, 74, 93–94, 96, 128,
  157
  *see also* German South West Africa
national interest, 82
  accomplishment of, 3, 10
Ndlovu-Gatsheni, Sabelo J., 138–139
neoliberalism, 28
  economic school of thought, 51
  ideological structures and forces, 2
  International Relations theory, 33
  socio-economic reform, 53, 128
neopatrimonialism, 38
  governmentality of, 58
  politics of, 41
neorealism, 33
  bandwagoning, 42, 143
  further questions on, 149–153
  subaltern, 42–45
  *see also* structural realism
NEPAD (New Partnership for Africa's
  Development), 59, 137
  establishment of, 127
  new threats, 16, 28, 34
  perception of, 54
  problems of, 55
Nigeria, 5, 59, 74, 81, 82, 119, 127,
  157
Nile Basin, 112, 146
  water of, 159
nongovernmental organisations, 2, 6,
  7, 20, 70, 74, 106, 114, 129
  in Ethiopia, 152
*normal* state
  smaller states as, 3, 4
North America, 25, 29, 42, 51, 146
Northern America, 114, 119
Northern Kenya, 9, 110
nuclear proliferation, 18

Obama, Barack (1961), 5
  administration, 8, 74, 120
  2008 election of, 89, 136
Ogaden, 120, 147, 152
  Liberation Front of, 121, 158

oil prices, 50
Organisation for African Unity, 40,
  59, 127
  *see* African Union
Oromia, 120, 121, 147, 152
orphans and vulnerable children, 7,
  70, 71, 77, 103, 118, 135, 148
  as threat to security, 81–82
Other
  as object of foreign policy, 58
  as object of public health, 23
overpopulation, 110

pan-Africanist agenda, 127
parastatal companies, 53, 138, 151
  definition of, 158
pariah state, 63
Paris Declaration on Aid Effectiveness
  (2005), 72, 153
partnership 9, 20, 27, 57, 72, 74,
  142
  choice of, 155
  compact, 7
  for development, 53
  ethic of, 76
  framework, 8, 76, 106, 15
  public-private, 2, 7, 19, 45, 62, 70,
  95, 97, 100, 143
  transnational, 37–38
Pascual, Carlos (1959), 56
Peace Corps, 6, 74, 95, 98
peacekeeping missions, 16, 64, 80,
  82, 128, 147
PEPFAR (President's Emergency Plan
  for AIDS Relief)
  emergency v sustainability, 68–74
  first phase (2004–2008), 5, 7, 10,
  68, 148
  measurement, 71, 104
  origins of, 66–68
  palliative care, 7, 135, 148
  private companies, 75, 138, 151
  second phase (2009–2013), 8, 10,
  12, 67, 71, 100, 153
  shared responsibility, 71–72, 91
  Stewardship and Oversight Act
  (2013), 6, 72
  supply chain systems, 70, 71, 103
  'wrap-around' character, 118

pharmaceutical companies, 19, 131
  services of, 118
  United States, 69
  Western, 25, 157
  *see* Big Pharma
post-apartheid
  government, 13, 126–129, 137, 139,
    151
  liberal-idealism, 130–132, 137, 141,
    147
  policy, 58, 59
  race relations, 131
  racial v class, 138
  regime, 138
post-Cold War, 2–3, 15–19, 24–25,
  28–29, 34, 58, 116, 137
postcolonial elites, 48–49, 150
postcolonial state
  comparative experience, 62–64
  domestic sphere of, 41
  functioning of, 43
  porosity of, 44, 76
  settlement, 48–49
postcolonial theory, 2–3, 38
post-Dergue, 111–113, 158
post-development, 36
poverty, 150–151
  in Africa, 8, 52, 67, 84
  in Botswana, 98, 105, 109
  elimination goal, 53, 61
  in Ethiopia, 113–116
  reversal of, 96
  in South Africa, 130, 138–140, 146,
    151
  urban and rural poverty, 116,
President's Malaria Initiative, 8, 54,
  74, 89
private companies, 1, 2, 19–20,
  26, 57
  in Africa, 52
private property
  institutions of, 97
progressive social movements, 138
Protestant Churches, 119
public goods, 57
  basic, 17
  global, 14
public health, 21, 84
  in Botswana, 100, 104, 144
  history of, 24
  new world order, 20
  schools of, 23
  securitisation of, 15, 17
  in South Africa, 125, 131
  public security, 17

quarantine, 21–22

rational action, 4, 10, 11, 12
recipient state, 27–28, 42
Red Cross, 23
refugee movements, 9, 110
Renewalist Churches, 86
rent-seeking behaviour, 51
Republic of Rhodesia, 63
  *see* Zimbabwe
resistance
  local, 3, 38
  values and ideas of, 131, 148
Rhodes, Cecil (1890–1896), 95, 97
Rhodesia, 96, 143
  *see* Zimbabwe
Ricci, James, 26
right-wing Catholics, 86
  *see* Christian Right
risk society, 18–19
  *see* also sociology of risk
Rockefeller Foundation, 23
Rosenberg, Justin, 44–45
  historical-sociological approach, 4,
    42–45
  state as social relation, 42–45
Rotberg, Robert (1935), 55–56
rule of law, 17, 27
Russia
  AIDS affecting the army, 82
  as emerging country, 126
  regional predominance, 24
  second wave country, 81, 119

SADC (Southern African Development
  Community), 128
Saudi Arabia, 65, 114, 146
  *see also* Arab states
'scientific imperialism', 76
securitisation
  in Ethiopia, 147
  statebuilding and, 53–62

Selassie, Haile (1882–1975), 115, 120, 122, 152, 158
self-help
  Botswanan foreign policy, 95, 99, 105
  Ethiopian regime behaviour, 110–124
  principle of, 31–33
Senegal, 59, 127
separate development, 63, 127, 134, 148
  *see* apartheid
severe acute respiratory syndrome (SARS), 19
Sidibé, Michel (1952), 26, 132
sleeping sickness, 22
smallpox, 22, 23
smart power, 33
  *see also* soft power
social constructivism, 17, 26, 29
social exclusion, 10
social mobilisation of the masses, 112
social welfare, 49, 52, 102, 116, 137
sociology of risk, 11, 15
  *see also* risk society
soft power, 33, 34, 54
  *see also* smart power
Somalia, 9, 110, 116, 120, 145
South Africa
  Asians, 139
  Black Economic Empowerment, 134, 137, 147, 151
  coloureds, 139
  foreign policy, 126–129
  HIV/AIDS advocacy in 125
  land reform in, 137–138
  National Planning Commission, 139, 151
  nationalisation, South Africa, 137–138, 152
  nativism, 139
  nuclear armament programme, 128
  regime transition, 127, 147
  regional hegemony, 59, 64, 126–127
  regional superpower, 126
  whites, 139, 159, 160
South Sudan, 9, 110

Southern Rhodesia, 93, 143
  *see* Zimbabwe
Soviet Union, 31, 32, 42, 49, 128, 143, 145
  in Botswana, 95
  demise of, 1, 54, 137
  in Ethiopia, 115
  in South Africa, 159
spill-over effects, 61
state failure, 9, 34
  categories of, 129
  consequences of, 17
  definition of, 55
  linkages to, 83
  literature, 153
  prevention of, 34
  in Somalia, 116
state interventionism, 137
  reduction of, 51
state paternalism, 104–108
state survivalism
statebuilding, 53–62
  project of, 38
  promotion of, 34
  West-led, 45
strategic infrastructures, 144
structural adjustment programmes, 12, 49–54, 59
  in Ethiopia, 112
structural realism, 4
  *see* neorealism
structural reforms, 5
subsistence agriculture, 63, 151
surplus populations, 55
Swaziland, 99, 107, 134

Tanzania, 74, 128, 157, 159
Taylor, Ian, 60
TCM (Total Community Mobilisation), 103, 158
terrorism
  networks of, 54
  recruitment for, 10, 82
Tigray People's Liberation Front, 111
Transvaal, 93
  *see also* Gauteng
Treatment Action Campaign, 131
Tshabalala-Msimang, Manto, 27, 131

Tswana Kings, 93
  Bathoen, 93
  Khama III, 93
  Sebele, 93
tuberculosis, 70, 83, 135
  epidemic of, 19
Turkey, 114, 146

Umlazi, Durban, 133
unemployment
  in Botswana, 98, 105
  in South Africa, 134, 140
United Arab Emirates, 65, 114, 146
  *see also* Arab states
United Kingdom Commission for
    Africa, 58, 146, 149
United Nations
  Development Program, 16, 113
  High Commissioner for Refugees, 74
  International Conference on
      Development's Financing, 72
  Millennium Development Goals,
      53, 113, 117, 153
  Millennium Summit (2000), 53
  Security Council, 80
  system, 1, 16, 26, 90, 154
United States
  Africa Command, 9, 129, 148
  bipartisanism, 87–89
  CIA (Central Intelligence Agency),
      81
  Congress, 7, 27, 66, 73, 74, 75, 89
  domestic constituencies, 84–87
  FDA (Food and Drug
      Administration), 69
  Foreign Assistance Act (1961), 69
  Global Health Initiative, 8, 71,
      83–89, 117–119
  Global Leadership Against HIV/
      AIDS, Tuberculosis and Malaria
      Reauthorization Act (2008), 6,
      71
  Leadership Against HIV/AIDS,
      Tuberculosis and Malaria Act
      (2003), 6, 89
  Millennium Challenge Account, 54
  Millennium Challenge Corporation,
      89

Strategic Concept, 81
USAID (Agency for International
    Development), 6, 66, 74–85,
    98, 115
various agencies, 6
United States foreign and strategic
    policy
  adventurism, 33
  anchors of, 9
  bilateralism v multilateralism, 91
University of Natal, 133
urban insecurity, 10, 18
urbanisation, 50

van de Walle, Nicholas, 50–51
Vaughan, Sarah and Tronvoll, Kjetil
    112–113
viral outbreaks, 18, 28
Voice of America, 115, 121

Walta Information Centre, 113
Waltz, Kenneth (1924–2013), 4,
    31–33
War on Terror, 5, 116
Washington Consensus (1989), 60,
    158
weaker state, 3–11, 142–143
weapons of mass destruction, 30, 54
Western Europe, 1, 4, 25, 33, 42, 51,
    90, 114
  donors, 119
  third way, 137
white minority regime, 63, 96
White, Ryan (1971–1990), 6
white supremacy, 23, 143, 151
whole-of-government approach,
    74–75
World Bank, 19, 24, 37, 51, 117, 128
  Poverty Reduction Programme, 112
World Food Programme, 74
World Health Organisation
  Alma-Ata Declaration (1978), 16
  International Regulations, 11, 15,
      18

yellow fever, 23

Zaffiro, James J., 94

Zambia, 74, 128, 157
  *see also* Lusaka
Zenawi, Meles (1955–2012)
  international standing, 114–115,
    146
  United States anti-terrorism
    cooperation, 116
  *See African Development, Dead Ends
    and New Beginnings*

Zimbabwe, 48, 111, 127–128, 159
  *see also* Republic of Rhodesia
  *see also* Rhodesia
  *see also* Southern Rhodesia
Zuma, Jacob (1942), 13, 126, 131,
    133
  administration (2009), 134, 148
  AIDS policy, 148
  architect for AIDS strategy, 132